Brand Building

ON THE INTERNET

Martin Lindström
Tim Frank Andersen

KOGAN
PAGE

First published in Denmark in 1997
By Børsen Publishing
Montergade 19
1140 København K

First published in Australia in 1999
By Hardie Grant Books
12 Claremont Street
South Yarra Victoria Australia 3141
First published in Great Britain in 2000 by Kogan Page Limited.
Reprinted in 2001

Kogan Page Limited
120 Pentonville Road
London N1 9JN, UK

Kogan Page (US) Limited
163 Central Ave, Suite 2
Dover NH 03820, USA

British Library Cataloguing in Publication Data

A CIP record for this book is available from the British Library.

ISBN 0 7494 3313 2

Text design, typesetting and cover revisions for new edition by Prowling Tiger Press
Translated by Patricia Harding in association with First Edition Translations Ltd., Cambridge, UK
Printed and bound by Creative Print and Design (Wales), Ebbw Vale

Thanks

Even though a distance of 24,000 kilometres between us should not have been a problem with the Internet and e-mail available, this book would not have happened without the assistance of Claus Hessner who has tirelessly co-ordinated the material and examined it critically, researched, checked sources and made sure we completed the manuscript. Therefore we owe Claus a huge debt of thanks. We would also like to thank Frederik Zoega, an expert in Internet traffic generation, for his help.

A very special thanks to Clare Strang, Bernadette & Glenn Williams and Rob Morgan – without your support this book would never have become a reality.

Lastly we would like to take this opportunity to thank our partners, friends, colleagues and families who have suffered patiently during the six months this book took to write.

Sydney and Copenhagen, March 2000.

Martin Lindström & Tim Frank Andersen

Visit www.brandbuilding.net for updated information about the book.

Contents

About this book

*"The only way
we're going to redevelop
trust in the Internet
is through the brands
that we know."*

Nicolas Negroponte

We live in a world where more than ever before competing products resemble each other.

Their lifecycle gets shorter every day. Huge amounts are invested in the development and maintenance of brands. The reason is that strong brands and consumer loyalty to them are the be-all and end-all for the owners of the products.

It is as simple as that.

The battle for the attention of the consumers is currently carried out via image campaigns in print, on television and via other traditional classical media. However, it is becoming more difficult and expensive to get the message across properly. And this is not assisted by the proliferation of media and channels of communication.

One of the reasons for this difficulty is that more disciplines need to be mastered than before. And it is more expensive because brands today need to be represented in more places in order to achieve the same results. In the USA, in the San Fransisco Bay area alone, an average .com start-up spends 25 million dollars per year on marketing and branding.

The development in the media in recent years shows that the level of noise has increased considerably. There are many more radio and television channels financed by advertising worldwide, and digital media have finally taken off. The public has embraced the medium of the Internet.

That is why we have written this book.

A new source of income

Up till now the Internet has been regarded by most companies as yet another marketing channel, an activity which did not involve potential income.

However, this image is undergoing a transformation. Today the Internet is being recognised as an underlying technology supporting the whole business: commerce, operation, customer service and marketing. The number of companies which in their daily business can show real earnings derived from their use of the medium has grown exponentially. A formula has finally been found that utilises a website to strengthen brand loyalty and generate sales. This is something which has become an expensive task via the traditional media.

Historically the Internet is the closest we have come to the perfect market. The new medium not only creates awareness, activates a need, helps the user to evaluate a product and creates the intention to buy, but also makes it possible for the user to buy the product there and then. In addition the Internet can make it possible for the product to be serviced.

What other media can provide such a market?

Restrictions such as a lack of overview, remoteness, inadequate information and excessive difficulty do not exist on the Internet. It has opened the door to myriad interesting possibilities, which we take pleasure in describing to you in this book.

From niche to mass medium

The Internet has already demonstrated its function as a mass medium:

- The 1996 presidential election in the USA will be regarded by many people as the last conventional election that did not take place online. The Internet stood for in-depth, elaborating comments, identification, topicality and factuality. This can be contrasted with the television which could only deal with the many themes of the election superficially. At the same time the Internet was able to make local election results available to the public much earlier than any other media. In the course of just 10 hours, 50 million Americans opted to follow the election on CNN's home page. Two years later 14 percent of the American population chose to download the Starr report about their president's activities.

- For one week at the end of 1997 more than 80 million people followed Pathfinder's travels on Mars via the Internet – a unique record for the non-commercial organisation NASA which proved that the public's desire for topical and factual information overcame the barrier of gaining access to the Internet.
- Shortly after Princess Diana's funeral thousands of people chose to express their sorrow by developing websites specially dedicated to 'England's Rose'. All official communications from the British Royal Family were also published on the Internet. The medium was no longer just a kind of plaything, but a meeting place for communication between the common people and the Royal Family.
- When the Albanian population of Kosovo were evicted by war, more than 4,000 websites were established around the world in only four weeks to financially support hundreds of thousands of refugees.

The Internet makes new demands on brands

In many areas the Internet is in the process of changing the buying habits of the individual consumer:

- Well over 10,000 people a day buy books from the world's largest bookshop, www.amazon.com
- More than 15,000 people monitor their courier deliveries every day via www.fedex.com and www.dhl.com
- More than 97 million people have downloaded the latest Flash version at www.macromedia.com
- More than 26,000 bunches of flowers are ordered

each day via www.interflora.com and www.1800flowers.com

- Dell Computers sells about five million dollars worth of computer equipment each day via www.dell.com
- Charles E. Schwab trades in over two billion dollars worth of securities each week on www.schwab.com
- In the USA, 20 percent of all new cars are now sold via the Internet on sites such as www.autobytel.com, www.carpoint.com and www.edmunds.com

All of this via the net or, to give it its more sexy name, cyberspace.

The enormous potential offered by the Internet also makes great demands of the producers of brands, who in the future will have to be able to develop integrated interactive communication that activates all levels of the sales process in the space of just a few minutes.

In this book we focus on what happens when a brand not only speaks but also listens, learns and understands; when a brand communicates individually to the consumer.

It should be noted that this medium is not based on communication with the lowest common denominator, which is what the traditional media offers. Instead the medium can adapt its content in response to each consumer's profile, requirements and expectations and can thus create a bond between the brand and the user.

This book shows how such a bond will change brand values and how it is possible to develop a dynamic online brand platform. We have chosen not to specifically focus on disciplines like Electronic Commerce (e-commerce) or Electronic Operations (e-operations). Rather we give most attention to the theory of creating strong inertacive branding (i-branding).

The Internet is not just a discipline, a parameter in the marketing plan, a gimmick or a new product off the shelf which advertising agencies can use. The Internet is a discipline which, in addition to building up a brand, is well on the way to changing the philosophy behind many companies.

LEGO is thus no longer just traditional plastic building blocks, but digital fantasies on the screen. Disney is no longer just cartoons and films, but living figures with which children can interact. Barbie has come alive and is more enjoyable, as it is now possible to design her clothes and follow her daily life on the screen. Yellow Pages is no longer just a reference book but a digital directory with undreamed-of search capabilities and a medium whereby the local butcher can not only show his telephone number but also the special offers for the day. Kodak is no longer photographic prints, but digital images which you can access on a separate website at AOL when you develop the 'ordinary' prints.

These are important factors at a time when it is a question of mattering to the consumers. This requires something more than just words and good intentions.

Eighty percent of all businesses in the USA and UK are already online

Practically all companies in the developed world are in the process of going on the net. Unfortunately this is often more out of necessity than desire.

Studies show that 80 percent of all companies with representation on the Internet are there because their competitors are also there. This means presence on the Internet is more often the result of a defensive rather than an offensive strategy.

This fact alone should give food for thought. After all, the Internet is an interactive medium. If the companies do not take the offensive in the battle for the attention of the consumers, a single click with the mouse will suffice: thank you and goodbye, new scene, new challenges, new opportunities.

A defensive strategy is problematical, as in the long term the Internet will change almost everything about a company: its organisation, the qualifications of individual employees, the core processes of the business and in many cases the company's products, sales and distribution.

In this book we offer suggestions for how an action-oriented strategy can be developed to point the company in the right direction.

Success provides experience

The following pages describe how brands are built up, developed and maintained on the Internet. We review over 70 websites and more than 40 international case studies which have been successful and provide examples of how a website can be integrated in a marketing plan.

In addition we take a look into the future to see how the medium will develop in the years to come and what significance these changes will have for both national and international producers of branded products.

Who will benefit from reading this book?

We have written this book for all those who are interested in the Internet and the future.

It is aimed in particular at those who are responsible for developing their company's Internet strategy. This involves traditional marketing and IT managers, and to an increasing extent upper management as the use of the medium begins to influence the development of the whole organisation.

The book is also relevant for all entrepreneurs who view the Internet as an opportunity for creating new companies, new brands and in particular innovative ways of thinking and acting.

Summary of chapters

The book presumes a knowledge of the Internet at a novice user level.

Chapters 1–2 introduce the Internet and its construction. The first chapter lays down a conceptual framework for the understanding of the Internet in a historic and media-related context, while the second chapter is aimed at those with little or no knowledge or experience of the Internet.

Chapters 3–4 focus on the Internet as an effective marketing tool. They describe how you can draw up a situation-oriented strategy incorporating the Internet in a marketing plan.

Chapter 5 defines the concept 'interactivity' and focuses on why good navigation and intelligent user design are fundamental for successful websites.

Chapter 6 explains how you can build up relations and create bonds between the brand and the user.

Chapters 7–9 focus on how a brand strategy can be made interactive and how to ensure that the interactive communication focuses on the brand and its set of values.

Chapter 10 examines the concept 'communities' and the commercial opportunities that arise when demographic, geographic or interest-based meeting places are developed on the Internet.

Chapters 11–12 discuss how traffic and awareness can

be generated by marketing the websites both via the Internet itself and via traditional media.

Chapters 13–15 investigate future prospects and the new opportunities that are arising in cyberspace today.

Breaking new ground

This book is the first ever to focus on the role of how to brand-build on the Internet.

We have written the book in order to give the reader effective methods for generating and maintaining the dialogue between the brand and the consumer. It also provides direction for strengthening and integrating the brand in the dialogue with consumers.

The book contains many tried and tested international examples which can save companies unnecessary development costs, repetition of tests that have already been carried out and, not least, bitter experience.

In addition, the book provides relevant links to successful websites, addresses of useful websites and links to websites containing valuable data for anyone planning to go on the Internet. At the end of the book there is a glossary for those still unfamiliar with the Internet's jargon.

We hope you will enjoy the book.

CHAPTER 1

The Internet in historic perspective

"All media are extensions of some human faculty — psychic or physical. The wheel is an extension of the foot — the book is an extension of the eye — clothing an extension of the skin. Media, by altering the environment, evoke in us unique ratios of sense perceptions. The extension of any one sense alters the way we think and act — the way we perceive the world. When these ratios change, men change."

Marshall McLuhan, *The Medium is the Message*

The Internet is the newest medium we have – the most recent breakthrough in communication technology. The Internet is still so new that we would be justified in asking whether today we understand the medium and its possibilities and characteristics, commercial as well as non-commercial. In many ways you could say that the Internet has reached only the black and white level of television.

The Internet is of course not the first medium that humans have created. We can therefore learn from how the generations before us regarded the media that they were presented with in their time, and go on from there.

By way of introduction it is, however, quite interesting to look at why the individual communication technologies arose. The popular conception is that technologies arise to meet human needs. According to this, the telephone would have been invented and accepted because people found that sending letters was too slow.

However, is it really true that 'necessity is the mother of invention'? No, because it does not seem reasonable or natural that we can recognise a need for something before we have actually been presented with that 'something'. No-one felt a need for cinema, radio, television or for that matter the Internet, before they became aware that those media existed.

Considering the media (communication technologies) that are known today, it is characteristic that the people who invented them – and those who first accepted them – often did not have any clear idea of what they would actually be used for. Alexander Graham Bell, who invented the telephone together with Thomas Watson in 1876, believed that the telephone would be used as a kind of hearing apparatus for the deaf. As a teacher in a school for the deaf this belief was natural.

The telephone was never used as a hearing apparatus and, like most media, its potential changed with time – or only became apparent after it was been put into use.

Alexander Graham Bell was not the only one who was on the wrong track when he tried to foresee the use of his invention. Thomas Watson, former IBM president said in 1943, "I think there is a world market for about five computers."

Introduction and development of electronic media

If you look a little simplistically at the electronic media today, most have passed through three stages regarding their introduction, acceptance and implementation:

Toy or novelty stage
The medium is presented as a kind of gimmick.

The mirror stage
The medium is no longer regarded as a gimmick, but is 'looked through' as a transparent reflection of reality.

The art form stage
The medium creates its own reality – a reality which is structured in a way which can be meaningful taking into account the medium's specific technology – that is, where the medium assumes a special unique form.

The three media stages

Source: Poul Levinson (adapted)

In 1878 pictures that moved, *motion pictures*, were seen for the first time. Edward Muybridge's 'Horse in Motion' created wonder and interest. The interest in the film sequence was not just due to the fact that it proved that a galloping horse has all four legs off the ground at the same time, but also because it was technically possible to show such moving pictures.

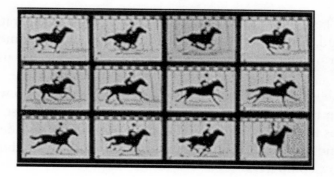

Film technology developed slowly and cinema became
a reflection of reality when it became technically possible to film in the dark. Filming was moved indoors and
a camera was placed in front of the stage in a theatre
and the whole play was filmed from the one viewpoint
without a break.

With the 'invention' of editing, the medium slowly
acquired its unique form. The cinema no longer
depicted a correct 'reality', understood as a true reproduction of time and place. In the cinema it was possible
instead to 'construct' a new reality – an illusion on

film – which was fascinating and convincing and, not least, unique to the medium.

Similarly, *radio* was a gimmick when first introduced. The first transmission of a voice occurred in 1906 and people were amazed that it was technically possible.

When the first 'proper' radio transmissions were broadcast in 1920 it was believed that the correct form for the medium had been found. The radio transmissions took the form of a radio announcer reading an item of news or a report – straight from a newspaper. How else was the medium to be used? Only when at a later date people started to use the radio for the transmission of music, plays and live reporting of important events, such as sporting occasions, did the medium acquire a form that was unique to it. In May 1937 the zeppelin *Hindenburg* exploded and caught fire shortly before landing. A radio reporter was on the scene and his live report of the disaster is still remembered as one of the most moving this medium has provided.

Television was officially launched in New York in 1939. Recognition of the unique characteristics of the medium took somewhat longer than a decade. The content of television consisted mainly of long feature films – just as the content of radio was initially made up of readings from the newspaper. Only when live transmissions began to be screened during the *Golden Age of Television* did the medium's unique form start to develop.

One of the brains behind the invention of television, Philo T. Farnsworth, was for a long time very critical of the medium he had spent more than 10 years developing. However, on 20 July 1969 when he – along with 600 million other viewers – watched man take his first steps on the moon, he declared, "It was all worth it for this."

Media made the world smaller

Common to all the media described is that they each made the world a little bit smaller – changed people's attitudes, contributed to the collective consciousness and changed the framework for people's perception of reality. The examples are innumerable. Here are just a few: Silent films and feature films showed exotic animals and foreign cultures. The radio brought the news of the attempt on the life of the Austro-Hungarian crown prince, news which is considered by many to have started the First World War. All those who were watching television in 1963 remember the pictures of the assassination of John F. Kennedy.

Utilisation of the media

As mentioned above, it has often taken quite a long time to find the unique form of a medium. The reason for this is that when they are introduced most media are utilised in accordance with the 'rear-view mirror principle'. New media were used to handle functions which one or more other existing media had previously fulfilled – for the reason that people try to understand the new media from the basis of a known conceptual framework. The medium gradually matures and its unique form is found. However, the further development and maturing of a medium are seldom the result of a conscious deliberate process, but rather the result of trial and error. The descriptions of the early utilisation – and later maturing – of radio and television exemplify this process.

The Internet viewed in the light of our experiences

Based on the principles outlined here, the Internet is yet another example of a technology whose application and use can be regarded as unintentional – and a technology which has furthermore changed form and content in the space of just a few years.

The question is whether we have progressed so far as to have attained an understanding of the Internet. There are strong indications that history is about to repeat itself, as once again the characteristics from previous media are transferred to a new medium. When communicating via the Internet this can be in the form of 'electronic mail' and if you have a 'favourite page' you insert a 'bookmark'. The starting point for a website is a home page – in spite of the fact that hyperlinks in principle have made one starting point superfluous and have opened the door to innumerable starting points. We are called visitors, but are we in fact not more than that? Would the description 'participants' not be more correct? There is nothing invidious about this situation but it sows the seed of suspicion that we still do not have a complete understanding of the Internet. For who can say whether today's Internet is at the gimmick stage, a transparent reflection of reality or whether someone has managed to turn the medium into an 'art form'? There is also the question of what needs the technology will create in the long term.

The way we see the Internet will change dramatically. Today, the Internet has just reached the equivalent of black and white television. So what is the 'colour version' of the Internet going to look like?

It is only a matter of time before we truly can say "One Home. Several Devices. One Voice." Forget only accessing the Internet from a PC in the future. The Internet is going to be everywhere – in your television, in your fridge, palm pilot, mobile phone, even in your fixed-line telephone. The Internet will soon be separated from any particular device – like the PC – and will connect everything. The Internet will also start to change its structure.

Brands in the future will talk together. The future is all about networks, and making devices talk together.

FACT

In 1950 three percent of Procter & Gamble's media spending went to television. By 1955, 80 percent of the total media budget was devoted to television.

FACT

In 1998 Procter & Gamble established their first worldwide online centre. The purpose: to ensure that Procter & Gamble would be prepared to move their television budget onto the net at the right time.

When Bang & Olufsen developed the world's first Stereo Link system in the 1980s – where the stereo could talk with other electronic devices such as the television, the phone, the light and the video recorder – it was a world sensation. A few months from now, the television will be talking to your fridge, summarising all relevant food commercials and ordering the items it knows you like, but at a discount rate. Extracts of this information will be available in all sorts of devices. Everything from the palm pilot to the mobile phone or the car will be able to inform you about what is going on.

Soon it will be possible to ask the phone or the palm pilot, when standing in a video store, what movies you have rented in the past and what movies it would recommend you watch.

So is this the colour version of the Internet? Yes, but remember that the development of television did not stop after it began broadcasting in colour.

Would you have been able to predict the World Wide Web six years ago? Well, that is how old it is.

CHAPTER 11

Introduction to the Internet

*"The Internet is so large,
so powerful and enveloping
that for some people
it is a splendid substitute for life."*

Andrew Brown

The origins of the Internet date back to 1969 when the United States Defense Department developed the so-called ARPAnet. The ARPAnet was intended to link military networks with a certain number of other networks in such a way that it could still function even though individual parts broke down, for example as a result of acts of war. The solution to this problem was to make all the connected computers able to communicate with each other, without having to communicate via one and the same central computer (server). The Internet itself became a reality in 1983 when, with the relaxing of tensions between the USA and the Soviet Union, the network became available for non-military purposes.

The National Science Foundation in the USA developed the network further so that it could be used by American universities for the exchanging of reports, research results, etc. Later the network was adopted successfully by European research establishments, as it was cheap and relatively easy to use. Since then the quality and capacity of the network has been continually improved and today the network comprises universities, local authorities and organisations as well as companies and private individuals.

What really provided the impetus for the development, use and penetration of the Internet was when employees at CERN (the European Laboratory for Particle Physics in Switzerland), led by Tim Berners-Lee, developed the World Wide Web (WWW) at the start of 1990. Today the Internet is like Pandora's box. There are millions of compartments containing information just waiting to be explored – and unimagined opportunities for communication.

Protocols, linguistic standards and programming – in brief

When two computers communicate with each other they do not use an open line such as when two people talk together over the telephone. Each requires the transfer of files and each file is divided into small data packages which are sent via a vast number of nodes from the sender to the recipient. The tools responsible for dividing and collecting the data packages are called communication protocols – or just protocols. A protocol can be regarded as a type of linguistic standard that enables the computers to 'talk' to each other.

The most commonly used protocols at present are SMTP (Simple Mail Transfer Protocol) used for e-mail communication, HTTP (Hyper Text Transfer Protocol) used for communication on the WWW, and NNTP (Network News Transfer Protocol) used for communication in news groups.

One of the more central elements in the technology underlying the Internet, from a marketing point of view, is the HTML document. HTML (Hyper Text Markup Language) is a specification of and a standard for how text and documents are to be constructed and coded so that they can be read by a browser (Netscape Navigator or Microsoft Internet Explorer). Using hypertext (hyperlinks) it is possible, by marking parts of a document, to point to underlying documents or even third-party documents provided by other servers.

In order for the Internet to function, underlying each hypertext (hyperlink) there is a precise specification of where the document in question is to be found – a so-called URL address. Everyone who provides documents on the Internet has a URL (Uniform Resource Locator), an address that makes possible the identification of a number of characteristics of the document.

A URL address is constructed of several elements and often looks something like the diagram overleaf.

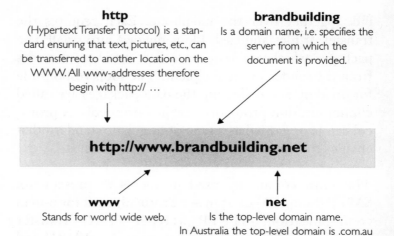

URL address.

http
(Hypertext Transfer Protocol) is a standard ensuring that text, pictures, etc., can be transferred to another location on the WWW. All www-addresses therefore begin with http:// …

brandbuilding
Is a domain name, i.e. specifies the server from which the document is provided.

http://www.brandbuilding.net

www
Stands for world wide web.

net
Is the top-level domain name.
In Australia the top-level domain is .com.au
In the USA .com signifies commercial servers, .org non-profit organisations, etc.

The three levels of the Internet

Today the Internet can be divided into three levels, each having millions of users all over the world: e-mail, news groups and mailing lists, and the world wide web.

The three Internet levels.

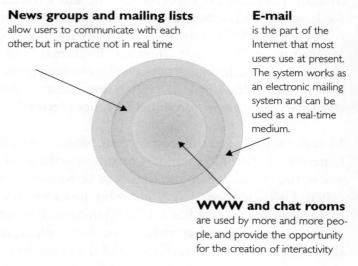

News groups and mailing lists
allow users to communicate with each other, but in practice not in real time

E-mail
is the part of the Internet that most users use at present. The system works as an electronic mailing system and can be used as a real-time medium.

WWW and chat rooms
are used by more and more people, and provide the opportunity for the creation of interactivity

Source: Peter Jakobsson (adapted)

The Internet is not just the world wide web – amusing, entertaining or serious websites. Electronic mail (e-mail) is the commonest communication tool on the Internet today. E-mail can also be regarded as the communication tool that really made the Internet popular. Today many more e-mails are sent than ordinary letters; soon Internet traffic will exceed telephone traffic.

An e-mail address can be recognised by the 'at' symbol @. If the address is glenn@williams.com.au, 'glenn' is a unique name for the recipient, 'williams' specifies the server to which the recipient belongs, '.com' is the category and '.au' the country where the server is.

It is not only possible to send messages via e-mail but also data files – text, pictures, sound, etc. – at the cost of a local telephone call. Now more and more 'alternative' ISPs are entering the market, offering completely free access to the Internet. A concept like www.freeonline.com.au offers users' four hours free surfing per day and unlimited free surfing within 4000 defined websites. Users pay with their personal data.

News groups (UseNet) and mailing lists

The purpose of news groups is to allow users to read and comment upon discussion items from other users and so widen their own horizons and/or share their own knowledge about a certain subject with others.

Another way to receive, or impart, new knowledge about a certain subject is via various mailing lists. When an e-mail is sent to the mailing list's own e-mail address, it is forwarded automatically to a number of e-mail addresses (persons) who have signed on the list. The difference between news groups and mailing lists is that you do not actively open and read a number of discussion documents in which you are interested as in a newsgroup, but instead you get e-mails sent straight to your computer. If the individual users on a particular mailing list are very active you can receive an enormous number of e-mails a day, possibly more than you can manage to read. However, there are now programs available that can sort the incoming post according to criteria which the user determines.

Interactive media:
IRC (chat rooms) and WWW, etc.

Today there are a number of interactive media on the Internet. The best known are WWW and IRC.

Chat rooms

With Internet Relay Chat (IRC) – popularly called a chat room or chat forum – users can communicate in real time. Chat forums work in principle the same way as news groups, but in real time and not necessarily with a predefined subject. There are many well-developed versions, such as the AOL-owned ICQ. Now a new generation of chat rooms is appearing, including uTOK; users here can post comments throughout sites on the Internet. These notes put the writer in touch with people of similar opinions.

WWW

Today when people hear about the Internet, most think immediately 'world wide web'. The above review of the many facets of the Internet is intended to show that the Internet is not just WWW, but that WWW is a part of the Internet. However, it is easy to understand why focus on the Internet today is directed principally at WWW, as it is here that users experience it in earnest.

HTML documents can be viewed on WWW as text, graphics, sound, pictures or animations, or combinations of these. WWW is thus the graphic part of the Internet. HTML programming makes it possible to develop websites where the users, via hypertext, can navigate between an immense number of documents and in this way define for themselves their supply of information.

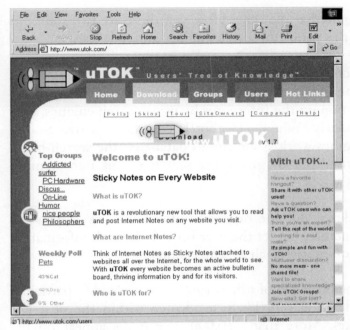

uTOK is one of the most popular chat post-it notes sites. It offers consumers a chance to share ideas; to stand on their own soapbox. Through uTOK.com, users can post and read notes on any website, turning sites into thriving global bulletin boards. Uniquely offering real-time polling, user-generated questionnaires and limitlessly diverse user-communities, uTOK.com introduces small voices to the roar of world discussion.

Up to a couple of years ago the majority of all websites consisted of 'flat' pages where it was only possible to read text or look at graphics and pictures. Within the past couple of years a new generation of tools for interactive programming has seen the light of day. These now make it possible to develop websites where the structure is not 'flat' but resembles multi-media presentations or interactive computer games.

One of the most important programs for interactive programming is Java, developed by Sun Microsystems. If you have a Java-compatible browser such as Netscape Navigator or Microsoft Internet Explorer, the program runs here. If a website is visited where certain effects have been created using Java, these will be displayed automatically.

Searching the Internet

As the Internet today consists of millions of computers and contains millions and millions of documents, it can be exceedingly difficult to find the information required at the time. However, there are two solutions to this problem: search engines and indexes.

Search engines and indexes

www.yahoo.com
www.hotbot.com
www.altavista.com
www.lycos.com

One of the most popular ways today of finding information on the Internet is by using search engines, particularly Yahoo!, Hotbot/Lycos and Excite. Search engines work as enormous databases, the search being carried out by giving the search engine one or more keywords.

Indexes do not organise information in a database structure, but let the user browse through information in categories such as 'entertainment'.

TIP

Want to get updated information about a specific country? Visit www.odci.gov/cia/ publications/factbook/ index.html – the service is free of charge.

The principle of using search engines and in particular indexes is very likely to change within the next few years. More than 250,000 new pages appear on the Internet every day. The huge number of pages already on the net now leads to confusing results from search engines, often producing more than a thousand link opportunities per search query. In the future it is very likely that 'infomediaries' will become the new generation of search engines. An infomediary is based on the idea of learning more and more about the consumer, until in the end it will become able to predict the consumer's need and behaviour even before the consumer has thought about it. More coverage of infomediaries can be found in Chapter 14.

The Internet as an effective marketing tool

"On the Internet, everything we know about marketing is out the window."

Michael Gerret, interactive marketing manager,
Chrysler Communications

It is doubtful whether it is really the case that all accumulated knowledge about marketing must be rethought in order to be able to be used on the Internet, but it is a fact that the Internet introduces new ways of solving old problems. It is equally clear that so far we have just seen the tip of the iceberg. Innovative and creative ways of using the Internet are continually arising and the ways of measuring success and failure are still being revealed. This chapter describes how a company can get started. We also summarise the 10 most important characteristics of the Internet which distinguish it from other more familiar media.

It's all about communication – not technology

One of the first things we need to understand is that the Internet is a channel of communication. It is very possible that for the time being it will remain the computer that provides access to the Internet and that the Internet will continue to contain an incredible number of technical facets. However, this focus on the technology which has applied so far on the Internet has drawn our attention in the wrong direction. From a marketing point of view the Internet should be used when it can provide value compared with the traditional ways of doing things – otherwise it should not.

Surprisingly, advertising agencies have turned out to be very conservative with regard to their understanding and use of this new medium. This is probably because the budgets for Internet development, in the beginning, were taken from the traditional marketing budget. It has therefore been a question of transferring money from one medium to another. And whether it is a question of the launch of a new product, a response activity or an advertisement for trainees, there will always be a traditional alternative to the use of the Internet. That is the reason why there is no great incentive to try new and risky methods.

However, it is now the case that the Internet has characteristics which mean that the use of the Internet in many respects not only makes sense but also gives better results. Before these are discussed, we will review the process of getting onto the Internet.

The three development stages

Regarding the many millions of companies currently on the Internet, their development can be divided into three stages, showing how far a company has gone in the process and what benefits the company is gaining from being on the Internet.

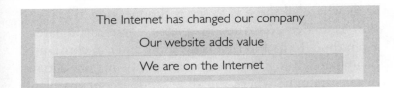

The Internet has changed our company

Our website adds value

We are on the Internet

The three development stages of a company on the Internet.

Stage 1. Hurrah! We are online!

In fact, not much is required to be represented on the net. For about $200 a month (and at present for considerably less in the case of small providers) a company can lease space in a web hotel (a shared Internet server which contains the company's website).

If the company's name has not already been reserved as an Internet address, this service can be obtained for a couple of hundred dollars more.

Most EDP (Electronic Data Processing) programs that are used in a normal office environment can be exported in a format (HTML) that can be used directly on the Internet, making the work of creating a number of static text pages minimal. And more and more programs are coming on the market, which make it possible to create a rational layout with logos and picture files without having to be an Internet expert.

A number of small, recently established web bureaux offer to create finished websites for companies for as little as $1,000 to $5,000.

You only get one chance on the Internet. If you disappoint the users they won't come back.

As a result, many companies have hurried to invest in a high-tech visiting card, a notice board or at least static company representation on the Internet. At best the return from such an activity is minimal, but it is a very dangerous strategy. Users can see whether the company really believes in the new medium and wishes to engage in serious communication with the user or is just testing the water. This has also led to many companies biting off more than they could chew, resulting in websites with areas where all there is to see is the message 'This section is under construction, please come again later'. Even though the Internet is dynamic and can constantly be updated, this gives a bad impression – imagine a mail-order catalogue where the shoe section contains blank pages with the message 'We are not quite ready, but we will try to have a selection ready next time.'

If the expectations of the company's target group are not fulfilled, the meeting with the company results in disappointment. The company has wasted an opportunity and the customers will be unlikely to pay a return visit.

However, there are many companies that choose to start here. The investment is visible and 'after all we can always opt out again'. But, as Internet developers, we are yet to see a company go on the net only to decide that this was after all not a place where it wanted to be represented.

Therefore if a company decides to be represented on the Internet, it must be with content that means something to the target group of current and potential customers and it must have a functionality that satisfies the target group. In other words, it must be in a way that leads the company in the direction of a solution which in the long term can give a satisfactory return in the form of a stronger brand and profile, or directly in the form of financial benefits through savings and sales.

Stage 2. Our website adds value

If the company's website is the result of a planned and rational strategy, then it will have been considered whether it is a good idea for the company to be on the net at all. How can we add value to the way we used to do things? How can we differentiate our company from the competitors by introducing new services through the Internet? These are some of the questions that need to be answered to find the real reasons for being online. There will still be many companies for which it is sensible to wait rather than to rush onto the Internet. But nevertheless it is at stage two that companies should begin. It may well be the case that the strategic benefits only become apparent at a later stage, but it is important that they are identified from the start – and there are many possibilities: insurance companies which give their customers the ability to file claims online, finance companies which permit online applications with an e-mail response the same day, airlines which offer online booking of flight tickets, petrol companies which make it possible to check up on bonus points earned, media which by means of dialogue let the readers be an active part of the product, or simply websites which provide the opportunity for trade. Common to all the examples above is the fact that the customer of the company concerned feels 'empowered', as they say in the USA.

Relevance is required!

By providing customers with tools via the Internet that make it possible for individuals to work with the company's products, to have the freedom to decide for themselves and to receive precisely the information that is needed when it is needed, the customers feel that they have received better service. The relations with the company and the product have thereby been improved. In other ways, the ability to solve a problem for the user in a more convenient, more effective, cheaper, funnier, easier way means that value has been added to the process.

And it is at this stage that a website starts to make sense. By providing a better service for the customers, creating new products and services and breaking down corporate barriers for the benefit of the customer, a platform is created which puts the company in a position to act in a customer-oriented way. Only at this point in time will the Internet be able to assist in strengthening the relationship between the customer and the company.

The days of 'under construction' are over.

There is currently no other real option than to start the company's web activity at stage two, bypassing stage one, as the time is past for websites that are the result of the 'experimental phase'. Customers expect and demand much more today, so if the company is not willing to come up with a solution which gives the customer a better experience and in this way is of strategic benefit, it should refrain from becoming involved.

In this book we will examine, with a number of case studies, those companies which have successfully created websites that have become yet another reason for choosing them rather than their competitors – the website itself has become a unique selling point.

Stage 3. The Internet has changed the company

More and more we think of the Internet as a business transformer. The Internet will not only impact on the marketing department but also sales and distribution, the customer service department and even product development. So we have to think of the Internet as an underlying technology that will affect the whole company and our value chains. And this cannot happen without changes being made.

The Internet as a strategic tool

The situation in 1997 & 1998

The situation in 1997 and 1998.

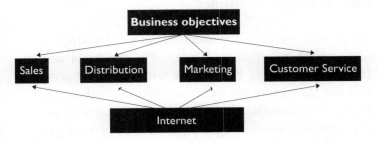

The situation in 2000 and beyond

The situation in 2000 and beyond.

So far only a few companies have reached this stage but there will be many more. It is quite possible to imagine the Internet as a digital branch of a bank where all the services that are to be found in an ordinary branch of a bank will be available. Even contact with a personal advisor will be possible by means of video conferences over the net. What role will the many branches which are only open from 10 a.m. to 4 p.m. on weekdays play in the future? When the consumers no longer regard the branch network as an important parameter and would rather make contact from home, there will be great structural changes. This will not happen overnight, but in the USA changes are already starting to take effect, for example in the travel and car industries, and these changes will probably take place everywhere at a rate acceptable to customers. When well-established value chains are destroyed, it means that a lot of intermediaries will disappear unless they succeed in redefining their role and finding new ways of justifying their existence. And it will be difficult because the Internet in many cases will be able to do the job better and cheaper because of its global presence and potential for reducing transaction costs.

A number of different industries, including those dealing with the type of product that can exist just as easily in a purely digital version, will notice the changes first: booksellers, libraries, music stores, newspapers and magazines, the film industry, the financial sector – have we forgotten anyone?

There will also be differences in the way in which companies with tangible and intangible products use the Internet. Whereas companies with tangible products will use the net to add value to existing products and to create integrated marketing campaigns linked closely to the product, the intangible products will to a greater extent be able to be traded, serviced, changed and distributed over the net. Here the Internet will have a more fundamental influence upon the company's way of doing business.

In addition, as far as the Internet is concerned, all companies should consider during their strategy planning what changes may affect them in the next two or three years. Only in this way can they be well prepared and ensure that the activities which are commenced now will take the company in the correct and desired direction.

The strategy must be
deeply rooted in the organisation

The further a company progresses in its Internet development, the more important it is that the solution is embraced by the company itself. It was easy with stage one websites. These could be both developed and managed by an external co-ordinator without any great input or involvement on the part of the company, which may as a result neglect to allocate sufficient resources for this work. However, from as early as stage two, much greater demands are made of the company if the web strategy is to be a success.

The company's website can easily be developed so that the company or the brand is depicted with the values which are required. These can be concepts such as dynamic, innovative, trustworthy or the like. However, unless the company assumes ownership of its Internet solution from and including stage two (enabling the users to work interactively with the company's products, enter into two-way dialogue and other things which characterise as a minimum a stage two solution) then there is a danger of a situation where there is a huge gap between the position/the promise the company has on the Internet, and the perception of the company in reality, and this can very easily have major negative repercussions.

It is important to remember that when we talk about companies having to change because of the Internet, this is a question of much more than just the company's marketing strategy. When it is used correctly the Internet can change a company's way of selling and distributing goods, the company's actual core processes, its organisation, the power situation between the different departments, its personnel policy, and the required qualifications of employees, etc. This is quite simply because the Internet clears away many barriers and creates the perfect market.

When we start to integrate the solutions into the company's backend systems, we immediately need to rethink a lot of logistic parameters. It is not enough for an online grocery webstore to have the perfect technical solution, if we haven't thought about how to deal with the fact that 80 percent of the orders will come between 2 p.m. and 5 p.m. on Friday with an expectation that they be delivered Saturday morning at the latest.

The solution must be rooted in the organisation

	ROI	Company's involvement
Stage 3	↑	controlled internally
Stage 2		
Stage 1		controlled externally

Companies must be intellectually committed to the net

In addition to an incredible number of aspects of the company being affected by the Internet, the speed at which these changes must be implemented will be brutal. Change of this magnitude makes great demands on the internal management and requires the solution to be accepted by and deeply embedded in the highest levels of the company, namely the board of directors.

It is equally important that these changes are communicated internally and that the consequences are discussed. Too many companies have already implemented Internet solutions without informing all the employees who have contact with the customer on a daily basis or whose work will be affected by the changes. This means not only that they cannot help the customer but also that there is a danger that they will be turned against this technological change.

In order to succeed with a stage three strategy all the frontline employees must be encouraged to understand the company's digital aim – they must be brought intellectually onto the net. This can be achieved by internal courses and seminars or, even better, by the company giving its employees access to the Internet, for example in their own homes.

When should we start?

Right now! That is the short answer and everything indicates that it is also the correct one. The penetration of the Internet has increased exponentially and, if this trend were to continue (which is unlikely), by the year 2005 there would be more people on the Internet than there are people on this planet! Whether it continues at this rate or not, the time has come to review the company's position. Experience shows that at best it takes about four to five months to prepare the correct basis for decision-making and to have it approved by the board. Following this there must be a development period which is seldom less than three months. If the solution is to be tested thoroughly, an extra month must be added to the timetable for testing and implementation.

In addition, experience shows that it takes a year before the use of the Internet is understood and has filtered down through the internal organisation. It is difficult to allocate internal resources to it before it has been demonstrated to be a success and it takes time to re-organise the internal procedures and routines to suit the opportunities provided by the Internet. Furthermore, the company will be forced to learn from its own experiences, both good and bad.

So, if the decision-makers in the company believe in the continued growth of the Internet, they should take the opportunity to gain experience and to make mistakes while the number of visitors is still relatively small.

Where should we start?

Whether the company is already on the Internet or is in the process of considering such a move, it is important to have a clear idea of what the company's mission is and should be in being on the net. This is a good place to start. The company should decide whether it is to be a question of a short-term network activity or a permanent website. Is the presence an expression of a desire for better communication with the company's customers or is it the result of a desire to sell goods via the net? Does the company only want to provide information or is it ready to enter into a dialogue? Will it be possible to attract users to the company's website or should the company instead go to where the users are already? There are many questions to consider, but by defining the reason for going on the Internet and by drawing up a basis for understanding, the company will already be much better equipped when it later calls a halt and asks questions concerning the return on the investment or concerning any changes of course.

When the LEGO group launched their website at the beginning of 1996 it was without having had many thoughts concerning its marketing value. Within the LEGO group it had been discovered that there were thousands of references on the net to the LEGO group's trademark. Many fans and major customers had created in their spare time their own personal versions of a LEGO website as the group apparently did not want to do so.

In this way the the LEGO group was well represented on the net without itself having any influence on what things were written and what tone and style were used. And, what was worse, several of these unofficial LEGO websites could easily be taken as being official, if the user was not aware of their status.

What is special about LEGO group's trademark is that

www.lego.com went online for the first time in 1996.

among net users are a disproportionately large number of (former) customers. Most of the early technology adepts played with LEGO a lot, and are expected to pass their enthusiasm on to their children. Douglas Coupland's book *Microserfs* describes this clearly. 'Have you ever noticed that LEGO plays a far more important role in the lives of computer people than in the general population? To a one, computer technicians spent huge portions of their youth heavily steeped in LEGO and its highly focused, solitude-promoting culture. LEGO was their common denominator toy.' At the millennium, LEGO was voted the best toy of the century, and one of its most important innovations.

Studies carried out by BBDO among Danish major consumers of the colourful bricks show that during the last few years the core values of the LEGO brand have changed in a negative direction. Eight- to 10-year-old boys with lots of LEGO talk about their LEGO like this:

"LEGO is something my parents played with ..."

"When I play with LEGO I am always by myself and I don't talk about it at school ..."

"There aren't enough options, so it is more fun to play with the computer, it's different all the time ..."

"It isn't all that smart to play with LEGO ..."

"If I had to choose between all my LEGO and my computer, then I would choose (long pause) ... my computer."

It therefore was and is extremely important for the LEGO Group to be on the net, but in the right context. For LEGO the Internet can be the ultimate channel of communication with children, while at the same time the difference between promotion and product is erased by means of various activities.

It was also a mistake that the LEGO group initially handed over the responsibility for the existence of the LEGO trademark in the digital universe to its IT department.

This resulted in a website which was not particularly well arranged, where it was difficult to tell whether the primary target group was the children (which would have been natural) or their parents (among other things because there were many long passages in English which the non-English-speaking children did not appreciate). In addition it was very difficult to catch sight of the LEGO group's range of products and primary messages such as 'A new toy every day'. The result was, in fact, not much better than the unofficial websites.

To cap it all, the LEGO group opted right from the start not to give children and adults the opportunity to enter into an e-mail dialogue with the company. And to emphasise that people should not expect to receive any reply from the LEGO group, all e-mails from the LEGO group were sent with the return address blindalley@lego.com.

The mistake of letting web strategy be decided in the EDP or IT department has unfortunately been repeated by many companies in the past three years, which has resulted in great attention being paid to the technical aspects while the content has been given a lower priority and treated almost as an irrelevance. However, this is all wrong. It is important to remember that a brand is based on content, not on technology!

Your web address will itself become a brand name

In spite of this sorry start the LEGO group has had fantastic success. Today the site is controlled by highly skilled marketing people. LEGO was lucky to be on the scene early and to secure an address – www.lego.com – which a four-year-old child can work out, even if they only know the basics about the net. It's a natural place to find the trademark LEGO. If a company has a well-known brand and manages to get an address reserved, the foundation stones are laid for success. LEGO is now the third most visited child website in the world.

The smartest thing available on the LEGO group's website from day one was their 'LEGO Web Club'. Here children could join and create their own primitive home pages. During the first eight months 100,000 children joined this LEGO club and more are joining all the time. LEGO can continuously monitor these members' interests and movement patterns and in time will be able to communicate with them in a targeted way concerning new products, special offers, etc.

Since then LEGO has given even higher priority to its Internet activities, so that www.lego.com today appears as a very inviting place for LEGO addicts and other interested parties. LEGO has made a good start on sales via the net, primarily via local websites where the dialogue with customers also takes place. In addition LEGO now aims to create one of the most visited websites for children and they have taken up the challenge of, for example, Disney Daily Blast which currently has several hundred employees – just to maintain the website! They can do so only because they have an extremely well-regarded and well-known brand where high quality in all areas is expected. Today it is one of the most succesful websites among children all over the world, but it took four years of trial and error to get there!

Be indispensable to the target group

An important parameter for knowing what a company should do on the Internet is to know the target group. It is of course possible to aim at several different segments, but experience shows that this is usually best achieved by means of different activities – via different value centres, if you will.

As the quality of the users' experience is what will bring them back again, analysis of the target group should include the following questions:

- Who are they?
- What is their existing experience of the brand?
- What expectations have they when encountering the brand?
- What demands do they make?
- What interests do they have?

- What needs do they have that the company can fulfil?

By knowing its target group in advance the company can form a clear idea of what user experience to give them.

Know and recognise your core skills

In 1996 a common model for the construction of websites was that large companies tried to construct a medium. Bristol-Myers Squibb created a cyberclub for women with sections on careers and finance specially aimed at women. Toyota created sections with cooking hints and lots for children. Levi's created lifestyle bazaars on the net. All because that was what interested their target group.

The problems with this policy have been twofold. Firstly, in many situations there was too great a gap between the content and the product, and, in addition, in practically all cases today they are competing with dedicated websites where a team of dedicated employees works exclusively with the subject matter concerned, whether it is sport, news, fashion, food or whatever. So the time when companies could play at creating media is past.

It is therefore important that everything the company does is based on the company's products and core skills. The company must recognise its niche and fit in where best it can.

Give the users something to take home – everytime!

When a user visits a website it is with the expectation of obtaining something from the visit, whether concrete information, an entertaining experience, a good bargain or contact with another person. The main thing is that the company must be clear about what it wants visitors to get from a visit – and also whether it is

"It's easier for us to do a site within our core-competencies rather than doing a section about women and careers or women and finance."
Peggy Kelly, vice-president of advertising, Bristol-Myers Squibb

their third visit in one week. Too many companies greet their customers with the same home page month after month. That's like publishing a newspaper without changing the front page – how exciting is that? The front page is the only page that users will see with certainty (unless they have put a bookmark in a special page in the website). It is interesting to think in terms of a session rather than a site. What will the result be of a user visit?

When a company starts to advertise, and as a result might pay 50 cents for a visit, then what the company has decided to offer users once they have landed on the website becomes even more important.

mini**CASE**

Libero

www.libero.dk

SCA – the Swedish competitor to Procter & Gamble – has to outsmart their much bigger rival, and do so on a much smaller budget. This has led to a very progressive Internet strategy. Through direct marketing (letters, print ads and brochures), SCA had already created strong links with expectant and new parents. With the Internet SCA saw an opportunity for real dialogue with their customers, but knew it had to be based on the customers' needs and interests.

Therefore www.libero.dk was created, as a community for parents. It has a large encyclopedia on parenting, plus tools like a 'baby namefinder', and how to choose the right diaper. The site hosts debates, with experts answering all kinds of questions. As a participant you can also buy and sell child-related equipment for free.

But Libero's real killer-app has been a 'baby's own website'. It doesn't take any special skills for parents to upload pictures, write small stories, child wishlists, etc. This enables relatives all over the world to follow the child's progress. It has been very popular, and the kind of loyalty and brand awareness created this way is a lot stronger than is possible with traditional methods.

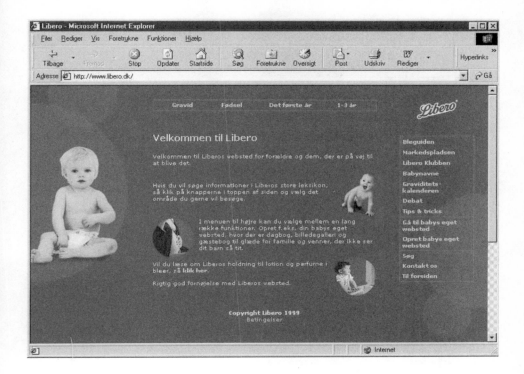

From mass communication to customisation

Everyone is an individual and wants to be treated as such. Internet users are in addition characterised by a marked restlessness. They hate to be bored and demand relevance. They want the company to demonstrate that it has an insight into their problems – they want to have personal advice. Therefore the more personal the communication becomes, the more relevant it is perceived to be and the more seriously it is taken. This has given many marketing people grey hair and led to complex database systems without the result being really regarded as personal. It lacked time – a dimension which was needed before there could be talk of building up relationships with the customers.

Due to its dynamic nature the Internet allows personal communication to occur in a natural way. Early experiments involved giving users their own customised

The front page of the Libero parents community website.

"The Internet Community doesn't consist of one segment of 50 million citizens, but of 50 million segments of one person!"

Howard Reingold, The Well

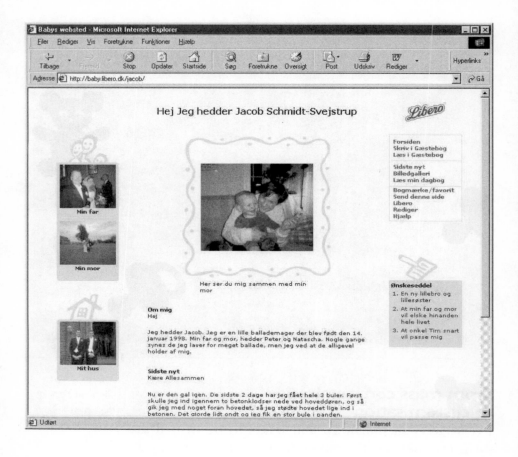

An example of a child's website created by the parents.

newspapers. Later more specialised experiments followed. Common to all these was that the website was gradually regarded more as a database than as a static medium and to an increasing extent the solutions took the wishes of the users as their starting point.

In fact the Internet can be described as a disloyal medium where a search engine or a CD-ROM shop is only the one preferred as long as it still works best and provides the most personal service. This is because it has never been easier to change supplier. Therefore there is still a battle in progress on the Internet; between travel agents, between estate agents, between mortgage credit institutes – in fact practically all the lines of business represented on the net. This is, at the same time, one of the most important reasons for this book focusing upon the building up of loyalty and brands – factors which in the future will be of considerable importance to companies in their fight for the customers.

Understand – and leverage on the strong points of the Internet

A lot has been written and said about the Internet and its strengths over the past 18 months. Some of it is correct but much is rumour and half-truth. Of course orders won't come flooding in from all over the world just because a company opens a website – in Swahili! But that is something that probably only very few hoped for.

Below are listed 10 special characteristics of the Internet, which from a marketing point of view make it a unique medium with some exceptional possibilities – if the medium is used correctly – namely, on its own terms.

1. The Internet is a global medium

One of the unique things about the Internet is that it can be reached from everywhere, regardless of where the computer with the website is physically located. To a company for which exports and foreign markets are important, the Internet offers fantastic opportunities for making available updated information such as manuals, sales material, documentation, etc. At the same time communication with people has never been easier, and it all is carried out at local rate call charges.

The Internet can be expected to give impetus to the gradual abolition of national boundaries in favour of regional differences.

2. The Internet is open 24 hours a day!

This is one of the aspects many financial institutions, such as Firstar, have chosen to concentrate on when launching their website. On the net a service (and a shop) can be open when it suits the customers. When FONA, Scandinavia's largest retail chain within music, video and radio/television, made it possible to apply for a cash loan directly over the net and to receive a reply the same day, it appeared that such an application obviously was something which was easier done in the evening in front of a computer screen rather than in a hectic and crowded FONA shop. That a reply was received the same day (if the application was sent before 7 p.m.) meant there were great advantages in using the Internet method.

3. The Internet is interactive

The concept of interactivity is discussed in more detail in Chapter 5. We will just mention here that when we, as users of the net, are permitted and prompted to take an active part in what is happening, the communication begins to concern us and our needs as users in a way which involves and engages us directly.

4. The Internet is individual

Ideally the activities on the net can be made to suit our needs rather than the company's. Eventually some companies will choose to go so far as to allow us to design the whole website to suit our own taste and preferences; it will become our own website from the moment we enter the first page. An example of this is the customising capabilities of the world's most popular search engine, Yahoo!. They have developed an entrance/portal which makes it possible to create a completely customised version called My Yahoo!.

5. From consumer to 'prosumer'

A lot is being said about mass-produced individuality. The best-known example of this is probably Levi's experiments in selling semi-customised jeans for women. This was a great success but something of a deception as it was only a question of a choice between

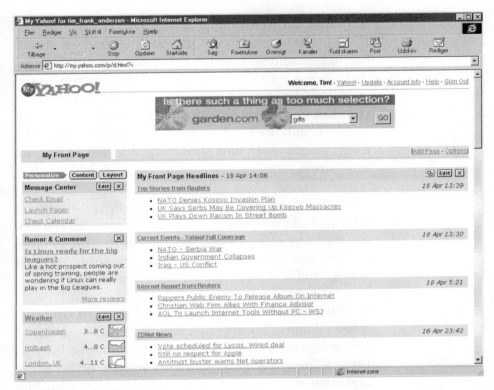

a number of predefined models, although considerably more than normal. However, the Internet does provide the opportunity for the customers to produce their own goods themselves, hence the term 'prosumers'. Dell Computers is one of the few EDP producers in the world which does not use any middlemen. All their computers are sold direct to the customers. Furthermore they are not manufactured until they have been ordered. In this way each computer is different and has an end-user lined up before it is assembled. On the Internet, Dell has developed a veritable smorgasbord so that customers can put together their dream computer in the comfort of their own homes with all the refinements they would wish for. And they can conclude the deal direct. The latest sales figures show that this has been a success. Dell has a turnover of more than five million dollars each day via its website!

Yahoo! was one of the first sites to promote customised club concepts.

Another example of the prosumer idea is found within BMW, which prior to the launch of their Z3 Roadster set up an impressive website where users could design their own dream roadster. The information was stored automatically in a database and as BMW has some of the most loyal customers the database could give a very accurate indication of which combinations were the most sought after and should therefore be put into production.

Along with the prosumer idea comes the possibility of involving the customer in the company's production apparatus by offering self-service, but in a much more inviting and attractive way. This can result in great savings and lead to increased customer loyalty.

6. The Internet is dynamic and easy to update

A few minutes after the tragic accident involving Princess Diana became public knowledge, thousands of Internet users all over the world sat down at their keyboards to comment, discuss and tell of their personal reaction. This is just one example out of many of how the Internet reflects events as they happen. Today, CNN is much more exciting to follow on the Internet than on television. It is important for a company to understand that precisely because it is in the nature of the Internet to be dynamic, relevant and always up to date, these are the requirements which users have of a company's website. There is a difference between a newspaper and a bank, but if the most recent press release is six months old and everything is figuratively covered in a layer of dust, what are things like at head office?

7. The Internet is both a sales and a distribution channel

Trade via the Internet will take off in a big way over the next few years. It is impossible to predict the extent of trade over the net, but a new IDC survey predicts that just the global trade between companies on the net will grow from $600 million in 1998 to $150 billion by the end of the century . However, as there is a wide spread between the predictions from the various analysis institutes, these predictions are often called 'guesstimates'.

For all companies in the market for virtual or digital products the Internet will also become an important channel of distribution, if not one which predominates entirely. Already today everything from software for fonts to digitally scanned-in pictures can be bought and downloaded, and this is increasing. This fact should also give the taxation office something to think about, as not only are the shelves in the virtual digital supermarket infinitely deep (you can download as many browser programs as you want, they are never sold out!), at the moment it is missing out on duties from this trade.

8. The Internet is a two-way medium

One of the fastest-growing activities on the net is 'chatting'. This is carried out in special chat rooms. AOL might be the best example of the success of letting people communicate with each other over the Internet. Its popularity is reflected in the visit statistics. But the Internet is also a two-way medium in many other ways.

On the Internet the user does not have to be satisfied with listening or looking, but can take an active part in the various activities and debates. And this is something that all companies ought to make use of, allowing users to have their say and thereby have an influence upon the design and prioritisation of the future content.

9. The Internet is feedback-oriented

The Internet continually gives users feedback on their actions. If a website is correctly designed the user is never in any doubt as to whether the system has understood the commands sent. In addition the Internet can reward and punish users depending on their behaviour patterns. Advanced websites even adapt themselves to the user's level of knowledge. Feedback is very important for a satisfactory and enjoyable user dialogue.

10. The Internet is everything – everywhere – anytime

Perhaps not yet, but soon. All over the world legislation is being passed to give access via schools, colleges and libraries. In addition the Internet is already available via mobile phone or personal digital assistant, like Palm 6. And before long it will also be possible to get on the Internet via the television and cable network. When the Internet finally becomes an integrated part of our every-day life the medium will be of even greater significance than it is possible to imagine today. Therefore all talk of the Internet's penetration will soon vanish. The major-ity of companies are therefore doing the right thing in defining their own role in this new virtual universe.

CHAPTER IV

Does your product or service suit the Internet?

*"To create a website
without providing the traffic to it,
would be like creating a direct mail campaign
without mailing it."*

Zeek Interactive

Why are 90 percent of all cinema-goers already in their seats by 7 p.m. when the first advertisement begins and why do they not wait until 7.25 p.m. when the feature film starts? Mainly because they regard the advertisements before the film as a bonus. This statistic illustrates very clearly that correct use of a medium is received positively by the user. This also applies in those cases where it is just a question of traditional advertising and where in principle the user pays, both in the form of time and money.

It is basically a matter of taking advantage of the strong aspects of the medium. Apart from the owner, no-one bothers to watch the slide show with the names of local shops that precedes the advertisements proper in the cinema, for the very reason that the slides do not make full use of the medium's unique characteristics. In the same way the Internet is not used in an optimal way at present. Scanning in a brochure and making it available on the Internet is in principle the same as giving a slide show in a cinema; it will never attract our attention. You can see this from everyday life; if you receive an e-mail of more than 20 lines the first thing you do is to print out the text. This is because you lack an overview of the received letter. All communication that can be printed off from the Internet without losing anything in the form of understanding or involvement is in principle not using the Internet optimally. It is very likely that people will print out an ordinary brochure which has merely been scanned in and put on the net. The user's perception of the company has in theory thereby become worse than if the brochure had been distributed in the traditional way. The picture quality is poorer and the overview more difficult, as the content is spread over several pages, with in some cases random page breaks. Of course the sender will experience a benefit in the short term in being able to distribute the brochure cheaply, but the recipient will not have benefited from the possible additional value that could have been gained had the 'brochure' been interactive. It can thus be very difficult to justify the distribution of such communications via the Internet, where the user's expectations about interactivity correspond to a cinema-goer's expectations concerning the use of the film medium by advertisers.

Visit www.frazier-deeter.com and see how a company of lawyers has chosen to use the medium creatively.

Television has proved particularly suited to product demonstration and comparison of two situations, e.g. clothes before and after being washed, or between washing powders A and B. This is perhaps why Proctor & Gamble – maker of some of the world's most successful washing products – is one of the world's leading television advertisers. Most of their television advertisements are based on comparative advertising.

TIP

What Internet game is the most popular at this very moment?

Visit www.arcadium. com

On the other hand, it would be difficult to make a case that television is suitable to advertise, say, bananas or spices. The additional value of using the medium's visual characteristics is limited. All the same, now and then we see advertisements for both on television. If a parallel is drawn with the Internet, it would not immediately appear appropriate to develop websites for toilet paper, bananas or tampons. And it is here that creativity – as in all other communication – comes into the picture.

Libra (in some countries called Libresse), a feminine protection brand, has established a website that hasn't lost the top position on health websites in countries where Libra is marketed since it was launched. Its case study, in Chapter 8, is a good example of how creativity can make a relatively low-interest product very interesting in a web format. On average a visitor spends 15 minutes on the Libragirl website, returning more than three times a year – a total of 45 minutes annually. Compared with an average television exposure of five minutes, this can be considered very high. Besides the big difference in the number of minutes exposed to the

www.libragirl.com.au

medium, a major difference is also that the consumer voluntarily participates on the Libragirl website. Users of the site searched for the address, waited for the pages to download and surfed through the Libragirl pages. This high involvement is not necessarily the case with regards to Libra television advertising.

mini CASE In 1998 MTV ran a campaign on their site claiming that unknown people had managed to gain access to the site and had left unauthorised messages. The hacker plot turned out to be a planned MTV action – introducing a new television show. The case is a good example of how creativity can generate the right momentum about a news story.

JoeBoxer is another good example of how creativity can justify why a product should appear on the Internet without any clear consumer benefits. When visiting the JoeBoxer site (www.joeboxer.com) the visitor will be asked to place the body in front of the screen and download a pair of virtual JoeBoxer underwear. The process, which continues in the same tone-of-voice over more than 30 pages, is pure fun but manages to add an extra dimension to the brand. A more detailed description of how to ensure brand-added value on the internet is described in Chapters 7 to 9.

Creativity was also the key word for one of the most acclaimed campaigns ever run on the Internet – in Brazil. The successful campaign, to promote a local Internet company, is best explained via the illustrations they used (and on the net these illustrations were in fact animated).

Creativity not only increased the click-through rate but ensured more than 10 international awards for this recent campaign promoting an Internet company in Brazil.

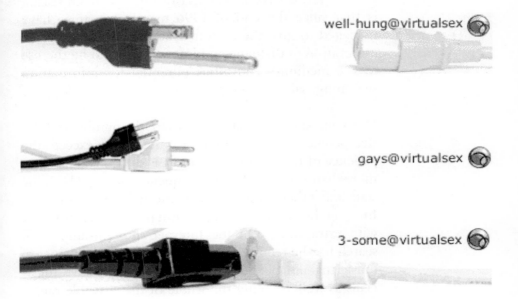

well-hung@virtualsex

gays@virtualsex

3-some@virtualsex

The product's interactive potential is decisive for its relevance on the Internet

Creativity is necessary for the successful integration of the product and the Internet on a branding site in the same way as creativity is the winning factor when it is a question of successful communication on television or in print. The more it is possible to use the medium in an untraditional way, perhaps by combining two familiar elements in a new way, the greater the success.

In principle all products are therefore suitable for exposure on the Internet. Certain lines of business and products are, however, more suitable than others, as they are of a kind which are better suited to the medium's communicative characteristics.

Which products are most suitable for the Internet?

Until three years ago only a few companies could show a positive return from their use of the Internet. However, this has changed drastically. The main reason is that since the end of 1996 many companies have managed to give the customer additional value by the integration of dialogue and interactivity and by the use of the medium's enormous potential for information searching, sales and distribution.

Everyone knows the situation where the number of CDs that people want to listen to in a music shop exceeds the patience of those around them. It is difficult to listen to more than a couple of CDs as a queue forms and both the staff and other customers become irritated. Using the Internet, however, the scenario can provide the customer with extra value. On the Internet the consumers can search for the required type of music, enter the names of musicians and obtain suggestions for alternative musicians as well as seeing the whole of the available range. The consumers can also listen to all the songs they want without being interrupted or feeling guilty. Ordering is carried out online, deliveries are made to the consumer's address and the charge only consists of the delivery costs. That consumers also receive a discount when buying CDs over the Internet is yet another advantage.

The introduction of RIO Diamond (www.diamondmm. com) has pushed the popularity of music on the Internet

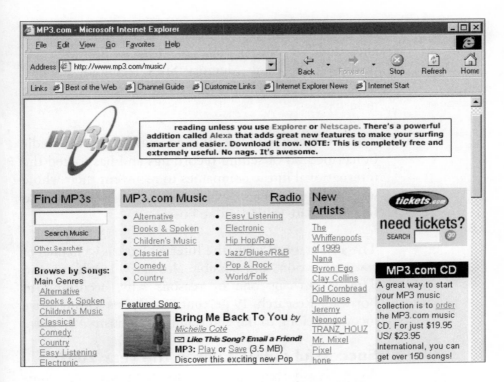

even further. More than 18 million songs are today available for download via the Internet, several hundred thousand are for free and all are of high sound quality. Downloading a song to RIO Diamond (a portable music device) only takes 10 to 15 minutes (depending on connection type). It is possible to store up to 60 minutes of sound on the RIO Diamond. The Diamond is based on MP3, a file format that stores audio files on a computer in such a way that the file size is relatively small, but the song sounds near perfect.

www.mp3.com is the key to more than 18 million songs on the Internet.

The technology has not only made life difficult for record companies and provoked the formation of an anti-MP3 organisation called Secure Digital Music Initiative, it has also opened the gates for a whole new world of music amateurs on the Internet. More than 100 amateur hit lists are today available on the Internet with thousands of hits created by 'ordinary' people around the world.

TIP

*Visit
www.mp3.com/new
artist/ and make
your dream of
becoming a pop-
star a reality!*

Sony is one of the companies trying to create an alternative to the popular MP3 technology, by introducing the Sony Memory Stick technology. Their hope is to avoid a cannibalisation of the music copyright industry.

The Internet has added value compared with the traditional method of selling recordings and has forced the international music companies to re-invent their whole way of doing business, which clearly has been shown to be out of date in the online business.

The advantage of using the Internet here as a channel of communication, and possibly also sales, is self-evident. This is perhaps one of reasons why, according to Forrester Research, 19 percent of websites with positive incomes belong to the entertainment industry.

Successful online sales in the year 2002

As previously stated in this chapter, almost every company has a reason for going online. By working with the Internet, however, we have learned that some product categories will gain more value by becoming online than others. In general, all product categories can be classified into three segments – Interactive branding (i-branding), Electronic commerce (e-commerce) and Electronic operations (e-operations) (a more detailed description of this model can be found in Chapter 9). Each segment represents either a way of 'saving' or 'earning' money by being on the Internet.

When deciding why a company should go online it is important to evaluate the site's online objectives. Is it to establish or build a brand, to earn money or to save money by implementing processes that cut existing costs in the organisation?

As is the case for traditional communication, very little research has been conducted to determine the value of

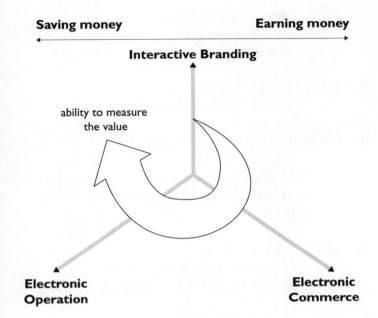

Saving money — **Earning money**

Interactive Branding

ability to measure the value

Electronic Operation

Electronic Commerce

I-branding sites are today the most difficult sites to measure in a quantitative way as there is no transaction involved.

online branding. It is a difficult task as a strong brand position does not necessarily mean a sales increase on a short-term basis.

The best way to get a verified indication of which companies today are more suitable on the Internet (within i-branding and e-commerce) than others is by looking at where tomorrow's online sales will be.

The list on the next page covers the projected six most successful revenue categories on the Internet for the year 2002. The research, interestingly enough, shows that only five product categories will cover 90 percent of all e-commerce on the Internet for the year 2002. This clearly indicates why so many websites haven't managed to become successful on the Internet today. The fact is that in far too many cases the 'real' added consumer value when buying online is too low compared with the 'risk' the consumer perceives when making an online purchase.

1. **32%** The computer industry
   Modems, computers,
   accessories and software

2. **24%** The travel industry
   Travel, hotels and events

3. **19%** The entertainment industry
   Interactive leisure products
   (edutainment, infotainment and games)
   Music and films (video, DVD and CD)
   Books

4. **10%** Gifts and flowers
   Chocolate, postcards, flowers,
   gimmicks, merchandising

5. **5%** Food and beverage
   Personal placing of orders and delivery
   Provisions (food, drink, etc.)

6. **10%** Apparel and other product categories
   Insurance and banking
   Search databases/reference works
   Transport, dispatch and communication
   News reporting, research, information

Below is a fuller explanation of each individual category, focusing on utilisation of the medium.

1. Computer-related products

Practically all the users of the Internet have a computer. Providing information about computer-related products and selling hardware and software via the Internet is therefore an obvious step. For example, if you want to upgrade a modem, one of the most appropriate places to look for information about it would be on the Internet. Software is one of the most rapidly growing product categories on the Internet today.

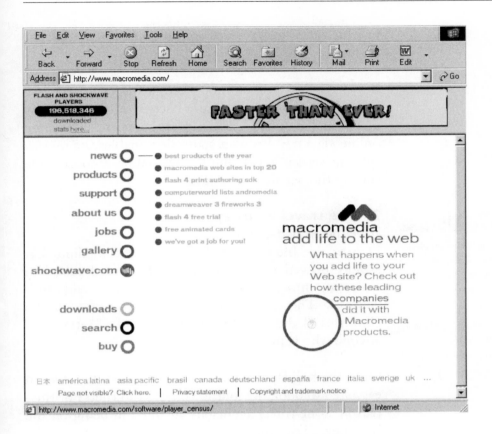

Macromedia, an American company that develops Internet software, stated in its conference in San Francisco in October 1999 that they have more than 500,000 visits to their website each day. Of the 500,000 visitors, 170,000 want to download programs. Macromedia therefore reached the break-even point with their website in the middle of 1997, even though their webmaster team already consists of more than 40 employees.

Purchase of hardware, such as what Dell offers its customers, is not the only type of service that has been shown to be successful on the Internet. Often a discount of 25 percent is offered if software is bought and downloaded directly via the Internet. If you want the coloured version of the instruction manual and the box

www.macromedia.com is one of the most visited software sites in the world, with more than 500,000 visitors per day.

TIP

Send an animated postcard free of charge — just visit www.shockrave.com/t/home_flashcards.html

in which the software was sold the price is 25 percent higher.

But the benefits don't stop here: a frequent and easy update of software has finally become a reality just by accepting 'yes' on the screen. User support can be done online via a new browser setup that enables the user to split the screen in two and receive online support while surfing the net simultaneously.

2. The travel industry
Travel, hotels and events

TIP

A website can often tell more about a country than lots of brochures.

Visit
odin.dep.no/ud/publ/ 96/norway – and visit Norway in a new way.

Due to the Internet's global spread the medium has rapidly proved itself to be particularly well suited to collecting information about other countries and other cultures. The amount of information about all the countries of the world is enormous and of interest to anyone who is planning a journey.

Once the holiday destination has been selected, it is an easy step to book the journey on the Internet. For this reason alone travel agents are justified in being on the Internet. The purchase process could almost be described as a chain reaction. Once the users have become accustomed to obtaining the first half of the information via the medium it seems natural to continue. The winners are the travel agents offering the users the required travel data online and ultimately also providing a booking service for tickets and hotel reservations via the Internet.

Many hotels make it possible to view the rooms and book them online. As far back as 1995 the city of San Francisco drew up a hotel guide which not only made it possible to book hotels but also to see what activities were available in the vicinity of the hotel. www.travelocity.com is another good example of how travel and hotel booking will be one and the same service in the future.

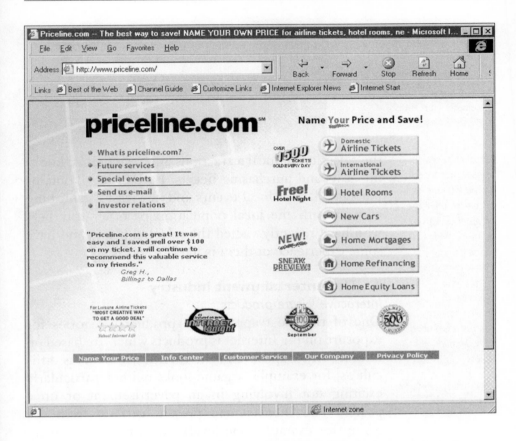

At the same time the Internet has started a war between the airlines, and as a result many US airlines offer standby prices to Internet users. The prices are often 200 to 300 percent lower than the prices obtained by contacting a travel agent in the normal way. By subscribing to a special airline e-mail list, customers are informed about low airfares on a daily basis. This will result in a dramatic change in today's role for travel agents. The traditional travel agency already suffers from substantial costs such as rent, personnel and paper-based infrastructure – costs which in a low-margin business can become life threatening when competing against Internet-based companies that can 'white-out' these burdens.

The next stage in the chain reaction will typically be

What do you want to pay for a trip from Sydney to Los Angeles? Type in the amount at www.priceline.com and become a part of the airline online auction.

Comparing Fares

City pair	Internet fare	Full-coach	Advance Purchase
Washington – Nashville	US Airways, (www.usairways.com), $79	**$598**	$414, $210, $158
Newark – Salt Lake City	Continental, (www.flycontinental.com), 179	**1,610**	785, 614, 408
Dallas – Cleveland	American, (www.americanair.com), 159	**1,296**	204, 204, 204
Memphis – Las Vegas	Northwest, (www.nwa.com), 149	**1,388**	463, 351, 351
Los Angeles – Vancouver	Air Canada, (www.aircanada.com), 197	**426**	337, 214, 214

Air ticket prices can usefully be studied on the Internet, as price-wise there are be great savings to be made. Many airline companies offer Internet users a chance to subscribe to a mailing list that informs them about daily discount tickets.

the selection of local attractions and restaurants, booking seats and purchasing tickets. Furthermore, obtaining calendars of local events and not least establishing contact with the local population or other travellers who have recently visited the selected places and have some experience of them is likely to occur.

3. The entertainment industry
Interactive leisure products

One of the most appropriate product categories for exposure on the Internet is products which are based on interactivity. Exposure in the traditional media is difficult as, for example, a game looks neither particularly exciting nor involving in an advertisement or on a poster. The Internet can present extracts from the game (for example, one level) which the user can try out, and can enable the user to download the whole game in return for payment. This means that users do not even need to leave their chairs. Often the price for downloading will be cheaper than the price users would pay for an identical product in a shop because on the Internet there are no costs such as packaging, retail trade distribution and advertising.

The latest methods also take care of automatic updating of new versions of software via the net.

Walt Disney's Disney Blast is an excellent example of how the Internet can be used as an entertainment medium. Disney Blast, the digital Donald Duck comic, is updated daily and 20 to 25 new games and stories are added each week.

Already products are marketed which are based on letting the user play the game free of charge. The games are constructed in such a way that the user has to buy equipment in order to make best use of the game. The price is often symbolic, but even if each player only spends a few cents on playing a game, experience shows that this form of payment is a goldmine for the provider. The number of players can be overwhelming due to the easy availability and the low price.

Disney (www.disneyblast. com) was one of the first really successful online entertainment concepts on the Internet which managed to charge money for its service.

Music and films (books, video, DVD and CD)

The world's largest bookshop – www.amazon.com – is probably one of the most famous success stories on the Internet. The bookshop today has three million books, CDs and video titles on its 'cyber shelves'. The typical delivery time is one week (including carriage by courier). Amazon.com not only specialises in book, CD and video sales but also offers many services linked to the sales process which in themselves can justify its existence on the Internet. Amazon.com's prices are estimated to be up to 40 percent lower than those of an ordinary retailer, primarily because of the lower costs of distribution and marketing.

At amazon.com the readers can write reviews of the books they have read and participate in a weekly competition for the best contribution. Amazon.com's services also include the opportunity to subscribe to a virtual news-list which is modified to suit the interests and profile of the user. You can also match your author or title taste with other amazon.com users' tastes and review suggestions for other titles which may match your taste. Today several hundred thousand users subscribe to this mailing list – an excellent alternative to the traditional book catalogue. Similarly www.amazon.com can recommend to their visitors relevant books on the basis of their existing favourite titles. This is possible because www.amazon.com records the readers' variations in taste each day and links these together with other readers' favourite titles.

4. Gifts and flowers
Chocolate, postcards, flowers, gimmicks, merchandising
www.interflora.com is a good example of excellent use of the Internet. If you order a bouquet of flowers to go from Sydney, Australia to Copenhagen in Denmark via Interflora in the traditional way it costs between $90 and $100 per bouquet including delivery. A bouquet of the same size ordered via Interflora's Internet website costs half as much. The higher price does not give you quicker delivery, more (or prettier) flowers or more lines of text on the greeting card. Another example could be a department store which in the run-up to Christmas might open a Christmas gift catalogue, where users could choose between selected gift ideas in varying price ranges, have their selection wrapped in their choice of wrapping paper and finally have the

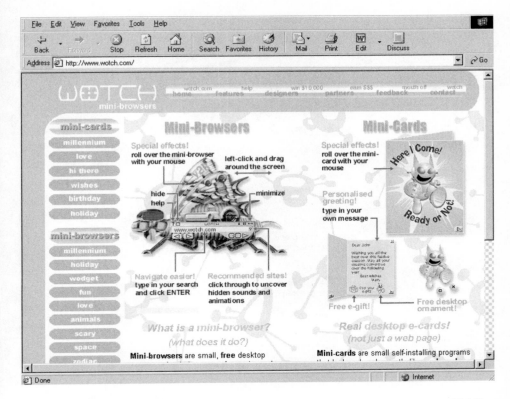

present delivered, all via the Internet.

New services have appeared on the Internet. www. 123greetings.com and www.e-greetings.com both offer free digital postcards. A newer online promotion is wotch.com, which offers a free download. It might be a reminder of your friends' birthdays or the weekly joke. Basically the more you interact with the application on your desktop the more valuable it becomes. More than 50,000 users download wotch.com per day, making it clear that the future is bright for such promotions.

More than 50,000 users daily download a wotch.

5. Food and drink products

This category includes, in principle, all types of ordered purchases, where the actual purchase process can be simplified via the Internet and thus give a particular company added value as a result of its existence on the net. One of the most successful websites in Scandinavia is ISO

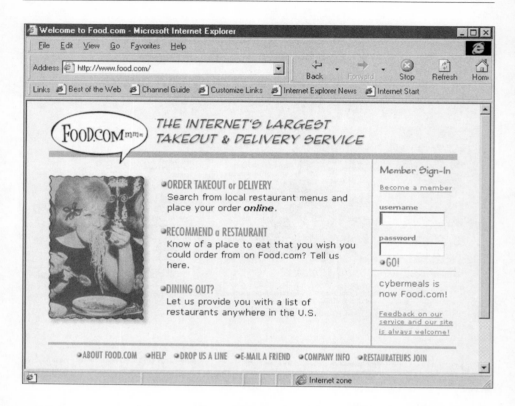

THE INTERNET'S LARGEST TAKEOUT & DELIVERY SERVICE

ORDER TAKEOUT or DELIVERY
Search from local restaurant menus and place your order *online*.

RECOMMEND a RESTAURANT
Know of a place to eat that you wish you could order from on Food.com? Tell us here.

DINING OUT?
Let us provide you with a list of restaurants anywhere in the U.S.

Member Sign-In

Become a member

username

password

GO!

cybermeals is now Food.com!

Feedback on our service and our site is always welcome!

ABOUT FOOD.COM   HELP   DROP US A LINE   E-MAIL A FRIEND   COMPANY INFO   RESTAURATEURS JOIN

www.food.com is one of the largest home delivery services on the Internet today.

(www.iso.dk), a Danish supermarket chain, where subscribers order provisions online. The Internet can complement smaller retailers too: HomeDelivery.com (www.homedelivery.com) lets New Yorkers browse local stores, order and get home delivery.

6. Apparel and other product categories
Insurances, brokerage, banking and credit companies
The financial sector should become a winner on the Internet. Already nearly all transactions between financial institutions are electronic. Most US-based banks offer 100 percent online banking for customers – a huge time-saver. Paying bills over the web can save hours of monthly paperwork (and postage). Eventually, billers will close the loop and invoice over the Internet. On the other hand, a PC still can't spit out $20 bills – the web has a way to go before it kills off the ATM. Initially consumers resist changes, but then find they

can't live without them. When ATM cash dispensers appeared in the 1970s, people distrusted them. Today ATMs are more popular than bank branches.

Insurers face more difficulties than banks. Many consumers rely on local agents to do policy shopping for them. Also, big insurers have aging computer hardware and rely on agents to sell their wares. Similar factors have slowed the progress of retail-oriented brokerage firms like Merrill Lynch onto the Web. If they're not careful traditional insurers, too, could find themselves losing share to Web-based discounters.

The Internet has revolutionised the once-staid investment world. In the 1970s, stock trades were completed on paper: bicycle messengers pedalled down streets with mountains of certificates and payments. Today a quarter of all retail trades are online. Upstarts like E-Trade have a lot of the market but older firms – notably Fidelity Investments and Charles Schwab – have a share, too.

In the long run, the distinction between online and offline financial services will fade away. Banks without websites will be as rare as banks without ATMs. Lenders with no web presence will lose market share. Insurers that don't provide services on the web will shrivel. Eventually, not enabling customers to check balances, originate loans and manage their financial lives over the web will cost institutions business. Financial service providers ignore the web at their peril.

Sixty-six percent of businesses in the West rate e-commerce as important in their overall strategy, according to IBM, while 35 percent of these businesses have an e-business strategy. However, only 31 percent of the US population, according to CDB Research & Consulting Inc., has bought products or services online.

The insurance and banking sectors are particularly suited

Most Important Reasons People Shop on the Web		What Information Do You Look For When Buying a Product on the Web?	
Easy to place an order	83%	Detailed information about the product itself	82%
Large selection of products	63%	Price comparisons	62%
Cheaper prices	63%	Detailed information about the vendor	21%
Faster service and delivery	52%		
Detailed and clear information about what is being offered	40%		
No sales pressure	39%		
Easy payment procedures	36%		

Survey conducted by Jacob Neilsen's Alertbox 1999

to the Internet as more and more people manage their finances from their home computer. A total integration with the bank and insurance company is therefore obvious. A survey conducted on 2,929 Internet users in February 1999 found that 83 percent state convenience as the major factor for preferring the Internet.

Not just transactions but also many forms of dialogue between the company and the customer can be carried out more easily via the Internet. In a typical situation where users need to contact their insurance companies, for example to claim on flood damage, they normally have to go through the following procedure: first the insurance company has to be contacted, then the company sends out a (sometimes incorrect) claims form. The claims form then has to be filled in and returned to the company. If the form is not filled in correctly then the whole process has to start again. The claim is processed and the company comes back with a reply. Typical processing time: four weeks.

On the Internet this can be carried out more quickly, easily and cheaply. The claims form can be displayed onscreen and while it is being completed it is possible to obtain supplementary information and ongoing verification of the data. The form is sent online and the reply

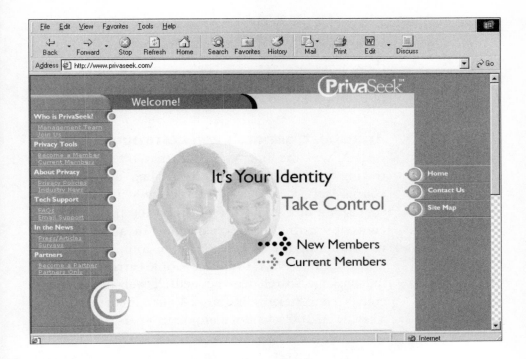

returns online. The Internet has thus given the company's service an extra dimension – justification for an insurance company or bank to be on the Internet.

Concepts like privaseek.com are likely to show the way for the future of online search engines.

Search databases

Search databases filter the chaos of information that is to be found on the Internet at present – for each day brings 250,000 new pages online. The next generation of search databases is very likely to be 'infomediaries'. An infomediary is a third-party search engine that collects data about its user and then acts on the user's behalf, to gain benefits on the Internet. An infomediary can choose relevant links, based on its profile of the user, from the thousands that may be thrown up by a search, thus creating true one-to-one communication.

The introduction of infomediaries is the first serious trend toward customised negotiation on the Internet. As a negotiator, the infomediary will gain discounts for a user by leveraging its store of your consumer details.

Leading search engines, like Yahoo! and excite@home, have acknowledged this recently by taking over some of the world's most respected data-mining companies. It is very likely that search engines and databases will become infomediaries to survive in the future.

Transport, dispatch and communication

FedEX was the first company that offered dispatch tracing of packages and letters. The integration of courier service and the Internet was in many ways something of a small revolution on the Internet as the concept was the first to create concrete added value by incorporating the medium into the company's product portfolio. In 1999 1.3 million people carried out a digital package search via the FedEX website. If this is converted to (telephone) work-hours, it corresponds to a saving of 200 telephone employees per year!

FedEX's newest technology makes it impossible to receive a package from the company unless the recipient signs for it on a digital signature pad. These signatures are then automatically put into a receipt database which is also available on the Internet. This puts an end to the old excuses from recipients who claim they never received something or other.

FedEX is systematically going about turning its problem areas in customer relations into strategic advantages, all by using the Internet. At the same time the basic processes in the company are being optimised and the customers are serving themselves, and are quite happy to do so. The traditional consumer has become a prosumer, who first produces and assembles the product and then orders it via the Internet. By letting the customer become part of the production apparatus, the company has the opportunity to make considerable savings.

At present, competing courier and transport companies are engaged in a scramble for position. Some have gone even further and by using GPS (Global Positioning System) are able to trace a package to the individual delivery vehicle and determine its exact position.

The future will offer even more advanced interaction. Tests were conducted in 1998 by BMW to enable online tracking of a car's exact position via the Internet. In addition they looked into transferring data about the car's current technical status to an individual website, which could mean that sometime in the future it may be possible for the car to book itself into a workshop and for the mechanic to have ordered the spare parts required before the car even arrives.

The integration between GPS and the Internet has only shown us the tip of the iceberg of what benefits we might gain by having this new technology available. One of the most tangible benefits available today is the ability for consumers to see the current position of the bus they are catching every morning to work. If it is delayed then an estimated arrival time will appear on the site. The system has so far been introduced in only two US cities but has proved to be a major success.

News reporting

The traditional mass media are struggling at the moment to find a balance between traditional news reporting (in newspapers, on radio and television) and news reporting via the Internet. The danger is that the new form of news reporting will cannibalise the original channels of communication. Experience shows that users of the Internet are not yet prepared to pay for this form of interactive service, and many news providers are therefore finding it difficult to justify why they should be on the Internet at all. A number of Internet-based concepts – like news.com – have, however, proved that news reporting on the Internet is justified. At present news.com and CNN.com are free for the end-users, but within a few years the companies will

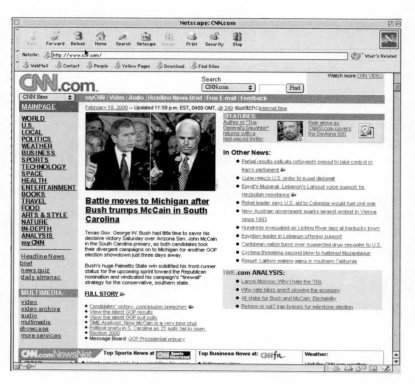

probably demand payment for their services. This will be the acid test of whether users are willing to pay to receive electronic news.

It all takes time …

As with all new technology, the Internet and the opportunities the medium offers will see major developments in the future. Not only will the medium have new technologies at its disposal which make the visual elements stronger, the interactivity more integrated and the flow of information faster, people will also become more familiar with how to utilise the unique characteristics of the medium.

The examples above all show that they have managed to link together the product, the brand and the Internet in a way which leaves the company more service- and user-oriented than before and which in the long term will help to differentiate them from their competitors.

CHAPTER V

From passivity to interactivity

*"A common myth about the
creation of web pages is,
'If you build it, they will come.'
I can tell you, they won't!"*

Tom Vassos, Internet strategies manager, IBM

The Internet has no conventions

You can be fairly sure that you will get what you expect when switching on the television or opening a newspaper. Of course the content varies from day to day, but you can be quite certain that the news will appear on the television screen at 9 p.m. and that the weather forecast will be in its usual place in the newspaper. The format is always the same.

Most media used on a daily basis present themselves in a well-organised and disciplined way, where it is easy to find the information in which we are interested. Changes are made gradually and at a speed which enables people to keep up.

However, the Internet is not like that. It is an uncontrollable entity where rules for the organisation of information are conspicuous by their absence. The problem with the Internet is that the celebrated technological development is taking place so quickly that there is an ever-increasing gulf between the producers' and users' understanding of the medium. There is enough work for a team of five people just to keep up with the developments for in-house use. Only professional web developers have their finger on the pulse. However, they are also the ones facing the problem. New technological possibilities become realities too quickly and these are uncritically incorporated in websites with results that are often light-years away from what the users really want.

The moment vanishes on the Internet

The Internet is intangible. Cyberspace has no physical appearance we can comprehend. The World Wide Web remains an abstract universe which it is difficult to imagine. However, the same imaginary nature is unfortunately a feature of most of its individual websites, as there are too few companies who go to the trouble of making it clear to the users precisely where they are on the website. In addition, companies make the mistake of inviting the users to immense websites where it is almost impossible to create an overview for them.

Most websites are unlike the familiar newspaper which has a unique and defined format. Regardless of what you are reading you always know where the article is situated in the newspaper and how far through the article you have read. If you want to jump from one article to another you only need to move your eyes or turn over the page. The well-arranged appearance of the newspaper provides such a good overview that it can be read from back to front without getting lost. It is undeniably more user-friendly than even the fastest modem and the best browser.

The Internet requires action

One of the first things that users notice when they first encounter the Internet is that nothing happens until they become involved themselves. The Internet is operated by interactivity. This word has, however, lately become as much of a buzzword as multimedia was at the beginning of the 1990s. Today everything is interactive if you are to believe the sales-talk and marketing for all kinds of products.

However, it is not so obvious what is behind the term 'interactivity'. An understanding of the importance of interactivity is essential for working with the Internet, as it is primarily the mechanisms surrounding interactivity that have put the Internet where it is today.

It is important for the construction of the profile of the company or the brand that the presentation of the opportunities which the company provides is carried out via an interface which is as well designed and user-friendly as possible. Those companies which succeed in this will find it much easier to create sympathy and get across the emotional values they want associated with their brand.

"Try giving a remote control to a kid and they think it is broken. Because all it can do is change channels. They want control over the content and TV doesn't give them that!"

Jake Winebaum, CEO, Disney Online

What is interactivity?

If you look the word up in a dictionary the first thing you will find is that it is not there. This is very characteristic of the Internet where a completely new lexicon is developing. However, the word is used frequently when the new digital media are being described. Just think of interactive television, the interactive cookbook, etc. It is therefore appropriate to define the meaning of the word. The word is derived from 'interaction' which means reciprocal action. In order for something to be interactive it is necessary for both parties to be involved – a two-way communication.

Interactivity, therefore, is a process where two or more parties mutually affect each other through communication.

If the computer is regarded as a medium, what the user sees on the screen is called the interface. It is this interface that enables the user to communicate with the underlying parts of the program which execute the user's commands. When talking about the interactivity between a computer program and a user, we mean the actions that are carried out between the program's interface and the user. The program is controlled by a number of selections carried out by the user and the way the program reacts depends upon which actions the user initiates – the selections have consequences. This is in contrast to other media which are self-propelled (slide shows, presentations, etc.) and which are not affected by the user, just like traditional television.

If this definition is transferred to the Internet, a static presentation of a company on the net will consist of a number of pages of information which it is possible to select between but which it is not possible to influence, whereas an interactive version is based on the customer's needs and wishes so that it can present the customer with solutions targeted at the individual user.

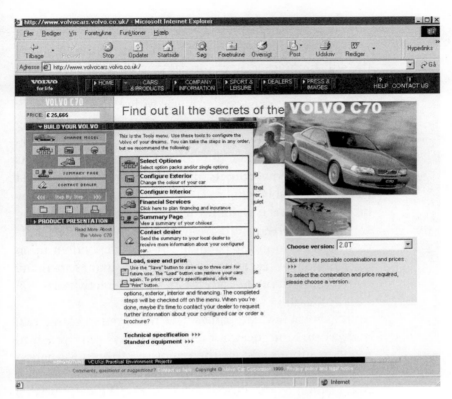

Users can order goods and services, assemble their own products and decide on optional extras to suit their price range. Static information about companies never comes in the top 10 of the most visited sites.

There are over 16 million different ways to build a C70, and it can be done directly over the Internet!

Using traditional media the presentation of the new Volvo C70 would be a product brochure with nice pictures and text giving details of individual models, but the C70 actually comes in 16 million different variations! This makes it perfect for the Internet. The online interactive presentation consists of small movies, and the ability to design and build your own Volvo directly on screen, with all the information brought to life, just waiting for your click to make a difference.

If the user wants a Nautic blue pearl C70 with Canisto alloy wheels, it just takes a few clicks and the price will be shown next to a picture of the desired variation. All the choices have immediate consequences via feedback in the picture which is continually updated and shows the user's choice. Users can stay as long as they want, remove the roof, try out the functions and the sound of different car stereo systems (provided the computer's loudspeakers are good enough!), find out the handling characteristics and fuel consumption in various scenarios. They can also give their own physical measurements and driving requirements and get the system to suggest the most suitable model. If the car is to be paid for by hire purchase, the system will also arrange this by letting the user propose the deposit and the term or alternatively a fixed monthly payment. It is all dependent upon the individual user. It is not surprising that many companies can see the advantages of interactivity.

Interactivity →
involvement →
commitment!

Today only a few companies have managed to convert an interest in and desire for interactivity into practical usable solutions. By far the majority of the information that is on the net is general and passive; it can be read but not adapted to the user's requirements. This is a wasted opportunity and one reason why companies do not get anything like the optimal return from their web activities.

The reason for the importance of interactivity for success on the Internet is to be found in the chain reaction: interactivity → involvement → commitment. The moment a user is asked to take part actively in an action, he must necessarily become involved. If the dialogue is meaningful and the experience continues to live up to his expectations, a commitment will be created which is very difficult to duplicate using other media.

Flow and the Internet

The majority of web sites are painful to use. Why? They don't focus on meeting users' goals or supporting visitors' needs. In the report *Why Most Websites Fail* by Forrester Research in September 1998, it was stated that for every one million unique vistors per month,

40 percent are driven away by hard-to-read text, slow performance or poor reliability. The same report shows that a person who has had a bad experience with a website will typically tell 10 others. Just think of the success of computer games. Here the involvement of the user can bring about a state of mind characterised by such great concentration that awareness of time and place vanish. This state is called 'flow' by the author M. Csikszentihalyi in his book *Flow – The Psychology of Optimal Experience*.

TIP

Nine out of ten mistakes in web design identified in May 1996 by Jakob Neilsen still cause severe usability problems and should be avoided in modern websites.

www.useit.com/alert box/990502.html

Csikszentihalyi believes that three things must be present at the same time in order to create flow:

1. A clearly defined aim or task
2. Quick and constant feedback
3. Continual balancing between challenges and ability

An example of a flow-creating activity is mountain climbing. The use of the Internet can also create this state. It is therefore worth looking more closely at the three parameters from the perspective of the Internet.

1. A clearly defined aim or task
It is important that a website immediately provides the user with an aim: an understanding of what it is possible to do on the website in question. The more freedom users have to define their aims, the more difficult they will find it, and the state of flow will never arise.

2. Quick and constant feedback
Although good interactivity results in involved users, if they do not constantly get feedback from their actions, anything that was gained is well on the way to being lost. A lack of feedback leads to uncertainty and makes the experience less satisfactory. A well-designed system or website reacts promptly to the user's actions. The more natural and visible the feedback, the more the

user will become involved. This is one of the reasons why computer games are so popular. The users are constantly being informed what is happening and how well they are succeeding.

Over the years many people have tried to carry over some of the principles of computer games to more ordinary business computer programs, but to date not with much success. The best examples are to be found within edutainment titles for children which teach them to read, spell and count in a format disguised as a game. In the future we will see more attempts on the net to use constant feedback to give users a more satisfying experience; and it is important that the feedback is unambiguous, constructive and cannot be misunderstood.

3. Continual balancing between challenges and ability

If the solution to a task is too easy, there is a danger of boredom and a resulting lack of flow. On the other hand if a task is too difficult, this creates stress and uncertainty which also lead to a lack of flow. By having the degree of difficulty of the interface increase as the user's ability increases, a balance can be retained between the user and the system so that the interaction continues to be exciting. This would be easy to implement on the net where additional and more advanced functions would only become available after a certain number of visits. This could in itself provide the motivation to return.

If these three principles are transferred to the Internet, they open up interesting possibilities for making customer service, product launches and other previously mundane tasks into inspiring experiences. Never before has it been possible to involve the user to such an extent in the search for information and in the design of products. As a user it is possible on the Internet to ask all the 'what if' questions and it will always be completely without obligation. The website will continue to answer correctly regardless. This is seldom the case in the real world where, for example, a maximum of three telephone numbers per call to Directory Enquiries may be requested and where most sales personnel become disinterested, annoyed and more vague in their replies after they have answered a certain number of questions about insurance, a coat, a toy or the like.

There is a difference between interactivity and navigation

When sitting at home with a video-recorder watching a film instead of going to the cinema, it is easy to think that in fast-forwarding through boring sections of the film the experience is interactive. However, this is not the case. Instead the remote control makes it possible to navigate within the information content. It is very important to distinguish between navigation – finding your way around in the information, whether it is a website, a CD-ROM or a videotape – and interactivity. Navigation does not itself add anything. It is like leafing through a book; the content remains the same and the choices do not affect the content in any way.

Only interactivity with the content counts.

That is not to say that navigation is unimportant. On the contrary, navigation is a basic requirement for a website to be used at all. If the structure, service and divisions are not logical and intuitive, most of the time users spend at the website can easily be spent trying to find their way around. Users will then be likely to leave the website as quickly as they arrived!

Focus-group discussions with both experienced and completely new users of the Internet have indicated that the main thing users demand of a good website is an overview of what they are able to do and a structure that is well arranged and logical. A user should always be able to get answers to four questions concerning the navigation:

Don't make the navigation a challenge.

- Where am I?
- Where have I been?
- Where do I go from here?
- How do I get out?

The problem is that there is a very fine balance between having as few options on the individual pages as possible and at the same time not having too many levels. Users also typically can't be bothered with content which is more than three clicks away. Studies of the way users learn show that people form a so-called cognitive model of how the user interface works. The more consistent the model – that is, when things always have the same name, look the same and are in the same position – the easier it is to learn to navigate. The same studies also showed that people can learn interfaces with about five different 'rooms' or areas so well that navigation is carried out without thinking about it. If there are more options than that, there will constantly be learning, necessitating an exploration and a subjective evaluation of where the information is to be found. This means that unnecessary energy is used for navigation instead of for the actual content.

The design of good websites makes great demands on good organisation of the content and a logical and uniform navigation. The aim for good websites must be that the navigation is so invisible that users have only to concentrate their energy on communicating, finding and looking for information or solving concrete problems.

Proper interactivity is achieved by actions that have an influence upon the content itself, regardless of whether it is a matter of booking a ferry ticket, amending a sales list, filling out a claims form or building a LEGO model directly onscreen.

One of the best examples of practically invisible navigation is found in the CD-ROM game 'You don't know

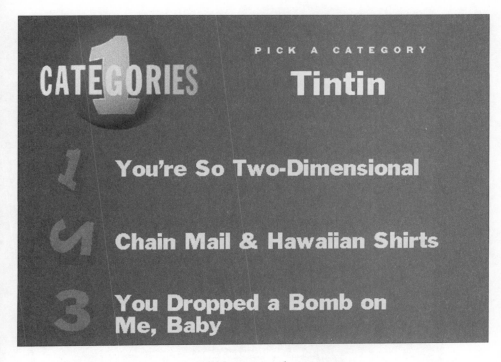

CATEGORIES 1

PICK A CATEGORY

Tintin

1 You're So Two-Dimensional

2 Chain Mail & Hawaiian Shirts

3 You Dropped a Bomb on Me, Baby

Jack'. The game is exceptional for several reasons:

- There is practically no learning curve; in just a few seconds everyone is under way.
- The game uses sound for a number of things, including the creation of a unique atmosphere and to give constructive feedback all the time.
- The game's actual concept can easily be adapted to other purposes and areas, including marketing.

'You don't know Jack' is designed as an interactive American game-show in the best wheel-of-fortune style, where the players are participants in the fast-moving race to win cash prizes.

This CD-ROM game is incredibly entertaining. At the same time there are innumerable commercial possibilities in the concept by transferring it to brand-building advertainments (an interactive combination of game, competition and marketing) on the net. The actual

The CD-ROM game 'You don't know Jack'.

CASE

'You don't know Jack' – The Net Show

CD-ROM and Website Berkeley Systems

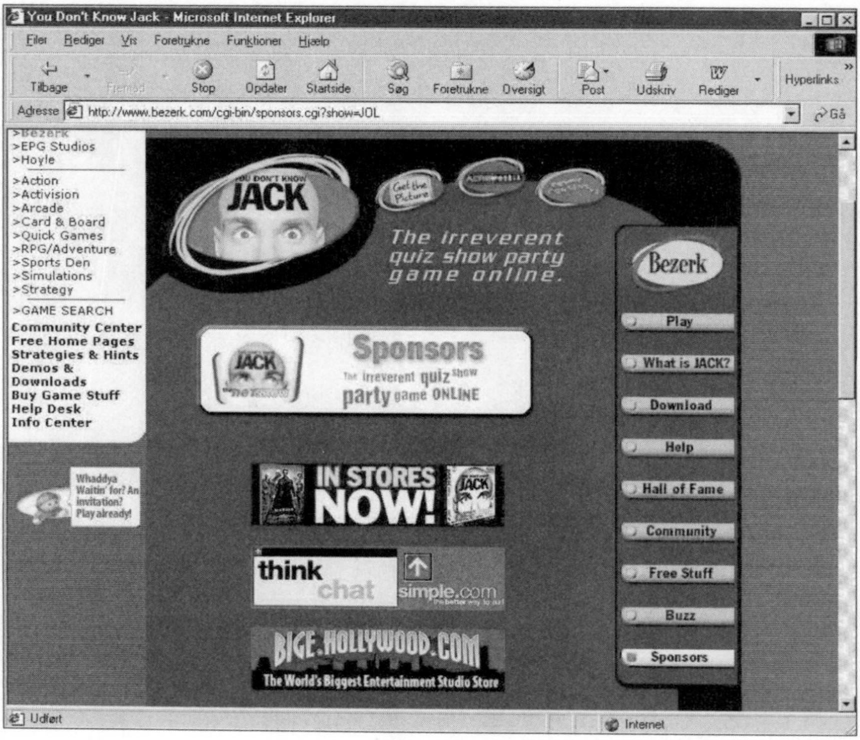
You Don't Know Jack - Microsoft Internet Explorer
Filer Rediger Vis Foretrukne Funktioner Hjælp
Tilbage Frem Stop Opdater Startside Søg Foretrukne Oversigt Post Udskriv Rediger Hyperlinks
Adresse http://www.bezerk.com/cgi-bin/sponsors.cgi?show=JOL
>EPG Studios
>Hoyle
>Action
>Activision
>Arcade
>Card & Board
>Quick Games
>RPG/Adventure
>Sports Den
>Simulations
>Strategy
>GAME SEARCH
Community Center
Free Home Pages
Strategies & Hints
Demos & Downloads
Buy Game Stuff
Help Desk
Info Center
Whaddya Waitin' for? An invitation? Play already!
JACK
The irreverent quiz show party game online.
Sponsors
The irreverent quiz show party game ONLINE
IN STORES NOW!
think chat
simple.com
BIGE.HOLLYWOOD.COM
The World's Biggest Entertainment Studio Store
Bezerk
Play
What is JACK?
Download
Help
Hall of Fame
Community
Free Stuff
Buzz
Sponsors
Udført
Internet

Having downloaded the engine, it is possible to play a lot of versions of 'Jack' online. The prizes are sponsored by different companies, and there are new episodes every Monday.

www.won.net/channels/bezerk/jack/jack-play.html

game is most reminiscent of a combination of 'Jeopardy' and 'Trivial Pursuit'. The CD-ROM has been a great success in the USA and new versions with up-to-the-minute questions about different subjects, including sport, are constantly being issued.

The navigation is practically transparent (invisible) to the users. This means that the players use all their energy in participating in the game instead of in learning to use it. The actual game is played with only one key per participant! In addition players have to press 1, 2 or 3 to select the correct answer to a given question. TheCD-ROM can easily result in several hours of amusing entertainment with enthusiastic involvement on the part, not just of the two or three participants, but also any spectators.

Now Berkeley Systems have moved the game to the

Internet, and at the same time made it possible to advertise in the show through a new form of advertising on the net called interstitials (see Chapter 12). You download a games engine and the questions are updated every Monday. You can then take part and win valuable prizes.

The game is basically the same and, most important of all, the interactivity is retained and the navigation is still invisible! It is incredible that the games idea has not already been copied for marketing concepts, as there is a great opportunity here waiting to be exploited.

Good user dialogue demands a well-designed interface

Unfortunately not all interfaces are equally well designed. In order to be a success with the users the interface must be developed so that the wishes, requirements and demands of users are satisfied, and in a meaningful and easily-understood dialogue which rapidly takes users where they want to be. This is not an easy task and at present there are many more examples of poor interfaces than there are of good functional solutions.

In order to be able to evaluate interface design it is necessary to have a definition which is measurable and some methods of measuring these criteria for success. The most frequently used methods range from group discussions to single-user studies. Focus groups are the best for giving a broad indication of the evaluation. In these groups several spontaneous reactions also arise and it is easier to discuss more emotional values. However, there are seldom two groups which come to the same result, so if you want to be able to quantify the results it is necessary to carry out studies with individual users.

Definition of user-friendliness

As a result of many years of research into interface design, it is now possible to draw up a list of criteria and design guidelines which lead to well-designed user-friendly interactivity.

Traditionally, user-friendliness has been defined by five parameters:

- Easy to learn
- Effective in use
- Easy to remember
- Low frequency of user errors
- Satisfying to use

Based on these parameters it is possible to draw up measurable criteria for the user-friendliness of a website, making it possible to evaluate the company's solution qualitatively. The traditional definition has, however, proved to be very expensive to apply in practice.

Instead we can work with a disaster-oriented analysis of a user-friendly interface:

It is the expectation of the user that an interface is free of disasters.

A disaster occurs:

- If users are unable to continue their work with the system without getting help from others.
- If users perceive the behaviour of the system to be very irritating or irrational.
- If there is a perceptible difference between what users believe the system is doing and what the system is actually doing.

In order for a problem to be called a disaster, it must be experienced by at least two independent users. Using this definition a website's user-friendliness is measured by the number of disasters in the interface.

There are very few web projects being seriously and objectively tested for user-friendliness. A test conducted by Forrester Research in September 1998 has indicated major usability problems. The test was adapted from software evaluation techniques and had as its objective to evaluate these underlying issues:

Payoff: Did content and function meet needs and expectations?

Courtesy: Did the interface respect time – and not waste it?

Trust: Did the site work consistently – and not fail easily?

Intelligence: Did the site proactively aid users to achieve goals?

Problems were found in all categories:
Payoff: Stumped by lack of information. In 50 percent of the cases the test panel couldn't find enough information to make a purchase decision.

Courtesy: Disappearing toolbars and unreadable buttons. Most sites were characterised by heavy inconstancy in use of navigation panels and navigation icons.

Trust: Broken links, failed function and unavailable content. 75 percent of all sites failed on basic reliability.

Intelligence: Unhelpful search engines reveal dirty secrets. 90 percent of all sites failed at least one of two search tests.

The same report shows that 15 percent of Fortune 1000 sites need to go through a quick fix process to ensure an optimal site. Seventy-five percent of all sites needs a rehabilitation of their site as they are characterised by having a poor information architecture surface.

Ten percent of all Fortune 1000 sites are currently so poor that it's time to consider drastic action.

Usually the problems are discovered much too late and at a time when they are very expensive to eliminate. However, by testing for user-friendliness at a very early stage in the design process, the design can be continually adapted to ensure a more successful course is taken. By confronting users from the target group with an early prototype of the design, it is possible to obtain quickly an impression of whether the interface contains any disastrous errors. It has been found that users are very bad at reasoning their way forward to something they do not understand. In addition many people perceive user-friendliness problems to be an expression of their own inadequacy. As all websites will be tested sooner or later – in operation if not before – it is strongly recommended that the users should be involved in the design at an early stage and that it is ensured that they can understand the structure and the terminology.

Ten design guidelines which lead to better dialogue

There are a limited number of good books written about the design of user-friendly interfaces on the Internet, but based on a review of the literature and many years' practical experience it is possible to draw up a set of principles that can be used in practice, all of which lead to a better design:

1. Design around the user

There is a lot talked today about being customer-oriented, but only a few companies have succeeded in this, as it is extremely difficult and usually requires great changes to be made. However, the Internet is the perfect place to make a start. Focus-group interviews show time and again that users demand relevant solutions that are designed around their needs and requirements rather than around the considerations of the company. This principle is described in greater detail in Chapter 6.

2. Don't make navigation the challenge

It's important to remember that users visit a given website because of the content, the functionality, the communication possibilities and so on, not because they find it interesting to navigate around. Therefore navigation should be as easy and intuitive as possible so it doesn't take the user's focus away. This means that designers should be extremely cautious with using different technologies like Java and Flash for the navigation, because if it doesn't work, the tour is over.

Many designers feel that it is logical to return to the first page of the website by clicking on the company's logo. However, this is a hidden function for most people (unless it becomes a convention!). Hidden possibilities will seldom be activated and can therefore often be removed if they are not important. So show the user's options clearly.

The choice of terminology is also decisive for whether a user understands what is hidden behind a concrete choice. It is therefore necessary to take the trouble to find the right words and to test how easy they are to understand on actual users.

When the Egmont group decided to relaunch their website, they also decided to jazz it up with fancy Flash animation and a whole new model for navigation.

CASE
www.egmont.com

On the right side of the screen there are five small pic-

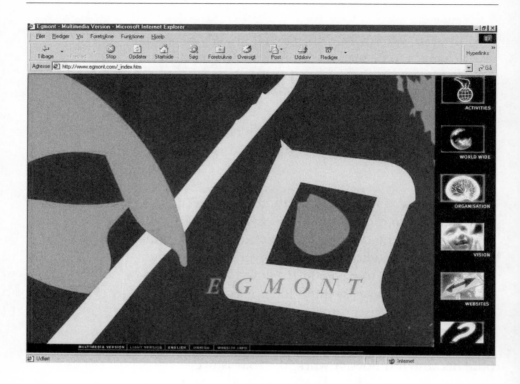

An example of a
website where
navigation is a
challenge! First, you
need to have
Shockwave installed
for the navigation to
work. Then you
discover the content
is moving when you
put the cursor on it,
so you must chase
the content. This
would be okay for a
site aimed at
gamers, but not for
a corporate one.

tures, but actually there are eight possibilities, you just can't see them all. If you move the mouse to the nav. Frame, the navigation pictures start to move, so you have to catch them. And they roll so you also have to wait for the picture to get back. This sure is fancy, but not very convenient. It has not been seen before, so you can't expect people to understand how it works. This is not an interface we would recommend.

3. Offer the user as few alternatives as possible

The more options there are on the screen, the more difficult it is for the user to make the right decision and to learn and remember where different things are found. It must be taken into account that to date the Internet has been populated by technically over-qualified users, which is why more complex interfaces have worked. As more and more 'ordinary' people start using the Internet, this design principle will become increasingly important.

4. Make it easy to revoke an action

There is nothing worse than a website where you cannot revoke an action. This is directly opposed to people's desire to try things out and satisfy their curiosity. As it becomes possible to carry out more and more actions on the net, such as the purchase of goods and the setting up of loans, it is increasingly important to be able to revoke. If it is not possible to revoke an action, the user must be clearly notified of this.

5. Demand few choices
of the user to reach the final goal

Experiments with different segments of Internet users have shown that regardless of whether they are raw beginners or experienced users, they want to get where they're going as quickly as possible. There is of course a trade-off between the number of options on the first page and the number of levels on a website, but no user will put up with much more than three clicks to reach the content. This is also the reason that the structure design is one of the most difficult parts of a website.

6. Be consistent

The terminology has proved to be crucial in understanding a website's structure. But it is equally important that the same things always have the same name and that basic options are always found in the same place. In addition consistency is required of other elements that are part of the interface. The ability to return to the front page must always be called the same thing and preferably be located in the same place. If, for example, the user can click on yellow elements, this choice of colour must be retained throughout the website, and so on.

It is also important that designers ensure visually that the consequence of an action is reflected graphically. That is to say that items that take the user to a completely different website are a different design to items that perform an action within the website.

7. Help the user who is experiencing difficulties

The more interactive a website, the more difficult it is to give the user the correct advice and the more things can go wrong. If the communication breaks down, the user should receive an error message. Only a few websites have understood how important it is to formulate the error message correctly. The design of good messages for the system requires the following to be taken into account:

- Error messages must in principle be constructive, polite and precise (see also Chapter 8), but must also suit the tone and style of the website, for which reason more youthful and humorous error messages can be fitting in the appropriate environment. It is

never the user that has made a mistake, but the system that has not given the correct information. A constructive error message ensures that the user is helped to continue.
- Never write anything that would not be appropriate to say if standing face to face with the user.

8. Beware of technology fixation

Even though more and more things can be done and new technological breakthroughs are daily occurrences, it usually takes a long time for these to be accepted by the majority of users on the net. This applies both to new versions of browsers and to various plug-in modules. A designer should always have a clear picture of what user experience is being offered to all of those who do not have sufficient technological equipment, including insufficient computing power and modem speed. Besides, the right idea can still go a long way.

A good creative idea should be able to be described on the back of an envelope!

In particular it can have disastrous consequences when new technology is used for the navigation itself. There are examples of websites that cannot be used at all if a particular piece of technology is not installed. And each time a new browser appears on the market, new opportunities arise to create advanced features that cannot be accessed by users with earlier versions.

9. Know the target group, and involve it in the design process at an early stage

A good website should reflect the fact that the developers have a sound knowledge of the target group, both in its tone and style and also in its whole structure. The better the design is able to satisfy the users, the greater success the website will have. The level of knowledge and requirements of the users must influence the design, both in the options available and in the design and language.

While the Internet is developing at the speed experienced today, it is essential to involve users from the target group in all design stages, but particularly in the early stages. The website should always be tested on individual users in order to ensure that the basic elements such as structure, language and design can be understood and are attractive. After all, every website will eventually be tested when it is put into operation, if not before. It is much cheaper and less risky to involve the users right from the outset. There is still only one way to find out what the users think of a given design and that is to ask them.

10. Speed is everything on the net

Users of the Internet are by nature restless and impatient. Therefore a website must not take too long to appear on the user's screen. It can be tempting to add impressive pictures and lots of animation, but it is seldom what the users want. The first page in particular needs to be quick to download and in general designers should aim for a layout where no page takes up more than 30kB, unless there are very good reasons for this. This limit will be raised in line with higher bandwidths, but the existing modems will probably be de facto standards for another couple of years.

Another important factor in web design is that it must take into account the multiplicity of recipient platforms that already exist. The factors below all affect what the user sees:
- Screen size
- Operating system and version
- Browser type and version
- Number of colours the monitor can display
- What plug-ins (additional modules) the individual user has (Realaudio, Flash, Shockwave, Java, etc.)

If a web designer wants to ensure that all the users will have the correct experience, tests must be carried out for all the above factors, which will require a very comprehensive test plan!

Without motivation, nothing is achieved

'What's in it for me?' This is an attitude that appears in practically all Internet-oriented user studies. It does not matter whether it is a question of business-to-business solutions or consumer-oriented tasks. The usefulness to the individual user decides whether the visit is regarded as being worth the trouble. The Internet is still regarded by many people as a huge time-waster, and when at the same time it is quite expensive for ordinary people to connect up from home (something which luckily should improve soon) the fuse is very short. If users cannot see any motivation to spend time in a company's website they will leave it before the first page has finished drawing itself. The following equation could be of interest:

The user's experience =

$$0 \times ? = 0$$

the quality of

(the design +

the content +

user experiences +

examples +

the interface +...) x the motivation

The web designer can improve and work with all the factors in parentheses. But even if the content is of a very high quality – nicely arranged with a good interface – this is no use if it is not the content that the user expects and is looking for. If the wrong content is presented and the motivation is therefore non-existent, then the result of the above equation will be zero and the user will stay away.

A great many companies are in the process of experiencing this on the net, where there are more examples of annual reports than of user-oriented content based on situations that are relevant to the customer. Consequently, however nicely the pictures of the factory and the managing director are presented, they are irrelevant to most users, who stay away.

The Internet as a creator of loyalty

*"If I am to succeed in leading a person
towards a particular goal, I must first find out where he is now and start
from there. If I cannot do this I am deluding myself when
I believe that I can help others. In order to help someone
it is true that I must know more than he does,
but primarily I must understand what he understands.
If I cannot do that, it is of little use that I can do more and know more.
If, however, I want to show how much I can do, that is because I am vain and
proud, because I really want to be admired by other people instead of helping
them. All true helpfulness starts with humility towards the person I want to
help, and for this I need to understand that helping is not wanting to
dominate, it is wanting to serve."*

Søren Kierkegaard

The experience of suddenly being able to talk with customers a company has had for years, hearing about their problems and their suggestions in a new and tangible way, has caused many people to regard the Internet as the natural medium for loyalty programs in the future. From talking to the customers, companies now have the opportunity to talk with the customers and to enter into constructive dialogue. However, to get the most benefit from the Internet as a loyalty tool it is necessary to understand the mental substance of loyalty; why some customers are loyal and others are not. What creates loyalty and why is it of interest from a financial point of view? That is what this chapter is about.

Loyalty as a fashion phenomenon

Once is not enough – that is the case in every market today. More than 99 percent of all companies are dependent upon their customers buying the company's products again and again. Even if heavyweights such as Rolls-Royce, Boeing and others in the exclusive category, where the customers have to pay a large amount to become members, have to be satisfied occasionally with one-off sales, there is one word more than any other that has come on the agenda of company management all over the world, and that word is 'loyalty'.

Purely linguistically, loyalty means that a person chooses a person or an object several times – even though there are feasible alternatives. Just as one can be loyal to a good friend with whom one keeps in touch faithfully over the years, so can there be loyalty to a product or a brand which is put in the shopping trolley more often than competing brands with the same generic characteristics.

So much for the linguistic meaning. The commercial meaning has only just become apparent to company management in recent years. Even if marketing managers have talked about the concept from time to time, loyalty was regarded as only one aspect out of many. As a rule companies have been more interested in winning new customers than in retaining old ones; these are already convinced after all. This attitude has in some cases even led to loyalty being penalised. For example, you have to stop subscribing to certain newspapers for a minimum of six months in order to obtain a discount! This is in spite of the fact that it is now well known that in an average company 20 percent of the customers account for 80 percent of the turnover.

In an average company 20 percent of the customers account for 80 percent of the turnover.

This is a natural result of some customers buying more often and in greater quantities than others. This is not surprising; in fact it would be more surprising if all customers bought exactly the same amount. Therefore it is much more interesting to look at how profitable the different customers are.

In the USA, Larry Light – former chairman of the Direct Marketing Association – who runs a consultant company specialising in branding issues, has taken the time to investigate what a company earns from its customers. In studies covering a broad section of US companies, Light came up with a rather interesting, and for some even rather unpleasant, rule of thumb. Namely, five percent of the customers accounted for more than 50 percent of the profits.

"Five percent of the customers account for more than 50 percent of the profits."
Larry Light

This fact alone makes it interesting to look at how the five percent can be persuaded to remain as customers – before they get ideas about finding competing companies or products to be faithful to.

Why are people loyal?
It is relatively easy to come up with a number of different reasons why people are loyal to something, whether another person, a product or a company. Below are listed a number of the common reasons, with discussion of

whether the Internet is a suitable way of influencing each of these reasons.

The object satisfies a physical or virtual need no other object can satisfy

For regulated markets like postal sevices, telecommunications and television (before the monopolies were abolished) it was not difficult to obtain loyalty. The same has been true for a number of the world's largest companies which were set up early with a product having unique characteristics. With increasing competition and the abolition of the monopolies, many of these companies have had to admit that it was not a question of really loyal customers, but rather an artificial hold over them. There will continue to be new companies that meet a need which no other has met to date. These are companies which are good at innovation. The Internet makes it possible to invent products that are not easy to copy because they do not actually exist. Furthermore suppliers are not dependent upon a large capital apparatus in order to get their products distributed. In contrast, imagine what it would cost to bring out a new cigarette or a new cola on the market, bypassing the market leaders. It is obvious how easy it is on the Internet. Search engines are a good example of companies on the net which came in and met a need no others had met. Today there are many search engines, but Yahoo! is still by far the most visited because, among other things, they keep adding functions and content other search engines do not have.

The object satisfies a physical need in a different way to other objects

In those product groups where all physical needs are met, producers are starting to meet the same needs in new ways. For example, for years Citroën has had a solid customer base which swore by the suspension system of the French cars. In the language of advertising this kind of unique characteristic is called a unique selling point (USP). Even though some companies want to use the Internet to create new USPs for existing products (whether home banking or claims notification) it is very difficult to imagine that any company will be able to retain the sole right to these functions. And therefore it will be something of an exaggeration to say that in the long run the Internet will create loyalty with such innovations, even though for a fairly long period of time it will be possible to attract new customers and retain them by using the possibilities of the Internet and the computer creatively.

It is to the customer's advantage

This form of 'loyalty' underlies most customer clubs, from the co-op dividend scheme to the ubiquitous petrol card and frequent-flyer schemes. However, this 'something for something' attitude runs the risk of creating loyalty to the price rather than to the company or the brand. This can lead to the customers always choosing to go for the best bargain. On the Internet, where transparency is increasing and it is easy to change supplier (a new one is never more than a click away!), it can be very dangerous to base a loyalty strategy on nothing more than that the customer can find it financially advantageous.

The object satisfies a psychological need

It is this form of loyalty that is covered by the concept 'brand-building'. It is the addition of emotional values to a brand in order to make the user identify with the brand and prefer it. As described in the introduction to this book, most products are becoming more and more alike and therefore brand-building will become increasingly important and a prerequisite for continued loyalty.

Just as any brochure, film and product the company sends out plays a part in building up (or destroying) the brand or the corporate image, in the same way the

Internet must help to build up the brand. The Internet has additional characteristics that are tailor-made for brand-building, more so than many other media.

1. Companies can use the Internet to become more accessible to the outside world, to let the customers get to know the company beneath its shiny polished exterior. In this way something is achieved reminiscent to friendship and for this purpose the Internet with its accessibility is better than any other medium.
2. The Internet also gives the company the ability to handle the customer in a more individual way. This is one of the foundation stones of creating strong loyalty. The customer is treated as an individual instead of as a tiny fraction of the target group.
3. Finally, there is the actual involvement which, as already mentioned, is a result of the interactivity itself. Apart from a face-to-face meeting with the company's employees, there is hardly any medium that can create involvement and build a brand as effectively as the Internet.

Loyalty is no longer an 'either/or' phenomenon

Back in the 1970s, young people were divided into a few archetypes – mods, rockers, punks, etc. They were totally loyal to the group to which they belonged and the relationship with the other groups bordered on hate. Whereas for the younger generation today, there are almost as many styles as there are young people. There are still fashions and trends, but there is no longer any unequivocal loyalty to a particular code. Different types of style and forms of expression are combined to form a personal style.

The same thing has happened with loyalty to brands. Today the talk is of a more realistic 'share of brand loyalty'. This is an acknowledgement that typical consumers have an accepted set of products to choose from, not just one product. Within the accepted group of products they can then choose more or less as the mood takes them, perhaps taking price into account. If it is brands of trousers, they have perhaps a set consisting of Gap, Levis and Calvin Klein, with each of these having a share of brand loyalty of between one and 100 percent.

It could of course be due to modesty that marketing people have started talking about share of brand loyalty instead of just loyalty, but it is more likely to be an expression of realism. Very few still have 100 percent loyal customers (other than a few exceptional brands such as Coca-Cola and Harley-Davidson).

We cannot say whether this is because customers have become unfaithful. However, as described previously, true loyalty goes beyond rationality and businesslike matter-of-factness. In the context of the Internet it can pay to look at loyalty in another light.

Think of loyalty as virtual love
Advertising agencies, which have many years of experience in building up loyalty programs and dialogue marketing, have gradually reached the conclusion that one thing in particular separates successful campaigns and concepts from those that are less successful. And this is by no means always to do with money or the type of product.

It is in fact sincerity. Just as true love cannot be bought, neither can customers' loyalty. Sometimes consumers let themselves be taken in for a while, or choose momentarily to suppress their feelings and instead make purchases based upon what are perceived to be the most rational reasons.

However, sooner or later they can no longer hold out against their feelings. Eventually they will decide not to select a supplier because they no longer want to be associated with the company's image, no matter how good the product or how attractive the brochures the company may produce. It is this effect that makes cola drinkers prefer Coca-Cola time and again, in spite of the fact that blind-tastings indicate that Pepsi Cola tastes better!

The Internet gives the brand personality

The Danish scientific journalist Tor Nørretranders has written a book about perceiving the world which mentions that it is in mistakes and imprecision that personality and charm are found.

He says that a straight line can be described using three dimensions: a point, a direction and a length. It is thus encoded and understood. A piece of string lying in loops on the floor is on the other hand not a straight line which we can encode in a moment. Three dimensions are not enough to describe the string. Each individual point must be described. Nørretranders says that the straight line is characterised by *ex*formation (information which has been thrown away), while the string is characterised by *in*formation.

And it is precisely this difference which means that in the long run most people prefer the string to the straight line, and that most people like Coca-Cola's rope-encircled logo and dumpy bottle better than the most minimalist logo with the name printed in Helvetica. People have an innate need for information. If the world is too much of a straight line, too clinical and disinfected, it becomes boring to live in. It is the little imprecisions, the lopsided angle, that win sympathy; in other words, personality.

After the tragic death of Diana Princess of Wales several media researchers noted that Diana's exceptional popularity was in fact due to her 'faults', the little imperfections. Diana did not appear as if seen through rose-coloured spectacles. She showed openly that she was a living human being for good and ill. She did not hide away her unhappy marriage or the fact that she suffered from bulimia. Diana was not a straight line who could be described in a few words. Diana was alive. And what did we have? A world which loved her dearly and an outpouring of grief greater than was seen after the assassination of J. F. Kennedy. Infoseek was able to find more than 500 websites developed and dedicated to Diana just 10 days after the accident.

Most advertisements and brochures have been carefully designed and they have gone through several approval stages and proofreadings before they reach the customer. Anything controversial is removed, all errors are corrected. Only correctness remains. Devoid of any personality.

In the dialogue-context of the Internet, this correctness can easily appear hollow. Without a heart and true commitment there is a great danger that it will all be perceived as a marketing gimmick which will be weighed and found wanting, sooner or later, regardless of how elegantly it may or may not be designed.

Commitment and openness are not sufficient by themselves. The Internet makes possible a much more nuanced dialogue with the customers when the actual content is considered. The aim must be to create a personal dialogue which, although it is controlled by a database, will at the same time be comparable to the dialogue that was known from the 'old-fashioned village store' – a dialogue characterised by intimacy and knowledge.

With the Internet you can reveal your company's personality.

❝ If you look at the supermarket of 1920, the grocer knew who you were, what day you got paid, how many kids you had, whether you were a drunk or a gambler – whatever. He fed your family and hired your kid to deliver the products. So he had complete customer knowledge.

Now we're coming full cycle. The virtual grocer should anticipate my needs better than a physical grocer. If, say, I have previously purchased significant numbers of earth-friendly products, he will send me an e-mail: 'Ryan, we've added 10 green products this week you might be interested in.' Because they've profiled me, it will expand the range of products they can sell me. The process becomes my intelligent purchasing agent. ❞
Ryan Matthews, editor in chief, *Progressive Grocer*

The basis for the loyalty program lies in the collection of data concerning the customers' behaviour. What they ask for, what they buy, what interests they have, where they can be found on the company's website, how often they visit – all kinds of demographical and action-oriented data. These user profiles govern what offers the customer receives, what dialogue is carried out, what the website looks like; in short, whether the solution is designed around the individual customer and is therefore perceived as relevant.

Whereas with a large company the customer is used to being passed around from one person to another, none of whom know the customer, the Internet can offer a different infrastructure which puts flesh and blood onto the bones of the person being communicated with.

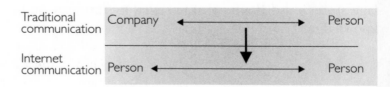

On the Internet it is no longer sufficient for the brand to talk to the individual consumer, it is now also expected to listen. This creates intimacy.

The Internet enables a company to communicate in a much more personal, dynamic and individual way than traditional marketing.

However, mutual intimacy also makes certain demands, so that it is important that the company recognises the consequences of starting to build up loyalty via the Internet. It both carries responsibilities and demands great resources. And if the promise and the position which the company establishes for itself on the net are not in accordance with the actual experience of the company outside cyberspace, it can have serious repercussions for the company.

The Internet brings the customers inside the distance where they can instinctively recognise whether a company is telling the truth or whether it is just a question of good marketing. The innate human lie-detector is very sensitive, as Richard Nixon found out to his cost…

Experience indicates that there is one condition in particular that has to be fulfilled in order to succeed in creating a really effective loyalty program which is based on more than the 'something for something' mentality. There must be at least one employee with customer loyalty as their sole area of responsibility and criterion of success. There must be one person who really cares about the customer without their hands being tied and without the commitment just being one of many items on their agenda.

Only if you dare to open up on the Internet are you using the medium on its own terms

In recent years a lot of energy has been devoted to developing visions and missions. And there is every reason for doing so. But where loyalty is concerned these cannot do all the work. As Jesper Kunde states in his book *Corporate Religion*, it is just as much a question of believing. Not to mention daring. If you don't dare, then the missions and visions all too often just remain a sheaf of paper or an inactive ring-binder in the cupboard. Just something to hide behind.

The Internet has been called many things. Not least 'the world's first democratic medium'. This is because it is the users who have the power (they also have power over television – they can switch it off – but that message never directly reaches the television executives). The real difference is that not everyone can broadcast their own opinion on television (not yet that is), whereas they can on the Internet.

On the Internet a direct measurement of whether anyone looks at your home page or not is obtained. There is no 'maybe' or the traditional advertising agent's estimate that the campaign has probably created a good image somewhere or other out in the real world. On the Internet there is an answer to the central question: Has there been anyone or hasn't there been anyone? There is no room for excuses or estimates.

The financial aspect soon makes it necessary to ask the question: Why should customers remain loyal to the company's home page? What kind of problems, tasks and assignments can be done easier, cheaper and more effectively on the website than in the real world? And here it appears that the customers' reasons for returning can be considered on three levels.

- Level 1
  To obtain concrete knowledge or entertainment. From encyclopaedia facts to pages of cyber sex.
- Level 2
  To carry out transactions (buy, sell, book, etc.).
- Level 3.
  To communicate and build up relations.

Every company can provide for level 1 more or less from its core data. This is just a question of facts about the product. Whether this is enough to get the customers to return is another matter altogether.

If you don't take care of your customer, somebody else will.

Level 2 is not so easy to put on the net as it must be integrated with existing systems. High demands are made of security and payment systems which work. These will probably come into being in the course of 1999 and then the majority of large companies will be able to offer these facilities – if they dare – as it requires the company to be brave enough to hand over the reins, enabling the customer to take over control of the sales process, the design of the product, and even in extreme cases decide what the goods are to cost.

As this suggests, level 3 also requires a lot of courage. The company is forced to abandon the old school with multiple proofreadings and polished brochures. Nowadays there are very few people who can be bothered to take part in a stiff and formal dialogue.

And what if the courage is lacking? Then hopefully the Internet is not essential for the survival of your company in the long term ...

The consumers' expectations in the future

Some companies are philosophically better equipped for this new involvement with the Internet. These are in particular those companies which already have some contact to a greater or lesser degree with their customers. Even though companies such as banks and insurance companies have worked to minimise the human contact with their customers over the years, they still have a more direct understanding of the fact that certain customers want direct contact. And they acknowledge that this contact has to take place to some extent on the customer's own terms, as far as timing, form and content are concerned. There are also other

A marketing person
is a salesperson
who is frightened of
the customers.

companies who are well prepared for what the consumers of the future expect.

❝ *One of our great advantages which we first discovered when we went on the net, was that we in DSB were used to writing to customers. It has always been the case that if a customer wrote to the director general of DSB then he got a written reply. We already had a well-functioning system of customer dialogue which true enough has become more busy, but which in fact worked well from practically the first day on the net. We have noticed that other large companies have a distinct fear of allowing customers to write to them.* **❞**
Henrik Gabel, Internet project leader, DSB (Danish National Railways)

It is much more difficult for all the companies that are used to communicating with their customers through an intermediary, whether a dealer or a supermarket chain. A toothpick manufacturer which has always sent its products to market via retailers will find it much more difficult to understand a company's requirements when it is in direct contact with its customers. However, this challenge also offers the unique opportunity for brands to communicate their brand values direct to the individual user on the net. This concept is called 'disintermediation' in the USA.

Many companies have relied on marketing and advertising instead of personal contact and sales. This has worked well enough as long as there have not been any other options. But now there are. If a customer wants to tell Nike that their new trainers are too narrow or that the heel is too soft, the widespread belief among Internet users is that it should be possible to send this message here and now. They do not want to have to go back to the sports shop. That should not be necessary.

This is the reality to which the world's consumers are becoming accustomed, but it is far from being the reality the producers of branded products have accepted. To date most of them have sent goods to market and backed them up with advertising. All their sales processes have been handled by others.

Front end is fun – back end is business.

The Internet's way of thinking is similar to traditional direct marketing. Direct marketing people have always concentrated on the actual sales process as they did not have a shop to hide behind. They were forced to think in processes all the time and to work out how they could guide customers through a number of stages without losing them on the way. The actual sales process is called 'the back-end' by direct marketing people. And it is not without good reason that it has always been said that 'Front-end is fun – back-end is business'.

It is fun to make advertisements but it is the response that puts money in the till. Similarly, it could be said about the Internet that it is fun to create a home page, but if people do not use it to build a relationship then it has failed. The back-end has gone wrong.

The good thing is that customers are only too happy to enter into a dialogue. They are enthusiastic about being able to talk directly with the company, without an intermediary:

Dear M&M's

We can't draw so we are sending you a joke instead.
Do you know why the blonde was sacked from the M&M factory?
– Because she threw out all the W&Ws!
Best wishes from Majken Fagerberg, Odense

Imagine the courage it takes for a company's management to encourage a free exchange of opinions. The person who replies to an e-mail suddenly becomes the representative for the whole company, whereas previously they just sent out a glossy brochure or referred to a million-dollar advertisement. Now it is the employee – Alice in Atlanta or Gorm in Glostrup – who is Coca-Cola. How can this dialogue with the customers be controlled? And should it be controlled at all?

There are some indications that companies should be very careful not to impose too rigid and restrictive rules concerning how employees communicate with the customers.

Tele Danmark's customer survey on the net

www.teledanmark.dk

When Tele Danmark (the Danish telephone company) wanted to define its new Internet strategy, it was decided first of all to find out what the users thought of the existing group website and what things they would like to find on Tele Danmark's website. A large questionnaire was set up on the website, with those who replied being entered in a draw for two portable phones as an incentive. It was expected that in the course of one month about 500 replies would be received. However, it only took three days to reach that figure! In less than two weeks they received more than 2,000 completed questionnaires, practically none of them anonymous. Suddenly they were in possession of a mass of relevant comments and a clear (although other than expected) picture of how they were to provide a better service for the customers via the Internet in the future.

The Internet brings a new intimacy

Anyone who has tried to communicate via an internal electronic mail system knows that it provides a new level of intimacy and a different dimension to both printed material and the telephone. And this must not be forgotten as it is this that is the very soul of the medium.

If a company tries to communicate 'by the book', in the same way as manuals are used when writing brochures and letters, then there will not be many Internet users who will bother to stay for very long. And conversely it is not possible to write exactly as we speak; it is somewhat different when it is on the customer's screen, without the tones and inflections of the voice.

In other words it is a question of finding a new voice for creating relationships. This is a voice which on the one hand provides fantastic opportunities and which on the other requires the company to dare to give it its head a little. As discussed earlier, the profound love for Diana, Princess of Wales was based on something that was not perfect. So if all e-mails are to undergo the same approval procedure as a brochure, the company's communication on the net will die out very quickly. Companies are therefore forced to take a different route. They are forced to find and train people who can master the art of keeping a dialogue with the customers going in such a way that it is both relevant for the customers as far as content is concerned and is in itself entertaining and brand-building in its form. This is the challenge.

Even companies with 3,000 - 4,000 employees feel that it is a big deal to have three or four people employed full-time to write to customers. They also feel the need to keep control of what is written.

The user is a radio station

The Internet is the place where relationships and loyalty are created. Everyone in the company becomes its sales staff, but the customers must be able to join in. This can take place through contributions to debate, by sending in anything from questions, drawings and poems to precise descriptions of their requirements. And customers really love this. This is one of the reasons why online meeting places on the net generally expect that in the long term approximately 80 percent of the content will be generated by the users themselves. Let the customers talk to each other, and listen in!

One of the greatest strengths of the Internet is that it makes it easier to make contact. Address, paper, stamps and biros are no longer needed to bring the customer in contact with a company. All that is needed is to key about 15 characters into an e-mail client. And unlike the telephone, the Internet does not require there to be a person at each end of the line. Internet communication works just as well asynchronously.

The medium imposes obligations

Can the company decline to be part of this dialogue and instead just use the Internet as a shop window? No, this is not to be recommended. Experience and studies show clearly that customers demand that companies which are market leaders in all other communication should also be in a position to use the Internet on its own terms. And these terms are simple enough:

1. The Internet has an informal jargon. Companies should (as always) think twice before weighing down their communication with formalities or stiffness. It is easy to appear stilted, old-fashioned and inflexible.
2. The medium is by definition rapid, so there is no use taking days or weeks to reply to a communication. It is all the same to the customer whether this is due to a lack of time or whether it is because the reply has to go the rounds of the legal department.

Ten pieces of advice
that can help to create loyalty

If the company is convinced that loyalty needs to be created via the Internet and if it is prepared to introduce the necessary changes, here are 10 pieces of advice that can point the company in the right direction.

1. The genuinely interested person

Engage or appoint one person in the company to be responsible for customer loyalty. Let the person concerned play a part in editing the company's website in close dialogue with the webmaster and the web editor (if these are different people).

2. The talents on the keyboard

Find and train a number of employees who will carry

on an informal but serious and individual dialogue with the customers. They must have the personal flair and judgement to be able to act in a customer-oriented way on everything from criticisms to enquiries. It may, for example, be a good idea to prepare an 'inspiration' presentation about how employees can write to the customers over the Internet. But let them each do their own thing, and trust them.

3. The tool
Create a home page which gives information and dialogue equal priority to the graphic presentation. Both the form and the content must play a part in building up the company's profile.

4. Tell the customers
what to talk about
Give the customers examples of what they can write e-mails about, instead of just creating an open module where they can think up subjects themselves. Ask questions for them to answer and to start their imagination working on finding similar questions. (When it is said that it is only imagination which sets limits, it turns out surprisingly often that these limits are narrower than many people believe.)

5. Save the customers' time
Make the questions that have already been answered available to the customers in the form of an FAQ area (frequently asked questions). Studies show that after two to three months of customer dialogue 70 to 80 percent of all question variants have been answered, which also means that the resources allocated to ordinary enquiries can gradually be used for more targeted and individual dialogue.

6. Proximity
Ensure that the dialogue on the net is made available to employees and to the management in particular. This

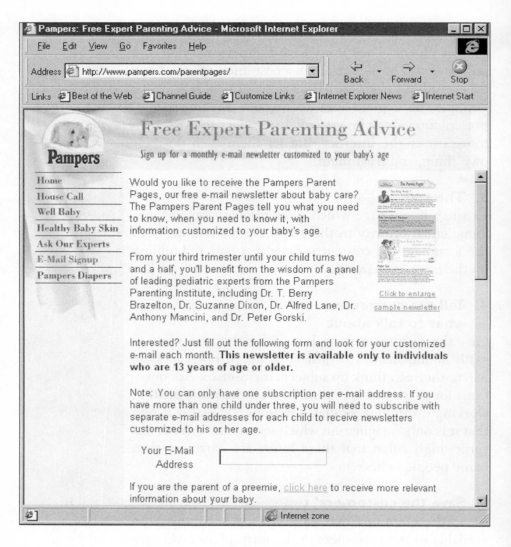

Pampers are already sending out personalised e-mails to new parents with all sorts of advice.

can, for example, be carried out via a 'war room' from which all first-time communications with the customers are handled. Position the room close to the management offices. It is quite healthy for the management to hear what the customers are actually saying to them. Just as the Internet is directing advertising agencies' attention towards customer dialogue, in the same way the Internet will be a significant influence in bringing the management back closer to the customers. There is a big difference between reading a customer survey from a reputable institute of analysis and seeing the customers' comments written directly on the home page. But take care, uncensored reality can be a great shock to a sensitive soul.

7. Be open and honest
Be honest with the customers. The Internet sets the stage for intimacy (as does all dialogue, and intimacy is a great creator of loyalty), so say things plainly. If the company has an altruistic and noble mission it is amazing how much the outside world can stand being told about it; also about the weaker aspects.

8. Let the customers make themselves heard
Use the opportunity to accommodate dialogue between the customers. Even if this is negative it is better that it takes place with the company's knowledge and co-operation. Allow users to influence and shape the presence of the company on the net. Utilise the interactivity to make the users visible on the website.

9. Let the customers make themselves known
If the knowledge which the company accumulates is used to customise and adapt the dialogue and the options for the individual user, it is amazing how much users can be persuaded to tell about themselves and their habits and wishes. This knowledge must under no circumstances be misused, but used correctly it is the driving force in the loyalty program and is therefore worth its weight in gold.

10. Be an optimist – but a realist
The Internet cannot at present replace either advertising films or printed material which is sent out to customers. Therefore it is necessary to have realistic goals and focus on the Internet in combination with other media.

The future of direct e-marketing
Spam (unsolicited junk e-mail) has always been seen as

one of the bad things that came along with the Internet, even though we are experiencing the same every day through our mail boxes. Nevertheless e-mails are still a very strong engine for creating awareness and traffic (see also Chapter 12). Companies just have to invent and learn the new rules. The first would be to use an opt-in model for sending out mail. This approach is broadly accepted. And the better companies learn to direct and personalise the mail they are sending towards the target customers, the higher value they will create. What is beginning to be seen is rich content e-mail, which over time will replace physical junk mail. The interesting part about such a mail is that it can even serve as a mini-store, where the customer will be able to buy products, get further information, get personal advice and communicate back easily and immediately. The potential is huge.

Why brand-build on the Internet?

"Brand is more than a name. It represents a relationship customers have come to know and value."

Regis McKenna

A brief introduction
to the concept of brand-building

Brands have existed in their present form for more than 100 years and products such as Kodak and Coca-Cola have been on the market for over a hundred years. The building up of a brand, brand-building, is therefore a relatively new communication discipline.

The traditional ideas concerning brand-building and the value of this have been challenged countless times and there have been many attempts to kill off brands. In spite of this, the value of most western companies is today worked out on the basis of the value of their brand; not the production apparatus, income or work-force. The value rises and falls in line with how much additional income the brand can provide for the company in comparison to a similar product that is sold generically – that is, without an identity.

Is there any value in online branding?

Since the Internet was used for the first time as a commercial medium, a constant debate has raged as to whether online branding has any effect or not. Forrester Research stated in their report *Branding On the Web*, in August 1997, that until 2000 the Internet won't be cost-efficient for major brands. The same report announced that by 2002 acceptable Internet penetration, functional e-commerce and bandwidth would boom the role of branding on the Internet.

Only one-and-a-half years after the report was published, it was clear that these projections were already outdated. Forrester Research stated in a survey conducted in March 1999 that 31 percent of the 52 top US advertisers said their core reason for going online was innovative ways to express brand benefits. The increase of direct e-marketing, a faster penetration than expected, stronger integration with television and better use of interactivity have caused this change. And according to another study, conducted by IBM in December 1998, 28 percent of all Western companies going online today stated branding was their main objective.

The value of a strong brand to the producer

The building of a brand, or a set of values, associated with the actual product provides it with an 'increase in value' or 'additional value'.

A strong brand has therefore great value for its owner, as it represents a means whereby turnover and income can be generated and at the same time it can be protected against attack or infringement of ownership by competitors.

To give an idea of the significance of a brand for a company, in 1991 Phillip Morris purchased Kraft Foods for about US$20 billion – estimated to be four times the value of the company's material assets.

The value of a strong brand to the customers

The relationship between the customers and the brand is reminiscent in many ways of a contract. The consumers know the advantages associated with buying a brand and rightly expect that the producer will deliver the full value. For example, the buyer of a Rolls-Royce expects that the car will be reliable, that it will be designed and manufactured to a very high standard and that the service network will work without a hitch. The buyer also expects that the more abstract emotional advantages – the psychological product – which he or she has bought will be retained. This means that Rolls-Royce must prevent the unauthorised use of the Rolls-Royce name, as misuse could detract from the high value of the abstract benefits of being a Rolls-Royce owner. It is therefore in the interest of every brand producer to look after these more abstract properties of the brand very carefully.

Brand advertising creates a distinctly favourable image that customers associate with a product at the moment they make a buying decision.

Successful brands stand for much more than smart values that attract the consumers only a single time. The values that create a brand are dynamic assets which have to be adapted and adjusted the whole time in order to retain the interest of the consumers.

When companies market themselves using traditional media, this takes place on the basis of well-prepared, well-defined and often also well-tested communication strategies. It is therefore astonishing that many companies have launched themselves out into cyberspace blindfolded, without having first carried out the usual strategic considerations concerning the fundamental purpose: the presentation of the company and its products.

Brands are about trust

A strong brand is invaluable, as the battle for customers is intensifying daily. When communication with users on the Internet is being developed it should be with a view to brand-building. It should not involve introspective company and product presentations, which is what a large proportion of all websites today amount to.

The future Internet generation doesn't trust the Internet at all – but they trust brands.

How much do you trust the information you get from:

	great deal	some what	not at all
your parents	83	16	1
teachers	61	35	3
religious leaders	55	32	11
friends	48	49	3
tv and newspapers	39	53	7
the Internet	13	62	24

source: Time/CNN 1999 from a survey carried out on teenagers between 13-17 years of age.

The enormous amount of websites and the resultant increasing confusion on the Internet mean that in the future the individual user will rely to an increasing extent on brand names, as they trust the names. It is not

A Model for Understanding Trust

As consumers interact with a site, they determine whether or not they trust it. Studio Archetype's study focussed on the first phase – building trust – but notes that the next phases, confirming and maintaining trust, are the bases of true customer loyalty.

As consumers interact with a site, they determine whether or not they trust it.

Levels of Trust

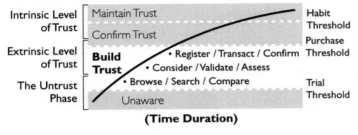

(Time Duration)

Source: Studio Archetype

surprising that consumers with access to the Internet tend to visit their preferred main brands on the Internet within a relatively short period of time, predominantly on account of curiosity but also because they already have a positive relationship with the product. In addition, they have expectations that they want fulfilled by their visit to the website.

For many users, brands will therefore act as a trusted 'consumer guide' on the Internet; a development which in the future will make much greater demands for the online brand. As the media will at the same time gradually merge into each other, for instance with the introduction of the Internet phone, the Internet mobile phone or the Internet-based television (a television set which can both show television and provide access to the Internet), such as the Microsoft-owned WebTV or its competitor NetTV, it is also of the greatest importance that work is carried out to create both synergy and recurrence in the brand's many activities connected with communication. Great differences between the communication concerning a brand using the traditional media compared to the Internet will become only too obvious when it is possible to 'change channel' from the television straight to a website. This could

... But TV Drives Traffic to Sites

Offline Sources to find URLs for Product and Service info

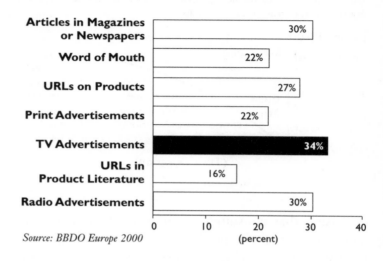

	percent
Articles in Magazines or Newspapers	30%
Word of Mouth	22%
URLs on Products	27%
Print Advertisements	22%
TV Advertisements	34%
URLs in Product Literature	16%
Radio Advertisements	30%

Source: BBDO Europe 2000

ultimately weaken the consumers' trust in the brand as the brand the consumer has known and loved for years no longer represents the well-known consistent image.

Leveraging real-world brand equity

One of the emerging problems of today's Internet world – and a major opportunity for offline brands – is the lack of trust consumers have in websites and online brands. People don't trust the information they are being exposed to on the net and are afraid of an invasion of their privacy online, in addition to being suspicious of the security of online purchasing systems.

The consumer's lack of trust is a symptom of weak brand management. Far too many websites tarnish their brand's image by bombarding the consumer with information they don't want or need, instead of using the intelligence gained from their site to restrict communications to that which is relevant.

A consumer may know and respect an online brand but their trust in that brand is what keeps them coming back.

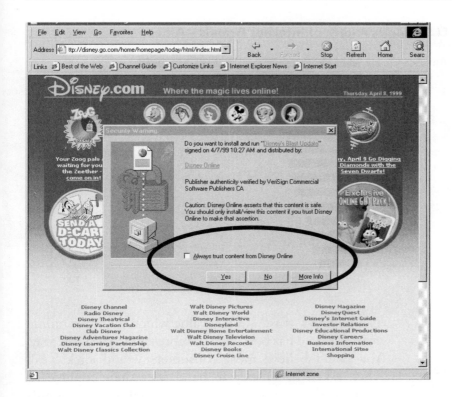

Maintaining the consumer's trust in a brand requires very defined guidelines for what the brand stands for and how it has to evolve in an online environment. This is what we define as brand-building. Companies wanting to form a relationship with their customers should employ appropriate rules to manage their brand-building relationship with their online customers.

Would you click 'yes' to this statement?

Global brands get a global medium

Only a few international brands have managed to transfer their offline brand values to the online world without either cannibalising the existing brand or establishing an online presence with very little added consumer value. Disney is one of the few 'real world' brands that has managed to control their brand image when they bridged the technology gap and extended their business online. The difference between Disney and online-only brands is that Disney not only represents a depth, but it

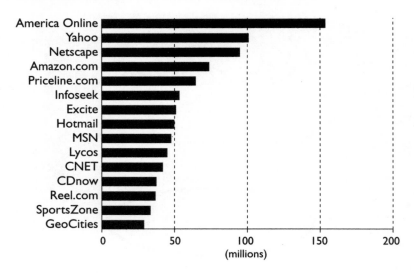

U.S. Adults Aware of Internet Brands – Aided*

Brand	(millions)
America Online	
Yahoo	
Netscape	
Amazon.com	
Priceline.com	
Infoseek	
Excite	
Hotmail	
MSN	
Lycos	
CNET	
CDnow	
Reel.com	
SportsZone	
GeoCities	

How famous is your company? A recent study identified seven 'Internet brands' recognisable by at least 50 million Americans – not bad for companies that are mostly five years old or less.
Source: Results are based on a telephone survey of 1,013 adults in September 1998, for opinion research by Priceline.com

also portrays 'trust' – a key value which no other online created brand has been able to represent in the same way. You could believe most consumers would click 'yes!' when asked by Disney to hand over their credit card number. Can the same be said for online-only brands such as the gambling site www.goldenpalace.com? At this stage, probably not, as there probably still would be a sense of hesitation by most consumers.

Goodwill and trust can't be bought, they are earned over time. Considering no online brand can represent more than a five-year history, there have been only a few online brands that have earned consumer trust, for example, Yahoo!, Amazon, AOL and Excite. It could be said that 'real world' trusted brands such as Disney have 'free tickets' to consumer web trust while the online brand market is still immature. However, established brands like Disney have realised they have to employ the same brand management respect for the customer that they'd have in the real world to maintain and extend that 'Disney-esque' trust from real world to online world. Disney takes all that is good about their company (family values, safe community, and trust) and transfers it online.

It is clear from current suspicions and a lack of online brand trust that future consumers will prefer the brands that respect the privacy of the individual and work to gain and maintain the consumer's trust in their brand. It comes back to the basic life principle of respect for the individual.

There is no doubt that when developing a brand-building strategy on the Internet it is possible to draw on experience gained from traditional brand-building in many areas and leverage on the values represented by existing brands. It is, however, important to remember that in just as many areas the nature of brand-building on the Internet differs from traditional brand-building, as the Internet must be used on its own terms. This is a matter of creating a dialogue with the consumers using interactivity, not mindlessly bombarding the consumers with the same advertising message day after day, week after week. Moving offline brands to the online world or establishing totally new online brands is a discipline that in many ways can result in 'brand suicide'.

The benefits of two-way brand-building

It is characteristic of today's brands that they have been primarily built up via one-way communication; that is, via mass media which are predominantly based on monologues, for example television, radio, the press (printed advertisements in newspapers, magazines and periodicals) and in the street (posters and advertisement display pillars). The reason for this is obvious: individual communication has to date been associated with very high costs and great difficulty.

However, no-one has ever doubted the value of individual or dialogue-based communication and there have been countless attempts to create such communication.

In 1991 an American publishing company launched an 'individual advertisement-based magazine' which made it possible for the first time for advertisers to address the individual consumer directly. The idea was simple but the technology was complex. In brief, the publishing company, via subscription-based magazines, divided the readers into sectors based on their interests. If an advertiser wanted to reach a particular target group, the advertisement in the magazine could be individualised by laser-printing the reader's own name and individual interests into the text.

The response was overwhelming but, not surprisingly, the technique proved to be too expensive in comparison with the contact price.

Telemarketing has similarly proved its worth for a long time. In several countries telephone canvassing (phoning a consumer for the sole purpose of making a sale) has been banned. Exceptions to this are the sale of magazine and newspaper subscriptions and sales on the business-to-business market. The reason is quite simply that the media is so effective in sales situations that the Consumer's Ombudsman recommended a ban in order to prevent the consumers being misled into making 'wrong' decisions.

Why is there an increasing interest in the individualisation of communication?

The numerous attempts to individualise communication within consumer marketing and to base it on dialogue are to be viewed primarily against the background of the radical changes in consumers' media habits during the 1980s and 1990s. The average television viewing time for consumers in Europe increased from 15.2 hours a week in 1990 to 25.2 hours in 2000. What is interesting is not so much the increase in viewing but the changes in behaviour which were noted at the same time. Today we have what every advertisement producer and advertiser has dreaded, namely the disloyal viewer. The viewer changed channels on average every two

User Growth

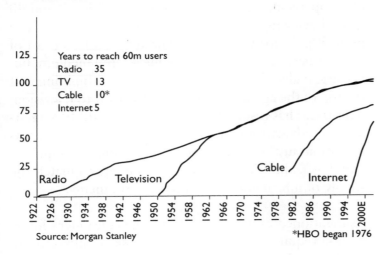

Years to reach 60m users
Radio 35
TV 13
Cable 10*
Internet 5

Source: Morgan Stanley

*HBO began 1976

The use of television and the Internet has risen sharply in the US.

minutes in 1999 against every six minutes in 1989. Viewers have no patience any more, they have become more restless, more critical and more selective. The whole population no longer sits glued to the set when a box-office hit is being shown, not because films have got worse but because viewers have divided themselves into sectors in comparison to just 10 years ago. The increasingly large selection of television channels and magazines means that to a greater extent than ever before consumers are able to select, and to reject.

Against this background many people have looked on the Internet as a glimmer of hope in the efforts to establish a more permanent individual contact with the consumers, and this hope is justified. According to an analysis carried out by BBDO, New York, in 1995 Americans watched on average 40.2 hours of television a week – while only 2.44 hours were spent in cyberspace. The relative amounts are changing quickly however. Three years later, in 1998, 5.02 hours a week were spent in cyberspace. BBDO's analysis also shows that on average people surf the Internet for 30-40 minutes at a time. The average duration of a visit to a

More and more retailers complain that television commercials aren't as effective as they were only five years ago.

website is estimated to be three to four minutes. By way of comparison, viewers spend only between 30 and 40 seconds viewing a particular brand on television. The figures speak for themselves. The Internet is not just of interest because it is a new and unexplored medium, but because it already constitutes, when brand-building is at the top of the agenda, a serious competitor to television. This trend has resulted in falling prices with the screening of advertisements on US television. Whereas television just lets the consumer change channel or switch off, the Internet allows consumers to match the supply of information with their requirements.

As mentioned in the introduction, the consumer's information requirements are seldom one-sided introspective product and company presentations and therefore some other fare must be served up when the aim is to communicate to, and especially with, consumers. The next chapter looks in greater detail at the strategic construction of this communication on a website.

CHAPTER **VIII**

Strategic building up of brands on the Internet

*"The difference between a product
and a brand is that the product has a physical existence
— the brand just exists somewhere in the consumer's mind."*

Anon.

M uch of the experience which has been gained over the years with the development of marketing strategies based on traditional channels of communication can, as mentioned in Chapter 7, be transferred to the Internet. Once the main aims of going on the net have been determined, the strategic planning of the marketing activities on the Internet can be divided into four stages:

As in all communication it is a question of knowing who is being communicated with. As the Internet provides excellent opportunities to carry out targeted communication, it is important to carry out a (web) segmentation of the potential users of a website and to define precisely the primary target group. Only when the target group has been defined can the next step be taken of outlining the framework for the communication, which will typically be focused on the brand attitude. The main thing is to decide which brand values the website is to communicate during a visit. In contrast to traditional marketing, with the Internet it is possible simultaneously to expose the users to many of the dimensions of the brand. This demands good organisation of the communication of the selected values – a special form of web brand-building. Finally, it is important to draw up a number of concrete goals for the website, in order subsequently to be able to evaluate the quality of the communication which has been developed.

It is important to stress that the four stages in the marketing planning described in the following pages cannot be implemented individually – they must be gone through sequentially. The process demands that we look forwards as well as backwards, as the four stages are integrated.

Going through the four stages leads on to the formulation of a well-planned web development strategy. This is dealt with separately in Chapter 9.

Web segmentation

Observing the many different websites that exist on the Internet today, it appears that many companies have made the mistake of believing that on the Internet they are communicating with everyone in the world. The Internet should instead be regarded as a very narrow channel of communication. Why is this?

Several car websites, most of them set up at the beginning of 1997, were based on comprehensive concepts which covered the interests of all car-owners. On the most wide-ranging websites everything from sports news, lists of cinemas and film reviews to the latest news from the gossip columns could be found. The level of ambition was high. The only problem was that those people who wanted information about the latest car models, or updated information about this, often looked in vain. Either the information did not exist, or it was too hard to find, or it was out of date, simply because the manufacturer did not have enough resources to keep it updated.

Car manufacturers were trying to communicate with all car owners at once – a target group which represents 50 to 60 percent of all the users on the Internet! It is impossible to build up an intensive dialogue or interaction with so large a target group at one time. One of the unique features of the Internet is that the medium's penetration covers a wide spectrum of the consumer sector, but from the point of view of marketing this is a disadvantage as it is impossible to enter into a dialogue with all the Internet's users at once. Dialogue is after all created by communicating in a targeted way with one or more recipients. The larger the number of different recipients of a message, the greater the danger that the communication will lose its direction and thus change character, from being dialogue-based to being mono-logue-based. If a precise target group can be defined, it is likely that a personal dialogue with the users can be achieved. This corresponds to a traditional dialogue, where the fewer the participants, the better the interaction and identification.

Experience with traditional media shows that the better the recipient of the communication is known, the better the communication can be adapted and individ-ualised. When it is a question of building up a personal lasting dialogue on the Internet, this parameter is par-ticularly important for the success of the website.

Embody the brand

A good way of defining a target group is to describe a particular person. What does the person look like, how does the person dress? Is it a family person with kids? What does he or she do for a living, and after work hours? What do this person's friends look like? Who would the person associate with at a dinner party?

A detailed description of the target group not only helps in determining the content of the site but also ensures that all people involved in the development process (concept developer, graphic designer, copywriter etc.) get a clear picture of who they are talking to.

An important part of strong brand-building is to ensure a harmony between the target group and the website. It is critical to know customers to be able to gain their confidence. If the content doesn't match their expecta-tions and speak the same language, the communication can do more harm than good. While constructing and planning a website, find out what requirements and expectations the users may have before, during and after the visit to the website. Do the users expect to be able to buy goods, test products, send e-mails or just obtain information? As in all other marketing, it is a question of knowing the actual and potential customers as well as possible. Knowing what interests they have, what they might decide to look for and why, then there is a good chance the dialogue built up via the website will be of interest and will involve the users. This is important on the Internet, not least because in the first instance it is the user who pays to be exposed to advertising material (via the telephone and subscription charges) and is therefore justified in having high expectations.

Segmentation of the users on the Internet

One of the features of the Internet is that it is possible to individualise the communication, without this necessarily leading to high unforeseeable costs. However, it is first necessary to carry out a segmentation of the users.

One of the more overlooked segmentation options which experience has shown to be particularly effective is the individualisation of a website's content in accordance with, for example, the user's age or gender – that is demographic criteria. As web technology develops further and its penetration increases, the segmentation criteria will become much more sophisticated, and geographic or demographic criteria will gradually lose their significance.

What do you want the consumer to gain on your site before, during and after their visit?

Before the visit	During the visit	After the visit	When receiving an e-mail from the site

Many products, such as Gillette, are aimed at a wide range of age groups on the Internet. However, communication aimed at different age groups should actually be very different – not to mention communication aimed at the two genders. Many companies could use further segmentation of their websites as a way to avoid 'genderless' websites.

The target group's psychographic characteristics (behaviour, preferences, life-style, etc.) can and should have an influence upon the design of a website. When marketing a car it is important to know whether the target group is primarily interested in the technology or makes a selection based primarily on design and/or various safety features. The three different dimensions will demand three different approaches to the product and will make different demands on the design of the website. As most websites today are database driven, it is fairly easy to segment the content to each of the different segments without major costs and without the visitor being aware of this. The result is a customised website that changes content automatically according to the consumer profile.

As the Internet is still a relatively new medium, the users have at present a number of psychographic characteristics in common. They are inquisitive, restless, hungry for information and innovative. There is no doubt that this profile will change in the years to come as the Internet's penetration increases. However, it will be worthwhile bearing in mind the above user characteristics and motivations for a while yet.

Relatively little information is required about the users in order to be able to reveal their areas of interest and thus obtain an indication of how the website is to be constructed. The development of the Internet has already made it possible to chart online a user's behaviour during a visit to the first pages of a website and then subsequently for this to determine what pages the user is to be exposed to and which site the user came from. If right at the start a user goes to a page with a lot of technical information about a particular product, the sequence of the subsequent pages can be reconfigured so that the focus of the website is upon more technical aspects. This subject is dealt with in greater detail in Chapter 14.

Selection of web values

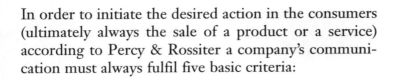

As described by way of introduction, the work concerning the brand's values consists primarily of identifying the framework for communication on the website; that is, what communicative function is the website to have in the buying decision process?

In order to initiate the desired action in the consumers (ultimately always the sale of a product or a service) according to Percy & Rossiter a company's communication must always fulfil five basic criteria:

The communication on the website must:

1. Activate a need for a particular product category.
2. Create brand awareness (recognition and recall of the product).
3. Make it possible to distinguish the product from competing products (evaluation of the product's ability to meet a particular need and comparison of the product and competing products).
4. Create the desire to buy in the consumer.
5. Indicate where the product can be bought (make a concrete consumer action possible).

1. Activation of the need for a particular product category

If the product is one which the target group only buys occasionally, product category need is not a communication aim. However, if the product is of a fairly new type, the first aim of the communication is to create a link between the product category and a particular motivation within the target group. This can, for example, be carried out by the website giving the users the opportunity to have the product demonstrated or to compare it with similar products.

2. Creation of awareness

In order to influence the consumer's attitude (perception of the product) it is absolutely vital to create awareness of the brand. The better the website is able to attract attention within the first 30 seconds, the greater the chance the user will not leave the website. In this regard many websites have started to construct tunnels – little interactive trailers aimed at attracting the attention of the users and motivating them to spend some time with the brand. A web tunnel will typically be an animated introduction. The animation is activated when the website is visited.

3. Creation of brand attitude

This is described in greater detail in the next section.

4. Creation of intention to buy

The creation of a conscious intention to buy is almost always an aim of communication with the customers. If the individual consumer is in the market for the product and the brand attitude is positive, the intention to buy will arise when the product is presented on the website. However, if the product is one where the involvement is low and where the motivation is positive (for example, products such as soda water, ice-cream, etc.), the intention to buy arises unconsciously at the last moment. In such cases the intention to buy will not be a communication aim on a website, unless the goods are to be sold online via the Internet.

5. Purchasing facility

It does not matter how good the communication may be

concerning a product if the consumer does not know where the product can be bought, how much it costs and whether it is the right product in a particular situation. If the product can be bought online, the communication must of course make this clear to the users. This should be obvious, for example with links to a sales page after all the product presentations. Many websites still suffer from having such complex navigation that users often abandon buying a product, even though both the opportunity and the motivation are present.

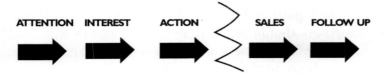

ATTENTION   INTEREST   ACTION   SALES   FOLLOW UP

This process can take less than five minutes in an online world compared with several weeks in the 'real world'. A major problem however, is that only very few sites today are able to lead action into sales.

The Internet is unique in that today it is the only medium – apart from a shop – which can independently handle all five functions in the communication process. The Internet can activate a need for a product category, create awareness, help the user to evaluate the product, create the intention to buy, make it possible for the user to buy the product and follow up after the sales. Both the time and distance parameters in the purchasing decision process are considerably shorter than for a 'traditional' marketing and sales situation, increasing the likelihood of rapid consumer action. Factors such as 'a lack of time', 'too great a distance' and 'too difficult' are eliminated. This is an important reason why in the future a website will be in many ways a much more effective tool in the sales process than traditional media.

As the above shows, it is extremely important that the whole presentation and sales process on the website is carefully planned. What action are the users to take during the visit? Is the website only intended to create interest – or is the visit to result in a concrete action in the form of product enquiries or a purchase? By considering the users' possible patterns of action and constructing the website based on these the situation can be avoided where a lack of the required content or difficult navigation stop the users in the middle of the course of action.

When the patterns of action have been determined on the site it is important to create a similar pattern outside the site to resolve where the consumers spend their time. Smart brands will get their messages off the corporate website and into the places their customers live. I-traffic did it for Disney when *101 Dalmatians* launched, putting dot spots all over the Internet. Wine advertisers should infiltrate recipe sections of sites like *Epicurious*. When users print the recipe, the brand message ends up on the kitchen counter.

Strategic considerations regarding brand attitude

Every brand consists of a network of associations; a structure of values which together make up the consumer's attitude to the brand. The brand attitude can thus be defined as the consumer's general evaluation of the product's ability to satisfy a particular motivation. Brand attitude will therefore always be a relative factor.

As the consumers always make a choice between several competing products on the basis of brand attitude, this must always be a goal of communication. Another reason for focusing strongly on brand attitude is that a visit to a website is practically always motivated by a knowledge of a product and by 'being in the market' for the product category.

Concerning brand attitude, one of the tasks listed below will always be relevant.

1. Create attitude (if the target group knows the name, web address or logo but cannot describe the characteristics of the product).

2. Increase attitude (if the attitude to the product is only slightly favourable).
3. Maintain attitude (if the target group's attitude to the brand is optimal this has only to be confirmed).
4. Modify attitude (reposition the product in the minds of the target group; for example, Pepsi tried to move from a diffuse target group to a well-defined younger target group by means of the concept 'GeneratioNEXT'). Modification of attitude will typically be required when the brand represents a number of 'old-fashioned' values or values which are not able to differentiate the brand's conceptual structure from that of its competitors.
5. Change the brand's attitude. This will typically be required when the brand has more negative than positive values.

Development of the brand platform

A brand consists of a range of different parameters, which all together create the total consumer perception of the product. The four categories below indicate the key elements, which create the basic brand platform or the brand 'DNA'. It is essential that the questions in each category have been thought through before the brand establishes an online presence, as a weak brand platform will be clearly reflected as a weak website.

Four brand key elements together create the brand platform.

The four brand key elements

This chapter will mainly concentrate on level 2 'brand personality', as this phase is the most vital level to clarify before establishing an online presence.

ROLE

The role of the brand:
1. What is the purpose of the brand?
2. How can it help the consumer?
3. What role do you expect the brand to have in the consumer's life?
4. What benefits (both emotional and rational) can the brand offer?

PERSONALITY

The personality of the brand:
1. What is the look and feel of the brand?
2. What tone-of-voice does the brand have?
3. What personality would the brand have if you should describe the brand as a real friend?

ACHIEVEMENT

What is the brand to achieve?
1. How is the brand differentiating from the competitors?
2. What unique benefits (emotional and rational) does the brand offer the consumer compared with the competitors?
3. How does the brand ensure it is different from the competitors in the future?

BRAND BACKUP

The brand backup:
1. What makes all the above claims credible?
2. What background, history or inventors prove that the brand clearly is trustworthy?

This listing should not be seen as a prioritisation of the importance of the above elements, as all four parameters are equally significant.

A brand not only talks – it listens, learns, reacts

To help crystallise the image of a brand, one can describe the (brand) personality users will interact with. The online brand should be seen as a person who talks, but also listens, learns, reacts. The better the brand is at this, the more opportunity there is to attach attractive values to it, so creating a positive brand attitude.

Orchestrating the brand

Sight is the key for online decisions. Think about it. The senses we use to buy a real product don't work in cyber-space: holding it in our hand isn't possible, smelling belongs to the past, and tasting – forget it. Our role will be to help consumers smell, taste and feel with the eye. Online marketing of products will be a huge challenge.

In the past, brand control covered the logo, graphic style, picture quality, typography and message. These are still important – but a brand 'voice' now includes the sound of a website, the tone of voice in e-mails, down-loading time, ease of navigation, security, colour scheme and the way a call centre handles enquiries. These add up to the perfect brand in the consumers' mind. Controlling all these elements will not only be a very important part in companies' future communication strategy, it will be critical to consumers' selection of products. The winners of the brand war will be those able to bring out every nuance locked within the orchestra, creating the perfect flow and the perfect impression in consumers' minds.

The world's most successful brands are characterised by a small but well-defined set of values, reflected in all communication from the brand. Below is a value propos-ition map, which helps to define a brand's value set. This useful model determines a brand's precise position on the consumer's value map. The closer are the chosen val-ues on the map, the stronger is the brand that has been created. If the values are spread all over the map it typi-cally indicates a weakness in the brand profile.

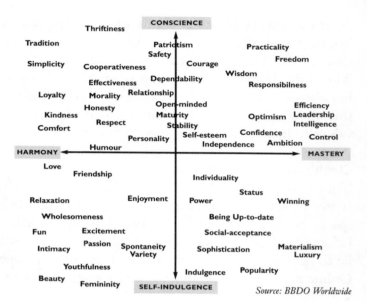

The brand is created by hundreds of different values. The closer values a brand represents, the stronger the brand is.

Source: BBDO Worldwide

The first time a user is exposed to a product in traditional media, the communication often just deals with a few product features – typically one or two USPs (unique selling points) or ESPs (emotional selling points). The set of values which is constructed based on this will also typically consist of two or three core values and will therefore not be very faceted.

In contrast, during a dialogue on the Internet the consumers will typically construct a nuanced network of associations consisting of a great many values all supporting the main set of values. These values would often be impossible to incorporate into traditional marketing due to a lack of time and interactivity.

If, for example, a website gives the users the opportunity to download actual product-related tools which can help to make tasks easier, quicker or more reliable to carry out (for example, if a bank lets the users download a budget plan), this will give the brand added value in the form of a positive attitude.

The brand has suddenly helped the individual user and thereby shown an openness and accessibility which was perhaps not previously experienced in connection with the company. This dimension will often be very difficult to convey via television or in print, as these media find it difficult to convince, involve and interact with the users over any long period of time.

But just as goodwill can be created via the Internet, 'badwill' can be easy to establish. If a bank website, for example, is difficult to use because of bad navigation, or the downloading time simply takes too long, this will indirectly reflect the brand's position. The intention might have been to be effective, easy and cheap, but might end up being slow, difficult and expensive, as this was the impression the consumer got after spending 10 minutes on the site.

Brand-building on the Internet is therefore not only about controlling all the 'classic' parameters, but also controlling the total consumer experience from start to end.

Below are the values that are associated with a feminine hygiene product, Libra pads. They indicate the attitude to the product, that is, the core values and the supporting values, which were created by earlier communication of the product's characteristics.

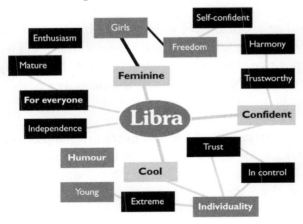

This diagram shows Libra's set of values. The predominant values in the network of associations surrounding Libra are shown in bold type.

Australia

Denmark

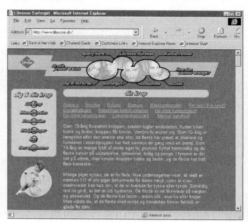

Same brand and same product, but in two different countries, representing two different cultures and approaches.

It is interesting that if the above web set of values for Libra is compared with, for example, the northern European version of the same product, the brand has a completely different brand profile, in spite of the products being identical. Great variations in a brand's profile are often due to historical factors, cultural differences or locally developed marketing strategies which over time have established an independent 'local' brand profile. The Libra example is clear proof that consumers in different markets often have widely differing perceptions of the same product, showing that, in spite of the Internet's world-encompassing philosophy, in many cases the markets should be handled individually using individual websites.

A brand exists in theory only in the mind of the consumer. A strong brand is often characterised by having many positive/innovative values attached. The stronger the brand, the higher the price the producer is able to ask for the product.

Whereas marketing of a brand in traditional media will often take as its starting point, and often limit itself to, the main values, it is possible to go a good deal further on a website.

The illustration below is given as an example of some of the values a brand might choose to be based on. The communication is not restricted to one, two or three core values, but consists of a great many values which together can create a nuanced positive attitude to the brand.

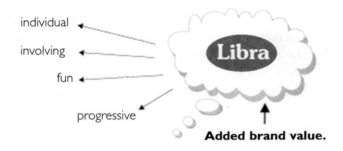

individual

involving

fun

progressive

Added brand value.

A brand is alive just like a person; it is expected to change character and attitude over time. All major brands have constantly been adjusting their brand platform to match changes in societal profile. In the future, the intensive growth in communication between people is expected to influence evaluation of brands even further. It is therefore important to have in mind how the brand should evolve over a period of one to three years to ensure a constant harmony between brand attitude and consumer profile.

The brand today	The brand in 1 year	The brand in 2 years

How is the brand expected to evolve over the next two years? Choose the five key brand values as you see them today and as you would like them to change within one and two years.

As described in Chapter 1, each medium has its advantages and therefore it will often be relevant to focus on different elements of the brand attitude in different media. The Internet still has its weaknesses; for example, television is better at showing large, attractive and atmospheric pictures. Therefore do not be tempted to try to communicate all values via the Internet without considering whether it is actually the best alternative.

Web brand-building

If a decision is made to let communication on a website deal with, for example, 10 to 15 values, there will often be several factors influencing the organisation of the communication of these values.

All behavioural research indicates that people, regardless of cultural and social differences, have only 10 to 20 basic values which control their actions. This means that there will often be considerable overlapping of the values that are to be communicated. A much more basic factor is that separate communication of so many values will spoil the good layout of the website and it is difficult to keep the visitors for the time this will require.

Organisation of values is known on a large scale from traditional marketing. Because of the brief and often incomplete exposure which the traditional media can offer at best, it has, as mentioned above, been considered necessary to develop advertisements that are based on composite topics with just a few brand values. This way of thinking has unfortunately also been brought onto the Internet, but it is a widespread

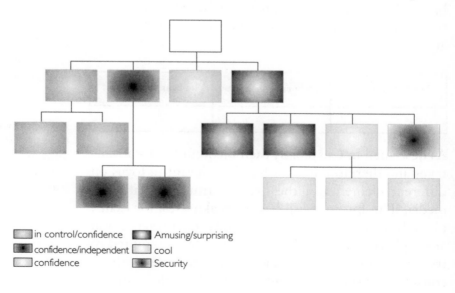

in control/confidence   Amusing/surprising
confidence/independent   cool
confidence   Security

misunderstanding that a website must at all costs be based on a composite topic.

The set of values or the attitude which it is wished to build up around the brand must be clearly supported by the many activities presented on a website. To combine all the activities, as with a television campaign, under, for example, one pay-off – a USP – however, will often be an obstacle to the subsequent development of new activities on the website. In theory each individual activity on the website should be regarded as a separate creative idea which is supported by an overall web concept, which in turn supports the brand's primary and secondary values.

Determination of the number of value centres

A number of values are gathered together in what are called value centres – centres which are supported by the associated 'attractions'.

In order to determine how many value centres the website should contain, be guided by the brand attitude and the brand's position in the market. In addition, take into consideration how long the consumer is expected to stay in the website and whether the product is a high- or low-involvement product.

If dealing with a low-involvement product where the consumers do not experience significant financial and/or psycho-social risk, it is seldom necessary to communicate many concrete product characteristics (if indeed there are any at all) and it could be questioned whether it is appropriate to develop a website for the product.

However, if the consumers feel there is considerable risk associated with the purchase, the communication of many, or all, of the product characteristics will often be necessary in order to create a positive attitude.

Building up knowledge of the many dimensions of the brand ensures the product can generate as many types of motivation as possible.

The number of value centres should therefore be consistent with the brand's value platform. A brand will typically represent about 10 to 15 core values, seldom more, and this will as a rule result in five to eight different value centres. However, it is impossible to draw up precise guidelines for how many value centres a brand website should contain, as this will depend upon the individual product and upon the present position of the brand in the market.

The website as an amusement park in cyberspace

A website can be compared to an amusement park, where a great many experiences or attractions are made available to visitors, but where it is up to the visitors to organise what they do on their visit. Walt Disney's amusement parks aim to build up and/or strengthen the many positive values that the brand stands for today. The synergy between the parks, the hotels and Walt Disney's films and merchandising is quite considerable. Walt Disney stands predominantly for soft values, and usually absent are the 'violent' attractions found in normal fairgrounds. The attractions are intended to support the overall experience the brand wants to represent. The more it is possible to predict the reaction of the visitors, the greater the likelihood that the visit will be a success, and that the position of the brand in the user's mind will be strengthened as a result.

How does this way of thinking affect understanding of how a website is to be constructed? Firstly, the sole aim is not to get as many people as possible to come to the main gate, but to make the park so attractive that the visitors will enter and stay inside for as long a time as possible and thereby build up a relationship with the brand by means of

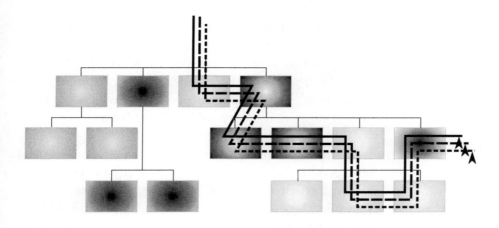

——————— 12-15 years (adult to child communication)
— — — 16-20 years (adult to adult communication)
•••••••• 21-24 years (adult to adult communication)

the many attractions. The aim is naturally that the positive experience will rub off on the brand and, not least, lead to a return visit a short while afterwards.

Web brand mapping

The starting point for a successful amusement park is a thorough knowledge of the expectations of the visitors. If the visitors expect the park to contain roller coasters, but can only find roundabouts, there is a great danger of creating a negative attitude to the brand.

However, if the park contains 10 roller coasters there is a great likelihood of a successful visit. A successful amusement park will typically have a number of main attractions and a number of smaller more individual attractions. The better a package of attractions is provided that matches the motivation of the visitors and which at the same time supports the park's overall vision, the greater success it will have.

In theory, all attractions communicate product characteristics, support values and/or build value. If the aim of the communication is to reinforce brand values such as independence, freedom, happiness and innovation,

The web value centres

The individual website:

In principle every single 'attraction' at the website represents many values. Some areas communicate serious, informative and confidence-giving product characteristics, other areas are amusing, humorous, innovative and surprising. The many value centres combine to create an overall experience of the brand. The Libra site's content (value centres) automatically changes according to the user's age.

each individual activity can and should represent/communicate one or more of these values. Of course the way to do this is not to write on the website, 'Dear visitor – here you will experience humour, happiness and innovation', but to provide activities which by their design support the core values of the brand.

It is important that the visitor is not just exposed to a few product characteristics, but experiences all the dimensions of the brand. In order to ensure this the visit must be planned in advance for the visitor. Which activities or messages should the visitor be exposed to as a minimum? What priorities should the subsequent activities have? Even if the aim is for the user to visit all the activities this is hardly realistic. Many amusement parks know the typical behaviour of a user. It should be the same with a website.

The strong attractions are the winners
Year after year the same attractions in amusement parks are among the most visited, as they represent something that the visitors find inviting. Other activities only survive for a single season. The number of visitors and the number of minutes the user has spent per attraction are typically the criteria for success. A parallel should be drawn from this for how the content of the website is to be structured and prioritised. The number of repeat visits and the number of minutes per visit to each individual section of the web should be evaluated carefully. If an 'attraction' is a success it should survive, and perhaps even be improved. 'Activities' which are seldom or never visited, or which only attract brief attention, should be evaluated based on their ability to communicate the desired brand values. If the quality is not high enough, the activities should be removed, as they may do more harm than good to the total experience of the brand.

A successful website is characterised by representing

Gay travel

↑
travel.com.au

Domestic Airfares
International Airfares
Hotel Accommodation
Tours & Package Holidays
Discount Travel Insurance
Gay Travel News
Bulletin Board

Gay Trippin'
Hot Specials

Join Gay Travel Club
Your Email
☐ Text Only
Join Now!

Gay Destination Info
General Destination Info
Gay Events Calendar
Transportation Info
Travel Toolshed
The Great OUT!doors
Email Booking Form
member of
aglta

SYDNEY GAY & LESBIAN
MARDI GRAS

We're here to help, give us a call on (02) 9249 5272 or fax us on (02) 9279 0244

many interactive activities, all of which support the website's primary concept and thereby support the values the brand wants to incorporate. The optimal website is only achieved when the website's concept is integrated so closely with the brand, the product or the service that the user feels the website is the brand.

www.travel.com.au represents a range of microsites covering everything from business, holiday, ski to gay travel.

Microsites as individual value centres

In line with the daily growth of commercial websites on the Internet, the use of microsites has become more common. Microsites, which are typically located in extensions of other theme-based websites, represent an extract of the company's or the brand's message. For example, if the user is looking for used cars, a microsite from an insurance company will appear – a microsite which focuses 100 percent on cars. Microsites are placed where the users are to be found, and they adapt their content according to what the user is looking for. This way ensures that the users are not snowed under by extensive, over-complicated commercial websites.

Often microsites are activated on the basis of the users' search behaviour. A company buys selected search words that are related to its brand's main profile. The result of this is that every time there is a search for 'cars', 'insurance' or 'claim' the brand will be displayed with tailor-made value centres relating directly to the subject searched for.

Microsites can be regarded as satellites of a company's website and also as independent websites representing just one of the brand's many value centres.

Microsites aim to elaborate upon selected values and give the user the experience that the brand offers trustworthy advice in each of these areas. The more the brand is able to bring itself in focus in a particular area, the greater credibility can be established. Presence and focus can thus act as credibility factors. Therefore the combination of microsites and company websites will often be a good Internet solution for many major branded goods manufacturers and service companies.

The Internet as a product benefit

If the use of the Internet is compared to the use of traditional media in marketing, there is no doubt that the Internet has advantages which can make the brand-building process especially effective. A good example of this is that the Internet can itself become a product benefit, a core value.

For FedEX users the Internet has become an important product benefit which they will ask for next time they send a package. The integration of brand, marketing, product and vision is slowly becoming a reality. The

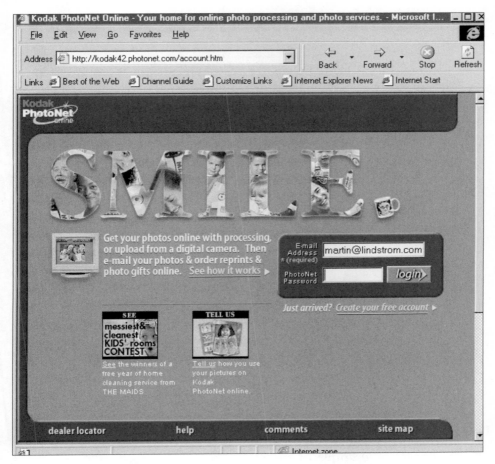

greater the integration, the greater the positive synergy and the more difficult it is for the user to change brand.

Another example is Kodak PhotoNet online. The concept offers consumers the opportunity to develop their film at a Kodak store and receive a digital version of the photos on their own Kodak page. The concept is unique as it not only manages to transfer positive values to the brand but also differentiates the brand from the competitors by clearly offering a unique service.

In 1997 Libra began the development of a comprehensive national website which had the aim of building up a closer dialogue between the brand and the users.

Drop off your film at any of 40,000 Kodak stores – and receive your photos both in print and as digital images online.

www.kodak42 .photonet.com

mini CASE

Libra

The user is
welcomed to the
website after she
has joined the Libra
club. Based on her
interests profiled
during the first visit,
the content is
configured so that
the most interesting
items "for her" are
mentioned in the
introduction.

In theory it is possible to make a website into a product benefit in all product categories, and Libra is a good example of this. Libra wanted to develop a number of activities on the Internet which would encourage a closer dialogue between the brand and the potential users. The communication task was interesting as the target group was extremely narrowly defined – girls between the ages of 12 and 17. It may seem at first that this target group was too narrowly defined, but analyses carried out on the Australian and New Zealand markets confirm that it is at this age that girls develop a very strong loyalty to a particular brand of feminine hygiene product. Because of large Internet penetration in Australia among the younger generation, where 43 percent of all Australians between 7-18 years has access to the Internet at home, it was a natural decision to use the Internet as a channel of communication to this narrowly defined target group.

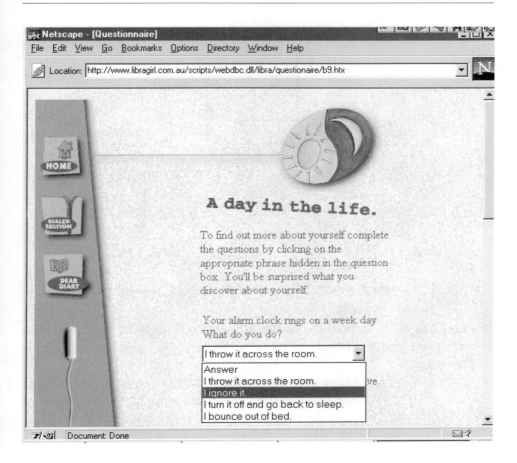

A day in the life.

To find out more about yourself complete
the questions by clicking on the
appropriate phrase hidden in the question
box. You'll be surprised what you
discover about yourself.

Your alarm clock rings on a week day.
What do you do?

I throw it across the room.

Answer
I throw it across the room.
I ignore it.
I turn it off and go back to sleep.
I bounce out of bed.

Howdey all at Libra,

Libragirl is the most coolest and grooviest website ever.
Far out! I'll have to tell all my friends now! Anyway that
D Day calendar for keeping track of 'that time of the
month' is the best. Now I won't have to advertise it on
my bedroom calendar.

Lots o love Karen

*The girl's individual
needs determine
the product.*

Instead of constructing a website which discussed various product advantages in the traditional way, the
scenario was reversed. The focus was upon the needs of
the girls rather than on the product characteristics.

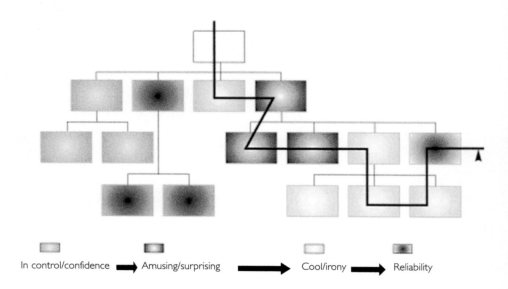

In control/confidence ➡	Amusing/surprising ➡	Cool/irony ➡	Reliability

The Libra web brand mapping.

The user's progress is mapped out on the basis of the values which it is wanted to add to the Libresse brand. Typical user behaviour will take the user through four value centres.

Aims of the Australian and New Zealand Libra website:

- The girl is to be in focus every single second she is visiting the website.
- There is to be interaction with her, we want to make her smile and feel that she is really at the centre of the Libra website.

All girls have individual needs when it is a question of feminine hygiene products – so why not start here, instead of taking the girls through a description of all 35 product variants? Such a description would be more likely to confuse them rather than help them towards a decision to buy.

When the user visits the website, she is asked for a description of her normal day. Text phrases can be selected, such as 'Every day I walk to school', 'I cycle to school' or 'I am driven to school in a car'. In all there are 12 different individual replies in the descriptive text which, when completed, provides a brief user profile of the girl. The profile results in a product recommendation. By utilising the medium's unique ability to interact with the consumer, the user is put at the centre

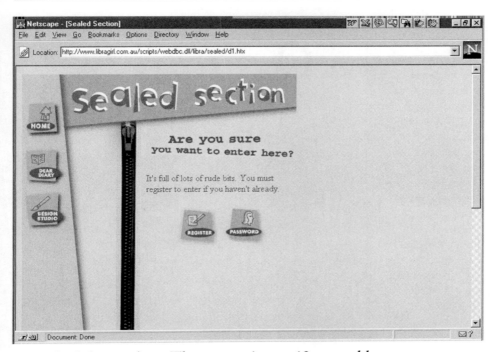

instead of the product. The uncertainty a 12-year-old girl must feel when she shops in the supermarket for the feminine hygiene product that suits her best is removed by the website and transformed into good (and extremely practical) advice. After the product recommendation the visitor is offered the chance to be reminded when her next period is due, based on the construction of a personal calendar. Two days before 'D-day' the calendar sends her an e-mail, reminding her about 'D-day'. If her period is late the girl can click on a panic button after which she will be given information about why a period can be delayed.

The website consists of 12 different activities, all based on six defined value centres. A number of the activities are placed in a 'sealed section' which is protected by a password and which requires the completion of a personal profile. It is possible to use the website without giving personal information, but the number of activities in which you can take part is then limited. Libra naturally wants to know as much about the girls as possible.

The secret password.

One of the core values at the Libra website is 'confident'. This core value (benefit) is reinforced countless times at the website, including in the 'sealed section' where the user is asked to key in her secret password.

Education in anatomy.

Based on the age of the user she can access a number of 'edutainments', all of which have the aim of making her confident about her body. The "E.R. Game" is only intended for girls in the age range 12-15. If the user is over 15, the game is automatically replaced by a game suited to an older age group.

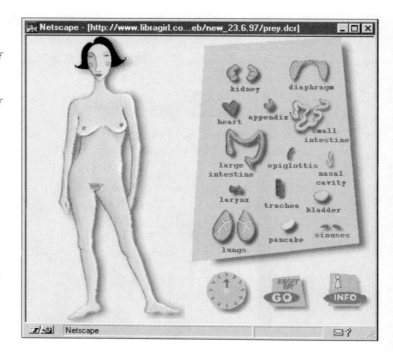

The 'sealed section' comprises a number of interactive activities which are all aimed at building up a dialogue with the girls and supporting the core values as cool, confident and feminine. The 'Kissing Game' is a test where the girls find out how good they are at kissing their boyfriends. 'Dream Date & Date from Hell' gives the girls the chance to dream about the perfect boyfriend and then vote on other suggestions sent in. The 'Gyno Game' gives the girls the opportunity to learn more about their own bodies by putting the right organs in the right places. All the activities aim to build up a relationship of trust between the brand and the user and to strengthen the core values associated with the brand.

Today the website is one of the most frequently visited Australian/New Zealand websites for girls within the target group 12-17 years old, receiving several thousand visitors a day, who on average spend 15 minutes per visit. The use of the Internet has therefore given

If the user forgets to enter her password, she is immediately presented with an amusing comment, reminding her to enter the password. The alternative would have been an error message which would have destroyed the overall experience of the brand.

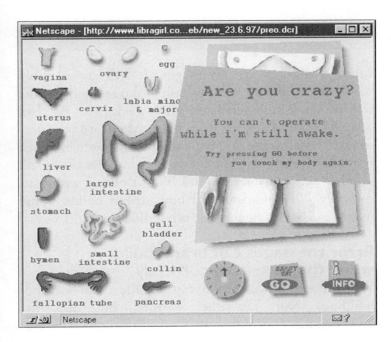

The 'Gyno Game' is only aimed at girls from 16 to 20 years old. If the girl forgets to click on the 'start' button before she moves the various parts of the body into the correct place, she receives an amusing message. The message reinforces the value centre 'cool and fun' and so helps to strengthen the overall experience of the brand.

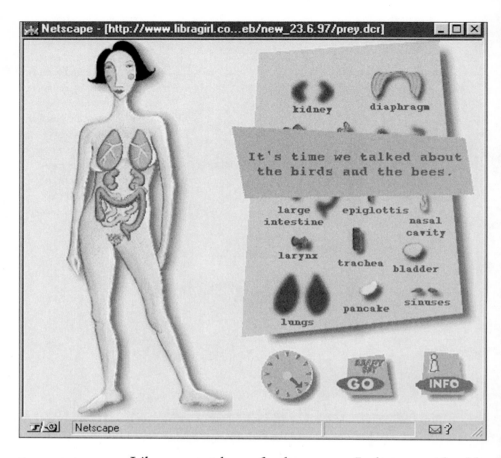

The messages change in character depending upon the age of the user.

Libra a number of advantages. It has considerably strengthened the brand's position in the market, and the website has a huge feedback. Each week Libra receives several hundred e-mails from users. Many are very personal in tone, so the original aim of the website has been fulfilled. Three years after it went online the site is still number one in Australia and New Zealand within its category – an indication of how strong online brand management can be when it is handled the right way.

Error messages can brand-build when they are used correctly

We have seen how a website can become a tool in brand-building. Not just the website, but also the error messages can, if they are used correctly, help to reinforce brands. How often does an error message appear on the screen when something wrong occurs: forgotten to fill in a coupon, forgotten to fill in a name or clicked on the wrong thing? These actions are usually perceived by the web designer as incorrect user actions, primarily because the action had not been foreseen. The response is an impersonal error message which often talks down to the consumer instead of up. But why should this be?

Incorrect navigation is the result of poor communication. Just imagine, for example, filling in a coupon in a magazine to find out more about a product and the letter is returned with the words 'Error 2323 – try again'. Would the writer know what had gone wrong and, more importantly, try again and ultimately evaluate the magazine and the company behind it positively after such an experience? Surely not. In spite of this several websites still manage to give the consumer impersonal, incomprehensible error messages.

There is not a great distance between a negative and a positive user experience. Error messages can be extremely good brand-building tools provided the opportunity is used properly. In the work with the Libra website the decision was made to use every opportunity to brand-build when a mistake was made. For every incorrect action a precisely planned reaction was prepared, often with a humorous twist.

The response to the brand-building error messages was overwhelming and is clear proof that at present we have just seen the tip of the iceberg in understanding the creative possibilities of the Internet.

Earn points by surfing with Pepsi

Pepsi is a good example of a product which primarily would belong to the i-branding category. The price of selling a bottle of Pepsi or even a case of Pepsi via the Internet would be expensive compared with the benefits the consumer would gain by just buying the brand offline.

So why should a brand like Pepsi invest money on the Internet? First of all because the match between the brand, the target group and the Internet penetration is perfect, and also because Pepsi positions itself as being 'the innovative brand' on the market – a statement which is well demonstrated via a presence on the Internet.

The Pepsi site's tone of voice is totally different from the competitors.

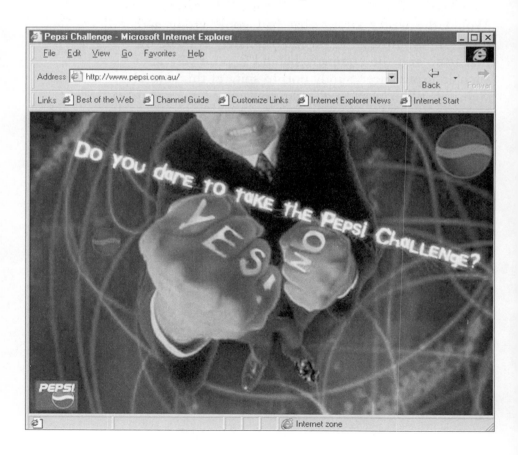

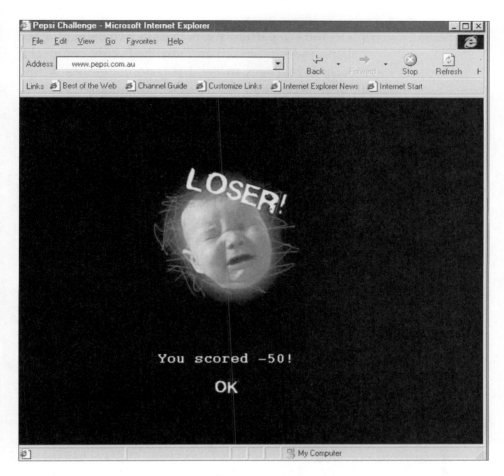

In parallel with all other i-branding sites the Pepsi site has had a major challenge to be both entertaining and, at the same time, loyal to the brand. This sounds like it should be simple but is probably the biggest challenge for brands on the Internet: What can soft drink, toilet paper, chocolate brands, etc. possibly say on the Internet without being boring or losing their core focus?

Visitors constantly receive a score status. If they aren't good enough they are asked to leave the site.

Pepsi managed to avoid this by creating the first site ever that was completely built on the concept that consumers earned points based on how well they were doing on the Pepsi website. The site, which was running until the end of 1999, was organised on the premise that it constantly offered consumers the opportunity to participate in 15 online challenges. Each challenge adds points to an individual score counter. If the visitor manages to get 1,000 points/globes during one visit, access to a lottery of several hundred valuable prizes is given. The main prize on the site is a trip to outer space, a prize worth US$98,000.

The site ignores many of the traditional brand-building rules by having a provocative and in some cases almost arrogant tone of voice. If visitors, for example, don't manage to earn enough points within a certain time limit the brand will ask them to leave the site immediately. If they get low point scores in one of the competitions – they are called 'losers'.

Sorry Martin,

I don't know how to break this to you but ...well...you lost.
Sorry about that but you're just going to have to toughen-up and try a bit harder....
Perhaps we will invite you back again - but no promise from our side.

Take care

Pepsi

A typical Pepsi direct e-mail

The site has managed to prove that the basic advertising rule, 'always talk positively to the consumer' doesn't have to be mandatory on the Internet. Pepsi's GeneratioNEXT has clearly indicated that the irony which Pepsi reflects both at the brand and also the visitors is able to win their hearts, probably because the obvious advertising message has faded out. And Pepsi's site has created a new equal tone of voice which matches this particular target group much better.

Web objectives

No matter what category the website belongs to – it will need a clearly defined set of goals. The objectives for e-operation (X-tra and Intranet) and e-commerce (online commerce) sites often are easier to define in quantitative goals than i-branding websites where the main focus is to build a stronger relationship with the consumer. It is important to stress that the guidelines on the next page are mainly dedicated to i-branding websites but can in some instances be used to measure the effectiveness of e-commerce sites.

The cardinal points in the development of a successful i-branding site is to carefully define a set of goals for what experience the consumer is to have of the brand during the visit to the website. Every page on the Internet represents an opportunity to attach and construct a set of values systematically around the brand. Therefore it is important that the decision to use the Internet is followed up by clear well-defined goals – if not quantitative, then qualitative – as this provides a significant opportunity to change the consumer's total experience of the brand.

Measurement of the communication value of the website

Unfortunately many companies have overlooked the research and evaluation elements offered by the Internet. These elements have to date been associated with considerable cost. However, the medium makes it possible to determine and measure many concrete user reactions which can give quantitative indications of the website's qualitative ability to communicate – not three weeks or three months after an exposure or an activity, but just a few seconds later!

To date the most frequently used quantitative measurement of a website's success has been the number of 'hits' or visits. However, these figures tell us nothing about the actual quality of the website. At a pinch they tell us something about how good the company has been at creating traffic on the Internet via traditional channels of communication. The quantitative goals should be based on a number of measurable parameters which can describe the quality of the communication on the website. On the Internet goals should, as a minimum, be set for:

1. The number of repeat visits.
2. The number of minutes the visitor spends per page and in total.
3. The number of minutes the visitor spends on average on the website's main activities.
4. The number of individual visitors.
5. The user's behaviour at the website.
6. The website that the user thinks of first.
7. The number of e-mails received from consumers.
8. The website's turnover and income.

1. The number of repeat visits

This parameter shows to what extent the website is able to live up to users' expectations. If the users have their needs for information, entertainment and/or communication satisfied, there is a strong possibility they will return. If the user found that the website offered far more than was expected, the probability the person concerned will return after a short period increases. If the consumer returns several times within a short period of time there is a strong possibility that the address of the brand has been added to the user's list of favourites (Bookmark), which is a feature of browsers such as Netscape Navigator or Microsoft Internet Explorer. The higher the brand comes on this 'mental' list, the better the website has been able to develop relevant communication with the visitors.

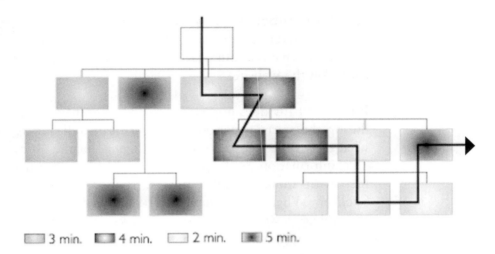

3 min.   4 min.   2 min.   5 min.

2. The number of minutes the visitor spends per page and in total

The longer the visitors spend at the website, the greater the probability that strong relationships are being built up between the users and the brand. A lot of time spent at a website will often be an expression of a high level of interactivity. However, users will often print out long texts (monologue-based communication) which will not be recorded by this type of measurement. If measurements are only taken of the total length of the visit, the subsequent evaluation will not show how the individual pages have managed to create a dialogue with the user. Therefore the measurement should include both parameters.

3. The number of minutes the visitor spends on average on the main activities of the website

The measurements per individual web page can be used to evaluate the attraction value of the main activities. For example, if two out of three pages in a main activity have resulted in long visits but not the third, this can be an indication that the creativity has come to a halt, but not the interest in the subject itself.

The web brand planning.

The more a customer's visit can be planned in advance, the better brand-building can be achieved. Are there activities/ values which the user 'must' experience as a minimum during a visit, and how long should the user spend in each 'value centre'? The answers form the basis of 'the Web Brand Mapping' - a model that maps out/illustrates the behaviour of the users at the website.

STRATEGIC BUILDING UP OF BRANDS ON THE INTERNET   173

4. The number of individual visitors

This parameter can give an indication of how successful the external communication has been in promoting traffic on the website.

If the company does not choose to advertise the website during the start-up period, this figure can indicate to what extent the website's address is logical for the users. This information can be particularly valuable to companies with more complex names, such as Marks & Spencer. What would the typical user search for and remember: www.ms.co.uk, www.marks-and-spencer.co .uk or www.marks-spencer.co.uk?

5. The user's behaviour at the website

How did the user react? Which activities were visited first and in what order were the subsequent activities selected? Is this in accordance with the messages and the values that were originally intended to be built up around the brand?

6. The website that the user thinks of first

With the way in which the two main browsers are constructed at present, it is not possible to view a user's list of favourites. However, it is possible to find out if the website was found via a search database or whether the address was keyed in/selected from a list of favourites. Indications are that in the future browsers will make it possible to view lists of favourites.

7. The number of e-mails received from consumers

Even though not everyone will acknowledge their visit to a website by sending an e-mail to the webmaster, the number of e-mails is often indicative of a website's quantitative success. Is the aim to provoke visitors so much that they send an e-mail or is the wish to avoid e-mails completely? In particular, for websites which offer product sampling or the delivery of a catalogue, the number of expected e-mails should be determined so that the subsequent internal routines can be prepared.

8. The website's sales and income

In theory, an i-branding site won't have any income although many brands today sell merchandising from their site as the products don't suit e-commerce. The more the website is based on Internet sales, the more important it is that goals should be set for sales, the rate of sales and the income. Many companies have set up e-commerce on their websites without developing a proper business plan for the website's sales in relation to the operating costs connected with e-commerce, such as the appointment of a webmaster, the setting up of routines for product deliveries, losses on false orders and the marketing of the website.

How are the concrete objectives set?

The setting of quantitative objectives for how many minutes users are to spend at a website, how many pages they are to visit, and how often they are to return can be extremely difficult, particularly if the company is using the medium for the first time and therefore has nothing to compare it with.

A good beginning is to consider the user's situation. How long will users be prepared to spend with the brand if it is telling them something really interesting? Two minutes, 10 minutes or what?

The initial aim should be to create such an interesting environment for the users that they never become bored and consider visiting a different website. Do the brand and the story the brand can tell have enough content for the user to stay in the website for 10 minutes? How often should the content be changed in order for it to be attractive to visit the website again? These questions can help us to view the content and structure of the website critically and thereby ensure that the users experience significant benefit from their visit to the website.

And last but not least, the setting of concrete objectives allows evaluation of the success of the website as a starting point.

[The source for the data in this chapter is from New 98 GenerAsians developed by AC Nielsen and Turner Entertainment March 1998]

Development of a Web Concept Briefing

*"Tell me and I will forget,
Show me and I might remember,
Involve me and I will understand."*

Benjamin Franklin

A concept on the Internet, as in traditional marketing, has two levels: the idea/strategy and the design. It involves not only getting a good idea but also finding out how the good idea can be executed creatively in the form of a user-friendly interface design.

To date most of the websites on the Internet have belonged to the category 'classic websites', primarily consisting of a company and product description, an employee presentation, a price list, a news page and the ability to send e-mails. This structure is now changing as the ability of such a website to generate traffic, and its subsequent relevance for the users, has proved to be limited.

Selection of a concept category

During the past year the most successful websites on the Internet have outlined a number of new paradigms. These websites can be categorised as belonging to one or more of the following three categories:

- **Interactive Branding websites (i-branding)**
  28% of all companies see themselves in
  this category

- **Commerce websites (e-commerce)**
  18% of all companies see themselves in
  this category

- **Operation websites (e-operations)**
  25% of all companies see themselves in
  this category

Single category websites will, for example, be M&M's, Libra or Pepsi, which all belong 100 percent in the i-branding category. On the other hand the LEGO website is a combination of both an i-branding and an e-commerce site as the consumer typically will be exposed to the brand's message and probably over time will consider buying some of the LEGO boxes online.

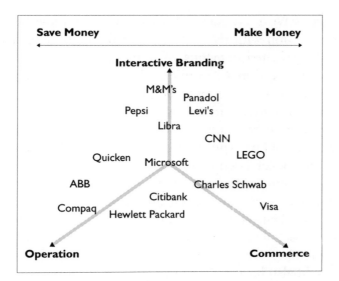

Examples of where some brands may categorise themselves in the concept triangle.

A website will often be a combination of the above categories. It is characteristic of the above three categories that they are intended to justify the existence of the website to the user and the company and to ensure than the user returns again and again.

The use of creativity on a website will change according to what concept category the site belongs to. Obviously the creative freedom when developing an i-branding website is much larger than that available when developing an e-operation site.

Below is a description of each of the three web categories. Based on what category the development of the site belongs to, the focus of the brief will have to change to ensure a balance between consumer expectations and what the site manages to deliver.

I-branding websites

Most of the world's best-known brands have very few new characteristics to publicise. Coca-Cola, Pepsi, M&M's, Moët et Chandon and Johnnie Walker have looked the same for decades, with just a few or no changes having been made since they were launched. If there have been changes, these have often just been in connection with the packaging or the logo. This makes much greater demands of a highly interactive brand communication. Consumers who visit a website which is characterised as being a 100 percent i-branding site will often have great (and often very undefined) expectations concerning the content of the website. For example, what would be expected from a visit to M&Ms website if it had never been visited before? Probably something entertaining? However, putting a game on the site will not necessarily mean that after the visit the consumer will associate the game with the M&Ms brand. A typical comment would be, "The games were fun, but I can't remember what brand they were advertising." There would also be a danger of the user associating the brand with the wrong values after having played the game.

The pure form of an i-branding website is also called advertainment. In his book *Ogilvy on Advertising*, David Ogilvy wrote, "If you can't tell the consumer about a concrete product benefit, if you don't have a concrete offer or if you can't launch something new, there is only one option left. Sing your message."

'Singing' on the Internet can be translated into the concept 'advertainment'. Advertainment, a combination of the words *advertising* and *entertainment*, aims to create interest by use of the medium's unique ability to interact with the users in order to promote a particular message. The fact that the product is not actually given a concrete added value does not matter so much in this context, as the user experiences an added value by being entertained by the brand.

Often advertainments are based on a strategic reworking of the brand's set of values. These can either be values which already exist but are weak, or values which are not yet associated with the product by the consumer.

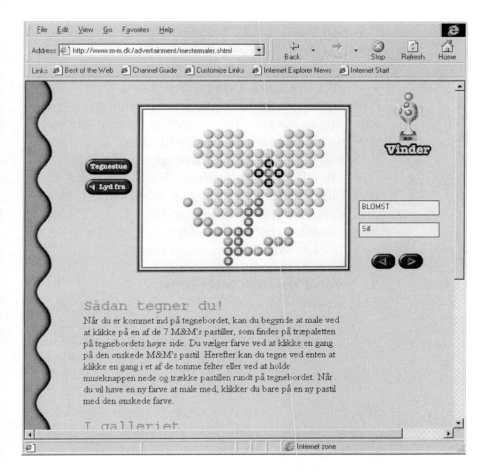

Success in the use of advertainments is usually correlated with the ability to integrate the product and message in the game. The greater the integration, the more positive the synergy – as in traditional marketing. Here the connection between, for example, an advertising film's story and the product must be clear in order for the advertisement to have any effect at all. All too often well-known actors have promoted a product without relevant context. The result has been that the viewers remembered the actor, but forgot the product.

It is therefore no use to create fun and games just for entertainment's sake without them being connected with the product's message and brand platform.

M&M's was one of the first products in the world to develop advertainments. The M&M's online drawing competition was created in Denmark back in 1995.

Creating a successful i-branding site on the Internet is based on these five critical success factors:

1. Build the brand, not a brochure

Nobody expects to see a brochure version of the brand when going online. Try to give eight-year-old kids a remote control – and they will think it is broken. Brands acting in an online environment are expected to not only talk but also to listen, learn and react. If the brand just manages to 'talk', or even worse 'talk' and 'listen', but forgets to show that it has 'learned' and can 'react' to what the consumer has said, then it is on the right track to committing brand suicide.

2. Involve through interactivity

Interactivity promotes involvement. For years creative people around the world have tried to generate stronger involvement with their audience on television, via the radio or billboards, but the real involvement never eventuated.

If a consumer spends 30 seconds being exposed to a commercial on television, the goal has to be to push the consumer from the television commercial on to the Internet and through interactivity generate, for example, a 15-minute dialogue. The only way this is possible is by using interactivity, as it ensures a customised and relevant dialogue with the consumer, and gives the brand a personal image in the consumer's mind.

3. Get intimate via dialogue

No other media has shown such strength creating an intimate dialogue with the consumer. The price of communicating with 10 or with 10,000 consumers via the Internet is in theory the same. The largest assets on the Internet in the future will not be the traffic on the site but the knowledge the site has collected about each of its users.

4. Expect results and measure them

Although it is difficult to measure the quality of an i-branding site, it is vital to establish objectives before creating it. What is the site to achieve? Can this be measured? These questions might be hard, but they are the keys to ensuring the site will become successful.

5. Give the consumer added value

A consumer with very high expectations of a brand will expect even more from the brand's website. If the site can't deliver, don't go online! The site has to offer some sort of added value to the consumer – help them save time, be entertained, be educated or earn money.

6. Monitor, evaluate and learn

To control the value of branding sites is very difficult – that is why it is imperative to constantly monitor them, evaluate the results and implement changes. Getting data about your site's performance can be costly. Very few businesses offer this service; one is www.hitwise. com, which helps small to medium-sized businesses compare performance with close competitors.

E-commerce websites

E-commerce websites are one of the most controversial categories on the net. They can be divided into two main types: business-to-consumer (e-tail) and business-to-business – this book focuses on the former. In each type three kinds of sites can be identified: *soft-delivery* (selling digital products), *hard-delivery* (non-digital products) and *service-delivery* (human services).

A company with a soft-delivery site has an advantage over other e-commerce sites, as the product can be supplied digitally, e.g. downloading programs or transferring money. Hard-delivery and service-delivery sites tend to represent products and services specially developed for the Internet – services not available via other sales outlets – or in a slightly different format.

Examples of e-commerce site types

	Soft-delivery	Hard-delivery	Service-delivery
B to C	Cnet	Dell	FedEX
B to B	DoubleClick	Microsoft	SAP

(Microsoft and FedEX cover several categories.)

E-tail sites

Nearly a third (31 percent) of US Internet users are buying online, and they are sticking to familiar, inexpensive goods, according to CDB Research & Consulting Inc. Books (33 percent of respondents), CDs (26 percent) and small gifts (20 percent) are most popular. Some more expensive items are accepted by online consumers: airline tickets had been bought by 21 percent and computer hardware by 13 percent.

Only 5.75 percent of all people shop online, but they spent $6 billion in November–December 1999, up from $3.1 billion for the same period in 1998, according to Jupiter Communications. This is just a fraction of the opportunity online shopping will present. By 2003, turnover is expected to be $78 billion.

There is a long way to go

Not everyone walks away from the keyboard smiling. Many online shoppers (32 percent) said there were sites they would be reluctant to shop at again.

∞ 43 percent of online shoppers were concerned whether online merchants would keep their financial/personal information secure and private
∞ 40 percent said that Internet retailers had run out of an item or had a disappointing selection
∞ 33 percent had trouble accessing the merchant or had other technical problems at the site
∞ 22 percent had a problem with shipping, or felt they were overcharged for shipping
∞ 5 percent felt the online merchant had lied to or deceived them in some way

Enquiry-to-sale conversion at e-tail sites

Item	Got information	Made purchase	Conversion
Flowers	14%	7%	50%
Computer h'ware	57	22	39
Books	40	14	35
Music CDs	35	10	29
Computer s'ware	60	16	27
Financial services	47	8	17
Movie tickets	13	1	7
Business travel	49	3	6
Telecommunications	17	1	5
Automobiles	43	1	2

Source: Milward Brown Interactive

Flowers currently have by far the highest conversion rate: 50% of all users visiting a flower site purchase the product.

Clicks & mortar – the survival kit

Organisations using traditional marketing rather than Internet-led strategies have become known as 'bricks & mortar' businesses. They have been regarded as the losers of the 1990s, as ever more e-commerce sites – 'clicks' companies – captured market share.

For example, bookstore Barnes & Noble, Toys'R'Us and HMV were shocked when Internet businesses captured several percent of turnover in five years – a share traditionally taking years to build. They hadn't anticipated the Net as a competitor and so bricks & mortar retailers seemed antiquated compared to the Internet. Recently, though, there has been a 'clicks-and-mortar' trend – mergers between the two; this is likely to be the way ahead for most e-tailers. One of the first to realise this was drugstore.com, which in 1999 merged with Rite Aid.

www.barnesandnoble.com

www.toysrus.com

www.hmv.com

See Lindström's new book *Clicks & Mortar* for a more detailed study of the above concepts. Published in December 2000 by Hardie Grant Books.

E-tail key guidelines

It is clear that becoming successful on the Internet is not only based on the strength of the brand, the quality of the website and the marketing budget. Some basic rules have to be followed to ensure a successful site.

1. It's about creating a business not a website

The Internet is exactly the same as any other business. Unfortunately, far too many forget to think about their website in this way. This often results in weak strategies, a bad marketing plan and a missing distribution strategy.

By treating the establishment of a site like a traditional business, which includes development of a business plan, a marketing plan and dedication of a separate ownership, a range of problems can be avoided.

2. Select and focus

As explained earlier, amazon.com has managed to keep a clear focus on what they are good at. Amazon, which was based on being a pure online bookstore, took more than three years to establish a detailed knowledge about their consumers, their preferences and the market before entering new markets. They first entered the music market in 1998 after they had acquired several music-related companies over the period of a year. Interestingly, they didn't sell classical CDs on their site in the beginning as they didn't feel sufficiently competent within this area.

The Amazon concept is a good example of how a clear focus has helped a company to survive on the Internet; and over time even managed to increase the business area. To be an expert within one particular area creates trust among consumers. To claim to be an expert in several areas is a much tougher mission which only very few brands have shown they are able to handle in a professional way.

3. Define a clear market position

The clearer the message is on the Internet, the greater the chance to capture market-share. The top 10 e-commerce sites are all characterised by having a very clear market position statement.

| **www.travelocity.com says:** | We have just as many destinations as airports. |
| **www.towerrecords.com says:** | Always top 1000 on sale. |

The statements are clear and easy to remember and certainly differentiate these companies from all competitors on the Internet.

4. Product information creates consumer empowerment

One of the major benefits of the Internet is that the space is free. In theory, the price for a 100-page site is similar to a 200-page site. When consumers are buying online the only three criteria they can relate to are: brand name, the price and the information about the product. This is one of the major reasons why information depth is essential for successful e-commerce sites. The more information provided about a certain product, the greater the chance the consumer won't leave the site in a desperate attempt to find an answer to a particular question. Today it is possible to visit a camera website that not only explains all features of the camera, but also shows how the camera works under water, how to clean the camera, the expected value of the camera after three years and compares the camera with nine other similar models on the market. Would a consumer even consider visiting another site to find more answers?

5. Create an ongoing relationship

In the final analysis it has everything to do with creating strong relationships. Why do people choose to visit the same store time after time when the product they are buying can be bought cheaper elsewhere in the city? Because of the relationship! Imagine the Internet as a shopping mall. One store may be incredibly service-minded where another hasn't even heard of the concept of service. The better the site is able to service consumer needs, and in some cases even predict these needs before they've been expressed, the likelier is a strong relationship with the customer. Many claim that the survivors on the Internet won't be sites with huge traffic, but ones that have systematically gathered data about customers, over time, so establishing a very strong one-to-one relationship with every visitor.

6. Think about a clicks-and-mortar strategy

Delivery is the key to success. More than 70 percent of .coms faced delivery problems in December 1999. Would your .com company work better if it had a 'brick & mortar' partner? If you are not sure of the answer ask yourself: "What bricks & mortar company would I hate to see teaming up with my biggest .com competitor?" This might help you find the answer.

E-operation websites

www.fedex.com annually tracks more than 1.3 million shipments worldwide.

One of the fastest growing areas on the Internet is that made up of the 'hidden sites', also called X-tranet. X-tranet is in reality an ordinary website – the only

difference is that it is password protected and therefore only accessible for a defined target group. Similarly restricted access also occurs with Intranet. Intranet is a website constructed on the same principles as a traditional website. The site is, however, placed on a local network with no external access from the Internet.

Both categories are predicted to become the fastest growing online data segments based on web technology, as they have proved to be extremely cost-efficient. Twenty-five percent of business-to-business companies said in a December 1998 survey conducted by IBM that the opportunity to cut costs was their primary reason for developing a website. Eleven percent of small businesses and 16 percent of medium businesses placed and took orders via the Internet, according to an Australian survey conducted by Yellow Pages Small Business Index in May 1999. Where the purpose of e-commerce sites is to earn money for the owner, the typical purpose of an e-operation site would be to save money for the owner. Often this will happen by moving various cost-intensive processes in the company to the net. These might be:

- Internal and external newsletters
- Handling of employee requests
- Digital updating of data-intensive catalogues
- Electronic invoicing
- Direct e-marketing
- Supply chain management
- Marketing support

Even though many of the roles fulfilled by an e-operation site will take place internally, the brand-building issue is just as important. The X-tranet and Intranet will increasingly get the role as the company's primary internal-branding tools, as all employees will have intensive access to the network. Product launches, internal messages, press clippings, competitor news, etc. will therefore create a key role on the site and this will create a strong demand for brand consistency with the external communication.

Five criteria for a successful e-operation strategy:

1. Focus on the business process, not the technology

Map down the whole business process and evaluate which phases are currently either too:

- time-consuming
- cost-heavy
- complex compared with the output.

Make sure that the business processes and not the technology are the driving forces when evaluating all cost-based activities. Far too often the real savings are to be found in processes that wouldn't appear on the list if technology were the driving force.

2. Find small replicable units and make them efficient

Mapping down the total business process will often result in hundreds of potential cost-cutting activities. The list can often stop the whole process as the number of activities may lead to a lack of focus on where to begin and end. Make sure to create an immediate internal success and use the process as a model for future implementations in the rest of the organisation.

3. Improve processes that benefit an (external) customer

FedEx and Dell are good examples of how it is possible to both save money and increase the (external) service level at the same time. In many cases a primary focus on the customer can create a double benefit reflected in better customer service and cost savings.

4. Promote improvements through behaviour change

Too frequently, implementation of complex cost-saving activities can result in huge plans but no cost savings, as the process never manages to start a behaviour change among staff or customers. An essential element in an e-operation plan is the development of an education program targeted at both staff and customers. Remember that behaviour changes are not only required of staff but also of customers, as they just as easily tend to establish cost-expensive routines.

5. Move from physical to virtual value chains

Sending a letter may be 500 percent more expensive than sending the same message via e-mail. By starting to move the physical value chain to a virtual-based value chain, large costs can be saved in a short time as most communication is based on one source with several channels.

Synchronous customer management

Based on the whole e-operation philosophy, a new standard for customer service called synchronous customer management has appeared. Forrester defines, in an April 1999 report, the new standard as consistent, high-quality customer support across all communication channels and business functions, based on a common, complete information shared by employees, their customers and business partners. The whole idea is to make the Internet a centrepiece of a customer management strategy. To enable synchronous customer management, companies will have to unlearn past practices and follow three new principles in all of their customer systems:

1. Employees, customers, and partners use the same customer data

To deliver excellent customer service, companies must ensure that their internal view of customers matches

TIP

Visit
www.alertbox.com
and subscribe to
Jacob Nielsen's
recent surveys
about good
navigation design.

what customers and business partners see on statements on the web or hear in conversations.

2. One customer system must lead

Companies must abandon today's practice of multiple, independent customer systems and create a single system that spans function, channels and audiences.

3. All other customer systems either fall into line or die

Sales, marketing and service will still use specialised systems for their unique needs, but these systems will leverage the common information that everyone else uses.

During the next two years, companies will feel intense new pressures as ever-increasing numbers of customers demand on-line-self-service. The Forrester report predicts that by the end of 2001 a separation between online function will fade, integration costs will devour IT resources and employees will discover the power of the online world.

Designing the website interface

Each of the three concept categories just explained represents a different level for use of creativity. Where the first category, i-branding websites, will have a high level of concept freedom, the last category, e-operation websites, will have a much tighter concept framework.

It is important that all three categories should be just as focused on strong branding. Employees are just as important ambassadors for the brand as the customers, so why expose them differently?

When the website's main concept has been developed and it has been decided which creative solution(s) the website is to present, there remains the creative execution, that is, the design of the interface/the universe which the users of the website are to experience. As already detailed in Chapter 5, it is important that the website is based on an easy and user-friendly design. The website must also be designed bearing in mind the following three criteria:

1. Graphic expression (colours, icons, etc)
2. The website's signal value
   (stopping power, overview)
3. Attitude/tone of voice

The creative utilisation of the Internet – or lack of it – has been the subject of discussion ever since the medium was first used for marketing purposes. Is it sufficient to develop a good website just the once and then sit back and watch for months on end while the users help themselves to the goodies? Or would the website lose its attraction as a result of a lack of updating?

1. Graphic expression (colours, icons, etc.)
Every single page on the website represents the brand. This makes great demands on the graphic profile as it must be able to support the brand's core values, the brand's graphic profile, and also be user-friendly and quick. A page should be so well designed that it could be recognised by the user without the logo. If this is the case, then it is likely that the design has a strong brand signal value.

Consistency is also essential for good graphic design. Are the icons the same on every page, are the illustrations created by the same designer and is the colour scheme consistent?

2. The website's stopping power
Experience shows that small details are often of great significance. Many newspapers manage to increase the day's sale of newspapers by 15 to 20 percent based on the news value. This is not surprising but it is food for thought as it shows the importance of presenting a

message the right way. A parallel can be drawn with the home page of a website. A boring and complex front page (perhaps combined with a long downloading time) can reduce the user's interest in spending time on an in-depth visit to the website. Another factor, which only a few companies have recognised, is the value of changing the front page each day. Imagine if *The New York Times'* front page was the same two days in a row – the same pictures, headline and news stories – with the date as the only difference. Would anyone buy the paper? Hardly. Only very few commercial websites change the front page from day to day or from visit to visit. Why should a websurfer then visit the same website again and again? If a company has changed the content of a website visitors should be made aware of this on the home page so that they are motivated to look at the site in depth again.

A website's home page should be regarded the same as the front page of a magazine. Certain elements are the same day after day, while other elements are changed each day to promote frequency of viewing. The more interesting the home page, the better it sells the content and the more traffic it generates. However, this is not to say that someone has to be permanently kept busy updating the front page. One solution could be that the front page referred to or advertised a new or different activity each time the user visited the website. The content remains unchanged, but the day's selected front-page reference varies. This ensures that the visitor is not satisfied just to knock on the main door of the 'amusement park', but is actually motivated to go in.

3. Attitude/tone of voice

This element will act as an integrated part of point 1. It is important that the graphic style matches the activities that both the brand and the actual content of the website represent. This is connected with the tone of voice of the text, which must also match the visual impression. It is a waste of time for a firm of lawyers to try to be innovative as far as the graphic presentation is concerned if they still use ponderous, obscure legal jargon when talking to their visitors.

Development of a Web Concept Briefing

As still only some companies view the Internet as a medium on an equal footing with traditional media, the work is unfortunately all too seldom based on a proper web briefing, that is, guidelines specially determined for the development team intended to ensure that the concept is developed in accordance with the strategy. Nonetheless, the briefing is fundamental for an effective website with strong brand-building and essential for the creation of a successful website. The briefing should take as its starting point the brand itself, the planned direction the brand will move in the future, and the defined communication aims. An understanding of the medium's unique characteristics is essential if a high level of creativity is to be achieved on the website. Many people believe that interactivity can only be achieved by the use of animation, complicated graphics, pictures, film and sound. Interactivity is not necessarily conditional on these effects. High levels of interactivity can be achieved by building up strong dialogue with the user. The more the users are involved in a creative way, focusing on the brand, the greater the success the website will achieve when all things are considered.

The basis of a successful online concept website lies in a well-thought-out Internet briefing. It is important to emphasise that a briefing for the Internet is not exactly the same as, for example, a briefing for television. The Internet briefing should cover everything that is in a traditional briefing, but the Internet offers a number of characteristics which should also be taken into consideration as the website often will involve several other activities in its construction.

As the required dialogue is to be interactive, the briefing must take this into account. It is therefore necessary to identify and define what form the dialogue is to take and how the interactivity is to occur. As an interactive website is by its nature controlled by the user, this functionality must be described before the actual creative work commences. Just consider the differences between the navigational requirements and expectations of an experienced computer user and those of a child!

On the next pages is a concept briefing, which can be used as an example when developing a website. The purpose of the briefing is to ensure a clear understanding of what to achieve and how to achieve this by developing the concept. The briefing will typically be the first of several briefings. These briefings, which will have to be developed later in the process, will typically have a more detailed focus on brand mandates, website content and technical guidelines.

Web Concept Briefing

Below is the web concept briefing, which can be use when developing the website. The briefing is divided into two different sections. The first section, which mainly is focused on the brands market position and perception, is based on which category you believe the site belongs to i-branding, e-commerce or e-operation. The second section is focused on the role of the brand, its personality and future direction. The purpose of the Web Concept Briefing is to ensure a clear understanding of what you want to achieve and how you want to achieve these goals via the concept. The functionality and production briefings, which later on will have to be developed, will typically have a more detailed focus on brand mandates (colour, typeface and illustration style use), web-site content and technical guidelines.

Part one: Market position and perception
Please rate the following out of a possible 10 points.
[10 being 'critical', 0 being 'irrelevant']

1. To what extent are each of the following issues a *current concern in your business?*
AND
2. To what extent do you currently believe an Internet solution may be *able to help you address these business concerns?* [Please indicate DK: for 'don't know']

I-branding
1a. How your brand is perceived by your market?
To what extent is this a
business concern?   `/10`

To what extent do you currently
believe an Internet solution can help?   `/10`

1b. The extent to which you know your customer?
To what extent is this a
business concern?   `/10`

To what extent do you currently
believe an Internet solution can help?   `/10`

1c. Your overall market share?
To what extent is this a
business concern? $\boxed{/10}$
To what extent do you currently
believe an Internet solution can help? $\boxed{/10}$

E-commerce
1d. Shifts and changes in your sales/distribution channel?
To what extent is this a
business concern? $\boxed{/10}$
To what extent do you currently
believe an Internet solution can help? $\boxed{/10}$

1e. Your sales growth rate?
To what extent is this a
business concern? $\boxed{/10}$
To what extent do you currently
believe an Internet solution can help? $\boxed{/10}$

1f. The emergence of potentially competitive Internet business models?
To what extent is this a
business concern? $\boxed{/10}$
To what extent do you currently
believe an Internet solution can help? $\boxed{/10}$

E-operation
1g. The overall costs of operating your business?
To what extent is this a
business concern? $\boxed{/10}$
To what extent do you currently
believe an Internet solution can help? $\boxed{/10}$

1h. Efficiency of operation between your company and your business partners?
To what extent is this a
business concern? $\boxed{/10}$

To what extent do you currently
believe an Internet solution can help? `/10`

1i. The productivity of your company or organisation?
To what extent is this a
business concern? `/10`
To what extent do you currently
believe an Internet solution can help? `/10`

Part two: Brand Platform
1. What are we developing?
Description:
What product is to be created?

Brand Core Values:
Type in the core values of the brand and the products.
Describe the brand personality.

2. What are the three key objectives?
Describe the three key objectives of the project?

3. Who are we talking to?
Describe the target audience/end user.

4. What is the key insight to how they behave/feel?
Describe briefly the way the target audience thinks/behaves.

5. What are the three key claims we want to make?
Describe the three key claims.

6. Why should prospects accept it?
Describe the key benefits of this product to the user.

7. Is there an existing site?
Site description:
Describe the existing site including the URL

What are the thoughts on the existing site?
Describe the thoughts on the existing site.

8. **What is the client's experience with the Internet to date?**
Describe the organisation's/company's online experience.

9. **Mandates or guidelines**
List any key aspects or compulsory elements.

10. **Attachments**
Is there any **brand** or **marketing** mandate which has to be kept?

CHAPTER

Online communities –
the virtual marketplaces of the future

"It takes a village to build a mall."

John Hagel III,
Harvard Business School

When Marshall McLuhan first wrote the term 'the Global Village' he could hardly have expected that in less than a decade his ideas would be realised in the form of online communities, digital meeting places on the Internet. Many experts believe that communities on the net are the websites of the future. This is associated with the fact that the behaviour on the net – called surfing – that is, jumping aimlessly around from website to website, is now being replaced by more directed use of the Internet. Users today have a fairly small number of favourite websites and they visit these frequently. The favourite websites are those which can best meet the needs of the user. These can be demographic, geographical or subject-oriented, but common to them all is that they can seldom be satisfied by just one company.

If the Internet is viewed as a meeting place with an unlimited number of rooms, an online community is the room where people with a common interest meet. Here novices and experts can gather, along with suppliers of goods and services within the area of interest concerned.

The basic need fulfilled by a community, physical or virtual, is to meet other people, preferably with a common interest.

Within the last century, the links to people's local community have become increasingly tenuous so that today most people have associations and relationships which are not necessarily centred on their geographical location. This has been made possible by various technologies such as the telegraph, radio and telephone, which enable people to forge relationships which cross geographical barriers and national frontiers. Along with this development the close contact with producers, and their individual knowledge about their customers, has also vanished.

The Internet is a very exciting medium in this area also, as it gives people a new opportunity to meet and be close to other people world-wide. In addition the Internet already contains information about practically every subject imaginable and provides opportunities for communication and access the like of which have not been seen before. The global village has become a reality.

Today most of us belong to a number of interest groups based on education, work, hobbies, social status, geographical location and interest in, even worship of, a brand. The Internet makes it possible to support and supplement these groups with a number of facilities to make the relationship easier to engender, more dynamic and more accessible.

By forming or participating in a community, companies gain a unique opportunity to be a natural part of the target group's dialogue and daily life, and possibly also preferences. The presence of the brand in a relevant context will be more acceptable and give better results than those obtained from purely commercial websites.

Why communities are so interesting to companies

There are several reasons for companies finding communities on the net so interesting. One of them is that no matter how much a company does to create an exciting commercial website, there must be a relevant reason, a motivation, for users to visit the company on the net. This is the case both for companies marketing low-interest products (nappies, washing powder, insurance, etc.) and for companies that are in contact with their customers (buyers of cars and houses) very infrequently. In these situations it is much more attractive to be where the customers are to be found when they are dealing with product-related subjects. These can be websites for parents (www.parentsoup.com) or for people interested in cars (www.edmunds.com). It suddenly becomes relevant to talk about nappies or a good buy in car insurance. The context makes the low-interest product suddenly become interesting.

Something for something

It is extremely useful to own these communities, as by their very presence the members provide a mass of relevant information which makes targeted marketing possible. They will only do this if they feel that the meeting place gives them something in return. They will expect the information to be used in a principled way to make the meeting place better and to ensure that the users get even more of what they want. Members' profiles tell a lot about their interests and needs, information which companies can utilise in their communication and product development, or which can be sold on. It is important that the members' trust is not lost by misusing this information and that there is ongoing development of the meeting place.

If you carry out a search for Volkswagen using one of the major search engines, you will find what huge interest in a brand there can be on the net. In addition to every conceivable fan website and amateur discussion group, there are lots of links to car clubs and to Volkswagen's official website www.vw.com.

Here great efforts have been made to attract and support the fans and the owners. There is a calendar of car shows and club events, an archive containing all VW's history and an area where fans can write about their favourite journeys and in this way help to build up a world-wide list of good driving routes. In the 'VW store' they can purchase all manner of VW equipment, and they can even apply for their own personal Beetle Visa card. This website is a good attempt at creating a community. The foundation is in order and there are enough people interested in the subject matter, should VW want to continue the work and develop a true VW community.

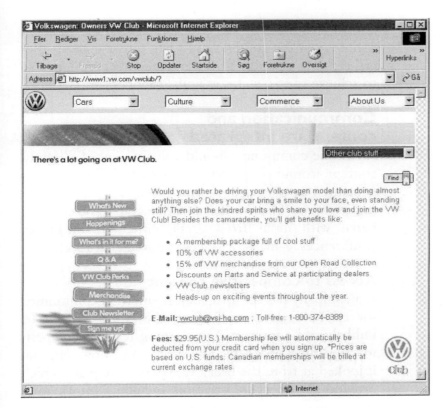

The browser window shows:

Volkswagen: Owners VW Club - Microsoft Internet Explorer

Filer Rediger Vis Foretrukne Funktioner Hjælp

Tilbage | Fremad | Stop | Opdater | Startside | Søg | Foretrukne | Oversigt | Hyperlinks

Adresse: http://www1.vw.com/vwclub/?

Cars ▼ | Culture ▼ | Commerce ▼ | About Us ▼

There's a lot going on at VW Club.

Other club stuff ▼

Find

What's New
Happenings
What's in it for me?
Q & A
VW Club Perks
Merchandise
Club Newsletter
Sign me up!

Would you rather be driving your Volkswagen model than doing almost anything else? Does your car bring a smile to your face, even standing still? Then join the kindred spirits who share your love and join the VW Club! Besides the camaraderie, you'll get benefits like:

- A membership package full of cool stuff
- 10% off VW accessories
- 15% off VW merchandise from our Open Road Collection
- Discounts on Parts and Service at participating dealers
- VW Club newsletters
- Heads-up on exciting events throughout the year.

E-Mail: vwclub@vsi-hq.com ; Toll-free: 1-800-374-8389

Fees: $29.95(U.S.) Membership fee will automatically be deducted from your credit card when you sign up. *Prices are based on U.S. funds. Canadian memberships will be billed at current exchange rates.

VW Club

What characteristics does a good community have?

Whether it is a question of a physical or a virtual meeting place, a well-functioning community has the following characteristics:

Volkswagen's site aims to create a vibrant online community.

Shared context

The people who are to be found in the meeting place are there on account of a shared interest, a common background or a shared set of values.

www.parentsoup. com

www.edmunds.com

Membership

In a community it is possible for users to reach a point where they feel part of the community and not just a group of onlookers. They can help new members and assist in developing the site via input and the generation of content. They know the jargon, the traditions and the 'codes' that are only understood by seasoned members of the community. They can also attain special rights as a member, and some members will be able to achieve special status as ambassadors or moderators.

Communication and content are integrated

An online community should contain a lot of different content around the selected subject, including content generated by participants with commercial or marketing interests. This content must be able to be co-ordinated with input from users, either by means of conferences, e-mails or subject-related chat rooms.

Access to competitive content

If a company has set up a subject-oriented community, for example about gardening, the company will be unlikely to be interested in opening it up to competitors and their products. The problem is, however, that if looked at from the user's viewpoint, the place which provides the most information, including information from competitors, will be the most attractive meeting place, all other things being equal. Therefore, instead of excluding competitors, the company owning the website should make use of the advantage it has in determining when the users are to be able to reach the competitors' pages. This also means that a company participating in a community can rarely get exclusive rights within its line of business.

The meeting place is based upon a business model

Many early communities were set up on a voluntary and non-commercial basis, like everything else on the net at the time. Thus the Manchester United Football Club's fansite was begun by volunteers, and you will still find amateur Manchester United communities that are very popular, but the main website is now run professionally because of the very large number of users. And this is the only feasible solution in the long term. Popular sites require resources on a much greater scale than amateurs can provide. Several millions may be invested in setting up and maintaining a brand-based community. Therefore these meeting places have to be based on a business model that is able to generate a profit. This can be achieved by means of sponsorship, advertising income or trade. Alternatively it can be achieved by other side-effects, such as improved brand-building or collection of information, which in combination can be so valuable that the site can be economically self-sufficient.

In order for a community to be judged to be working well, it must have the same characteristics as a physical community. It must be lively, well visited and pulsating. There must be a clear impression that the users are well acquainted and the tone of the dialogue must be pleasant. It is these characteristics that a company should look for when it is considering becoming an active part of an already existing site.

Users are not all alike!

When observing the patterns of use in existing communities it becomes clear that, as in the real world, there are several different types of user and some are more valuable to the 'community' than others. At The Well (www.thewell.com), which for a long time was a very well-functioning American online community with a defined target group among the well educated, it was even possible to observe a rowdy element, which deliberately antagonised other members and made extremely provocative contributions. These proved to be quite valuable for The Well as debates always flared up around these contributions and at the same time new participants were provoked to contribute. The antagonists' contribution was to bring the community to life online.

www.thewell.com

Typically, new users seldom take a particularly active part. However, if the meeting place succeeds in retaining the interest of new users, with time they will develop into more seasoned users who also become increasingly valuable each time they return.

People who are 'just looking'

The first few times people visit a community, they will only be onlookers. At this stage they will not participate actively in conferences or chats. It takes time to find one's feet and to learn the jargon of the new meeting place.

Users and buyers

If the site succeeds in retaining the onlookers, after a while they will begin to take a more active part in the various options. If transactions are an option, some users will turn into buyers. They will not be content just to find information and communicate, but will also buy products. The reason why buyers are more interesting than users is that they are a source of income, both through any transaction income and through increased advertising income.

Ambassadors/super users

www.tripod.com

These will typically be among the most faithful members. Some of them will have participated right from the start. They are among the keenest participants in debates and often make contributions. They spend a lot of time at the website and can help new users to get started. This type of user is so important to a community that it can actually make sense to pay them for their participation.

At www.tripod.com they are constantly looking for participants for the Tripod Panel. These users are allocated tasks but at the same time play a part in influencing the further development of the site. The company Village, which develops three communities,

www.parentsoup.com, www.aboutwork.com and www
.betterhealth.com, has over 500 unpaid users who work
as online custodians and moderators of debate forums
and assist the meeting places to operate smoothly.

It is important for community owners to have a plan for
how to receive new members and how to try to retain
them. It could be a question of a development plan for
online members: how often they receive new information, how they obtain new roles, how the more experienced members help the less experienced – just like in
the physical world.

There are many different kinds of community

Today a number of different types of community are
appearing on the net. They have a number of characteristics in common but also have some unique characteristics. If a company wants to set up a new community
it is as well for it to know what type it should be.

Geographical communities

These are communities which deal primarily with a
physical place in which all the visitors have a shared
interest. It could be Mauritius (www.mauritius.net) or
Copenhagen (www.aok.dk). Common to all these communities is the fact that they make information available about a physical place. The information can be
anything from restaurants to theatre performances.
These geographical communities are very popular in
the USA. There is an intensive battle in progress concerning city websites. Microsoft is at present developing its own city guides under the name Sidewalk (for
example, www.newyork.sidewalk.com) in serious competition with Citysearch. This is because many experts
believe that the Internet will also play an important role
on a local scale.

www.newyork. sidewalk.com

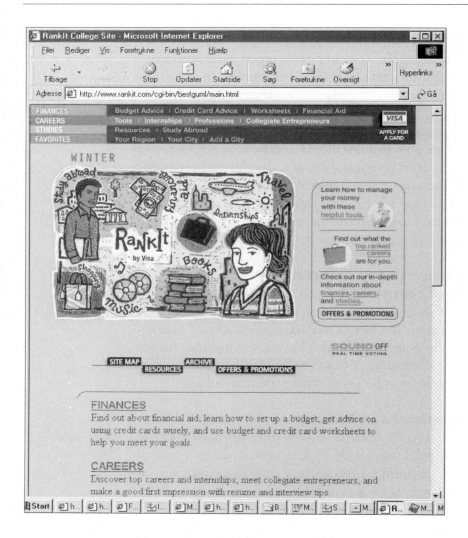

Rankit is a successful community for young students, owned by Visa.

www.thirdage.com

Demographical communities

These meeting places are aimed at different age groups. In Denmark there are a number of youth communities: www.kult.dk and www.chilinet.dk are two of the best-known examples. One of the USA's most successful communities is www.tripod.com. The target group here is young people in the age range 25–35 years. Communities have also been developed for the sector called 'woopies' in the USA (Well-Off Older People). A good example is www.thirdage.com. Parents are another demographic group receiving special treatment, with communities such as www.par-entsoup.com and www.parentsplace.com. Visa has launched a very successful community called www.rankit.com, which is narrowly targeted at young students having their own place for the first time, either on campus or independently. Here they can find good advice on how to stretch their money. This is done by the users constantly voting on which restaurant, music venue, etc. they like the best.

Subject-oriented communities

This type of community is focused on a concrete subject. It can, for example, be music or art but can also be a belief or political conviction. It is in this category that the various forms of activist communities are found.

Within the travel area there are a number of communities where it is possible to find relevant information on destinations and buy tickets at the same time. One of the better examples is www.travelocity.com. Other subject-oriented communities include ESPN, a very large sports-oriented website.

www.travelocity.com

www.espn.com

Branch-oriented communities

Various organisations and associations can create communities on the net of a more business-to-business type. In Finland there is a very successful community for the building industry called Duuninet (www.duuninet.fi). Another example is www.freight-market.dk, a community targeted at companies interested in transporting goods over longer distances.

Function-oriented communities

Communities aimed at various job functions have also been known for a while, primarily within the field of IT where a website such as www.cnet.com has been a source and starting point for many IT employees. Within marketing, websites are also starting to appear, with various studies and tools related to this job function. An interesting example of a function-oriented community is www.monster.com.

What is interesting about communities is that with time they can divide and form sub-communities. In a geographical community there can perhaps arise a subject-oriented sub-community and in the same way a demographic community can develop into a geographic one, etc. This is called a community's fractal breadth. In the same way very broad subjects can be subdivided into more specific subjects and in this way create new meeting places. This is called a community's fractal depth. The greater these two parameters, the more interesting a site, and the greater its economic potential.

The five basic needs

Even though meeting places are able to develop and even though it is important to get started quickly, there are some important parameters that have to be in place right from the start. In order for a community to be successful, five user requirements need to be satisfied:

Interest

It is vital that the meeting place covers a shared area of interest. This can either be professional or aimed at private individuals. In order to attract the group of people who are interested in or who have expertise within the field concerned, the level of cover must be so interesting that there are no other places that deal with the subject better at the present time. The subject can be anything from diving or stamp-collecting to speculation in shares.

Information

Within the area concerned, the meeting place must cover as many aspects as possible and make available the information that is required. Much of the information can come from the users, but they must not be the only source of information. It is a good idea to research the subject on the net and ensure that there are relevant links to other sources of information on the subject. However, it must be ensured that the site does not end up as a link station without any actual content, in contrast to a gateway website which by its functionality helps the user to find the correct information.

It may not always be a question of hard facts. The areas of fantasy and dreams are important aspects that can be covered. The net provides users with the ability to find their dream house and to furnish it according to their wishes rather than their purse. And of course the same applies to cars. It is also possible to put together your own dream football team or a cycle team for the 'Virtual Tour de France'. Finally, there are many communities which are engaged in role playing, on the lines of Dungeons and Dragons, where you can act out a role or assume a character (also called 'avatars' on the net) and in this way escape from the daily grind for a while.

Interaction

The ability to work interactively with the content of a meeting place helps to give it value. At www.tripod.com under the subject 'Careers' you can work with an 'interactive résumé builder', which gives the members good advice and guidance on drawing up a CV and also provides assistance in constructing a personal online application. At www.parentsoup.com you can use the program 'Baby namefinder' to find the name that is just right for your child and also discover its origin and what it means. In the Internet version of the women's magazine *Women's Week* (www.alt.eon.dk) there is a vote each week on topics covered by the magazine so that it is possible to gauge the attitude of the users to the subjects. All these interactive measures help to create involvement in the meeting place.

www.tripod.com

www.parentsoup. com

www.alt.eon.dk

When the world's largest producer of insulin for diabetes patients decided to start communicating directly with its end-users, it developed and implemented a community called www.diabetes.dk. As a service, visitors get their own area, complete with diary, calendar, and a place to put their own diabetic data. It has been such a huge success that the drug company is now in the process of rolling out local versions in over 25 markets – all built on the same platform.

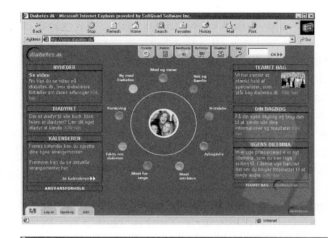

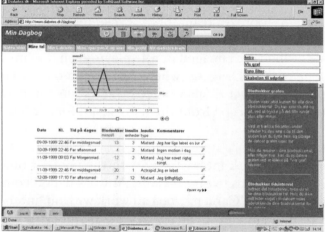

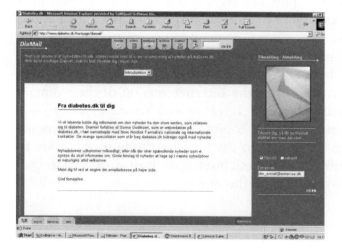

Communication

One of the most important aspects of online communities is the communication which is carried on at the website, both between the members and between the creators of the community and the members. This exchange of views and personalisation is essential in order to retain users and to make them feel at home and a part of the online meeting place. On CompuServe there is, for example, an online meeting place for people who have either contracted cancer themselves or who have encountered it in someone close to them. Here there is an opportunity to exchange experience and information about different treatments and research. In addition, relevant literature can be downloaded, but the most important thing is the ability of the meeting place to bring these users closer together by means of personal accounts and contact and in this way create a feeling of fellowship.

Transaction

Traditionally transactions on the net have been in the form of 'barter economy'. As trade proper has not been able to take place there has been talk about the exchange of and trade in knowledge and information as well as other forms of digital products such as software, demos, etc. However, the Internet is on the brink of a breakthrough for trading via the net, with transaction-oriented services being connected to online communities. A meeting place about cinema should also provide the opportunity for sales and booking tickets. Similarly, a highly specialised community dealing with, for example, the Spice Girls is also the best possible place to sell Spice Girls merchandising products.

If these five user requirements can be successfully fulfilled, a company will be well on the way to setting up a website with great community potential.

Benefits of communities for companies

In comparison with a traditional commercial website communities have a number of specific advantages which make it sensible to think along these lines, whether the company wants to invest in the establishment of a community or only wants to be a part of a community as a step in its online marketing.

Easier access to the customers

Because a community is the relevant environment for people with the same company-related interests, this benefits the company. It is easier to be where the customers are already to be found, than to try to entice them over to the company's own site. However, this presupposes that there is a community in which the relevant target group is to be found in sufficient numbers.

Greater willingness to buy

In a community that is well known, it seems less risky to make a purchase. There is good access to relevant information about the products and a customer can even discuss the product with other people who have bought it, prior to purchase.

Targeting and matching

With time, online communities will amass a lot of information about the individual members and their interests, needs and wishes. This information makes possible much more accurate targeting and tailoring of offers and services in accordance with individual needs. As a result of dialogue with members, special products and bundles can be customised. This can make it possible to increase the number of customers and to increase the revenue from each individual customer.

The middleman can be eliminated

By communicating directly with the end-user and building up relationships, many producers are in fact able to omit the middle stages represented by distributors, wholesalers and retailers. This will not take place overnight, but the tendencies are already evident; for example, most airlines are busy setting up direct booking systems for customers via the Internet, bypassing the traditional travel agents.

Overall there is a very important difference between traditional commercial websites and communities. They are not mutually exclusive, but it is essential to understand that more than anything else it is the users who hold the reins in a community. Company functions that are in direct contact with the customer will be the first to change when the company seriously attempts to be customer-oriented on the net. The problem is that there are still no relevant community websites for many companies, but this can provide a potential business opportunity.

How do you build up a community?

If a company is considering setting up a community instead of a traditional commercial website, there are a number of things it needs to consider. First and foremost, it is vital that the subject is appropriate for both the company and its products.

There is still no tried and tested recipe, but the procedure described here contains some basic analyses, guidelines and priorities that have led to success for other communities.

Define the target group for the community

It is clear that a community aimed at butterfly collectors will find it more difficult to achieve commercial success than a meeting place aimed at young people in the age range 25–35 years. When the target group has been defined, demographic statistics can help to determine the number of potential users now and in the future.

Define what values the meeting place provides
It is just as relevant to define where the website provides value in comparison to the offline alternative. Is it quicker, cheaper, more precise, easier, more amusing or does it impose less obligation? For most communities it is contact with like-minded people that is most important. It is generally a unique experience to be able to exchange stories, tips and tricks and to have questions answered by experts in a particular field, sometimes from all over the world.

Determine what resources the company has as its starting point
There are a number of resources a company can make use of straight away in connection with the establishment of a community:

- *The company's brand name.* If the company already has a strong and familiar brand, this gives immediate credibility and recognition on the net, particularly at this time when many companies are trying to set themselves up on the net. However, care must be taken not to use the brand in a context which is completely new to the users. There must be a connection between the communication on the net and other offline marketing.
- *The company's customer contacts.* These can be used both to research what things are wanted and to inform about the existence of the community when the company has made a start. If it can make sure that these existing customers are involved right from the start, then it will have a number of potential users right from day one.
- *Already existing material.* It is impossible to kick-start a community without any content. If the company is in possession of any material which can be used on the Internet immediately, a lot of work can be saved.

The fact that a company has these resources does not necessarily mean that it will be successful with a community. These only help to create traffic at the start.

A community typically passes through three stages during the establishment phase, all of which will decide whether it will be a success in the long term. If one of these stages is unsuccessful, there is a great danger the meeting place will never be a success.

Stage 1: Traffic, traffic, traffic!

During the establishment phase the most critical factor is to create traffic – and preferably lots of it. There is nothing more boring than a community where the conferences and the chat rooms are empty. And it is not particularly exciting taking part in a debate when there are no other participants. It will always be easier to set up the first community of its genre, while for the subsequent ones it is considerably more difficult. This is a good reason for not wasting any time, even if the potential target group is still only small. For example, this applies to communities aimed at women.

Chapter 11 discusses in greater depth how traffic can generally be created on a website, but a few guidelines will be mentioned here:

"The growth in women has been faster than projected. They've gone from about 20 percent of the net's population to 40 percent in just two years. And there are expected to be 30 million new women coming online in the next two and a half years."

Candice Carpenter, CEO iVillage

- The content is vital – the net is full of it, so make use of the opportunities!
- Attract attention.
- Build up the site by means of alliances with market leaders.
- Be very careful of asking for subscriptions.

Stage 2: Expansion

During this phase the most important thing is to get to know the users better and to find out the easiest way to give them what they want. What parts of the community do the users use most, and what do they feel is missing from the website? Improving the community attracts even more potential customers. Involve the users in the decision-making, so they feel that they are helping to determine what happens on the website. It is during this phase that onlookers are converted into users and users into ambassadors.

When these parameters are in place, start to consider how to use knowledge about the customers to create turnover via the meeting place, either through sponsorship, sale of advertising, sales income or membership fee.

Stage 3: Consolidation

At this point in time much of the content should be created by the users. There will now (hopefully) be so many of them that the company only needs to throw in the ball and they will then take over. Therefore maintenance starts to consist to a greater extent of managing the content and making it easily accessible to the users. It will now be appropriate to provide special online facilities and improve the means of communication between the users, for example by improving the interface, providing new and better search facilities, better structuring and better editing. At this stage the company should also start to individualise the access for the individual user. This can be carried out by recognition functions and personal agents which ensure that the user is always informed of anything that is of particular interest.

"There's a basic metric that says it takes $20 million to get the first one million page views per day."

Candice Carpenter, CEO iVillage

Optimally a community will go into a self-sustaining spiral where exciting content brings in new users who create exciting content which in turn leads to greater loyalty towards the community.

Where will the income come from?

On account of the positive spiral that can be attained by the operation of a community, there are strong indications that the development in the number of members, content, traffic and finances will follow an exponential curve rather than be constant growth. This means that ROI (return on investment) cannot be expected right from the start, but that the investor needs to have patience. On the other hand it can go really well once the community has attained the critical mass.

Sources of income in a community will typically be:

Advertising income
Sale of advertisements is the most obvious source of income. As knowledge about the members is accumulated, the advertisements can be more targeted with the possibility of greater income as a result.

Sponsorship
As many communities will have special areas of interest, it is appropriate to think of sponsorship. iVillage has a 40–60 split between sponsorship and banner advertising income, but they much prefer the sponsorship as this is normally arranged in such a way that it provides the meeting place with new functionality and content (see also Chapter 12).

Alliance income
The partners who take part at commencement or who join later can either pay a fixed rent or help to cover the establishment costs. By making basic electronic objects available (shopping basket, payment mechanism, keyboard interface, conference facilities, etc.) and by providing shared advertising, a product can be put together which can be very attractive to alliance partners and can therefore yield a revenue.

Membership income

This is the most difficult to obtain as it frightens many users away. There are a number of models for how to ask for a fee. It can be a fixed subscription which gives access to additional functions or it can be per use or per function. It is most important that the content is of a very high quality before a monthly fee can be charged. In Denmark the financial newspaper *Børsen* has been successful in asking for a subscription for its online services, just like the *Financial Times*, and Disney has also been successful abroad with its children's community, www.disneyblast.com – but here the quality of the content is very high.

Profile income

"Two million dollars will get you in the game – today, that is."

John Hagel III and Arthur G. Armstrong

If a community is set up successfully with a good proportion of a particular target group and if information is accumulated about the profile and behaviour patterns of the individual members, this will offer enormous potential for targeted marketing. External companies will be interested in paying even a very high price for contacts with a specific target group. If a community for the building trade can supply 1000 contacts who have shown an interest in a new kitchen, the price per contact that a kitchen company would be willing to pay would be very high.

It is in these profiles that the true value of a community lies hidden, whether the company is responsible for establishing the community or is only participating as one of many alliance partners. However, it is important that the unwritten code of ethics of the Internet is observed, which forbids uncontrolled sale and misuse of such information.

A community can become a brandname in itself

The building up of these virtual online communities requires a lot more resources than many companies are prepared to invest at present, but the decision to wait may in itself be dangerous. There is at any rate no doubt that a successful community with a strong brand will finish up by being worth a lot of money. It is here that the battle is raging in the USA at the moment. The CEO of iVillage, Candice Carpenter, believes that if a company has not created an online community brand within the next 12 months, then it has no chance of doing so.

Not making a decision can prove to be the riskiest decision of all.

Communities as companies listed on the stock exchange

In order to be successful, companies should regard the operation and development of a serious and viable community as an independent business with its own organisation. The Norwegian media company Schibsted has recognised this. Right from the start it employed 10 people to run the Danish version of the community Scandinavian OnLine which has now increased to over 100 people. In Sweden there are more than 80 people employed just to run www.torget.se. In the USA a great many of the large, successful communities went public by listing on the Nasdaq exchange for high-technology stocks during 1999, and this trend looks set to continue.

It can appear to be a brave decision to allocate resources to run a professional community at a time when at most 35 percent of the population over 18 years old has access to the Internet (even lower in large parts of the world). A development and operation budget of between one and three million US dollars is not far off the mark. On the other hand it can be just as dangerous to wait.

The mechanisms in the development of a community are not linear, but exponential. This means that once a community attains a critical mass of content, functionality and members, a positive spiral effect is put in motion, which makes it incredibly difficult and expensive for successors to break into the market. There are many advantages in being the first, but it requires the belief that the present trend will continue. In the USA there are no doubts. There entrepreneurs are busy getting in on the act before it is too late.

How do I create traffic on my website?

*"The only factor becoming scarce in
a world of abundance is human attention."*

Kevin Kelly, executive editor, *Wired*

During the first years of the Internet the word-of-mouth method was practically the only marketing method there was. And this has meant that rather curious websites such as The Museum of Dirt (www.planet.com) have had many more visitors than most companies will ever get. This method is, however, in the main impossible to manage and control. Many companies have without doubt thought that when their website was up and running everything in the garden would be rosy. Only a few had foreseen that they would have to invest several hundred thousand dollars a year just to advertise their web activities, but for many this is indeed the case. This is because a company is more or less invisible on the Internet until it has told its target group that the company can now also be found in cyberspace. People do not just come across a new website by chance, as they sometimes may happen on a new shop – particularly as several thousand are opening each week! A number of measures must be taken before the company becomes visible on the net and can thereby create the traffic which is a necessary precondition for the company's Internet strategy to be successful.

PR and the press

In 1996 and 1997 it was relatively easy to get a good website mentioned in the press. There were many column centimetres dealing with the Internet and if a company was the first in a line of business or if the website contained innovative elements, then the company could be reasonably sure of being mentioned. This is no longer the case. That is not to say that newspapers are not interested in writing about a company's web activities. It just requires more professional PR than before. When a company is the seventh insurance company or the fifth bank to go on the Internet, it will have to find a new angle which makes it interesting for a journalist to write about its activities. If the company can't do that, there is the danger that the users will not find the site very interesting either. As described in

Chapter 9, every website should be different from those of its competitors and should contain innovative elements – it is here that the interest lies.

The company is invisible on the net...!

In addition to targeting the press, there are many things a company can do to spread the word about the existence of its website that do not necessarily cost a lot of money, but there is also the danger that the result will be correspondingly low.

Market the web address everywhere

It is obvious that the web address should be everywhere the physical address is also to be found.

- Business cards
- Letterheads
- Brochures
- Annual reports
- Telephone directories and other reference books
- Television and radio advertisements
- Advertisements
- Hoardings and billboards
- Packaging
- Point-of-sale material

The problem with these references is that the company cannot at the same time give the users an incentive to visit on the Internet. However, these references help to create awareness of the company's web address and in the long term make it into a brand in itself.

Direct mail and enclosures
(free rides) to existing customers

If the company is aiming to create increased loyalty among its existing customers and the functionality of the website also reflects this, an appropriate idea would be to send all the recorded users in the target group a letter detailing what new opportunities are now being made available on the net. In this way the whole story can be told and can be adapted to suit the needs of different sectors. This method was used by Scandinavian Airlines when they launched their website providing the facility for users to check the current number of frequent flyer points earned.

If the company regularly sends out invoices or statements to its customers there will, if the company is geared up for this, also be the opportunity to design a special Internet enclosure which can go in the envelope without needing extra postage to be paid – these are called free rides.

Register the address on every search engine

Most websites are still found via search engines and Internet indexes. In order for a company's website to be found during a search, it is necessary for the company to be registered. This work is usually carried out by those who have developed the website or by companies who specialise in registration and metatags, but it must not be taken as a matter of course. The number of search engines is increasing as rapidly as everything else on the net and they are becoming more and more specialised. The more places the company is registered the better. However, if there is a product- or branch-specific search engine in the field the company represents (for example the travel industry or the pharmaceutical industry) a presence there will probably be more important. These will sometimes require a payment to be made and, if this is the case, documentation of traffic should be provided.

Exchange links

A simple form of network alliance is when two parties enter into a reciprocal agreement to provide links to each other's pages. In order to find out what companies may be interested in such an exchange deal, think of the companies that are in the company's value chain.

These can include:

- Shareholders
- Business associates
- Suppliers
- Dealers
- Companies offering complementary products.

There can also be situations where it makes sense to exchange links with competitors. The company can be reasonably certain that the target group is right, and if it is stronger on the net or offers better service, lower prices or just has a stronger brand, it will probably emerge victorious from such an exchange deal.

Vertical portals

Within many industries entrepreneurs will sooner or later create web marketplaces – also known as vertical portals – so users do not need to visit all the relevant industry websites. This can lead to an industry-specific community (as described in Chapter 10) but it can also develop into a so-called vertical portal. A good example of this is www.autobytel.com. Here the user can find offers from car dealers, distributors, etc. instead of having to visit each one. If there are relevant portals for the industry that the company belongs to, it should seriously consider being represented there.

If there is not yet a relevant portal, it could make sense to set up links to all competitors without necessarily getting links from their sites in return. In this way the company's website can develop into the place where people interested in the industry start browsing, and eventually the site can become the gateway for the industry. This needs to be planned and developed in such a way that visitors are not just sent to another address as soon as they arrive at your website, but instead the company makes good use of the opportunity to present its information – being the first and the best.

Travelocity's order page.

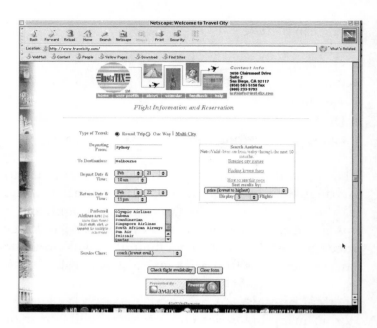

There was a similar situation in the 1970s in air traffic. The first airlines that developed online reservation systems and then installed terminals in travel agents had great success. However, it was not possible for the travel agents to have terminals to/from every single airline at each workstation. So when American Airlines was the first to introduce a joint system, which could not only find suitable American Airline tickets but also tickets from competing airlines, this system, SABRE, quickly became the sole source of travel information and reservations for many travel agents.

The benefit for American Airlines was obvious. The system first tried to find an American Airlines ticket, before looking for competing flights.

Today SABRE plays a major role in the airlines' efforts to make the travel agents superfluous and allow the users to book tickets themselves directly via the net. This can already be done, for example, at the huge website Travelocity, which is linked directly to the SABRE system.

Internet marketing

To generate traffic to the company's website requires dedicated marketing and of course this can be carried out directly on the Internet combined with traditional marketing. The advantage of advertising directly on the net is the certainty that those who see the advertisement also have access to the Internet.

In addition, it is very easy for the user to react to an Internet advertisement, compared to traditional response advertising. The aim of Internet advertisements, also called banner ads or banners, is to create so much interest that the user clicks on the advertisement and thereby gets to the place where the company can provide further information.

During the past year the market for Internet advertising has undergone a huge increase, and there are no signs that this development will slacken off in the years to come, rather the reverse. The number of competing websites is increasing at the same rate as the advertising budgets and, even though the number of users is also growing at a fast pace, the battle for visits to a company's website will intensify.

According to the Internet Advertising Bureau's latest statistics (3 November 1999), in the US Internet market alone the advertising revenue was worth US$934 million during the first 6 months of 1999. This is an increase of more than 100 percent when compared to the same period in 1998. Of this turnover, about 59 percent of the $934 million was generated by banner ads, while about 28 percent of the advertising resources was devoted to various sponsorship agreements. It is expected that in 2000 the total Internet advertising budget in the USA will amount to about 4.7 billion dollars.

Advertisers on the net

The number of advertisers who are either already advertising or are interested in advertising on the Internet is increasing rapidly. One of the main motivations for advertising on the net is the ability to directly measure the results on the bottom line through increased sales. Among other things, the aggressive growth in the number of users making online business transactions has contributed to the increased interest in Internet advertisement.

At present the advertising market in the USA can be divided into the following categories. The market share for each is given as a percentage of the whole:

- Consumer-related 29%
- Computing   22%
- Financial services 20%
- Business services 9%
- Telecom   6%
- Others   14%

Source: IAB, November 1999.

It is to be expected that the US development will be repeated in other geographical areas.

Advertising opportunities at present

In the past two years advertising opportunities on the Internet have undergone a dramatic development from simple statistical advertising columns with fixed locations to dynamic, interactive and user-sensitive advertisements with a form and location that can vary depending upon the wishes of the advertiser. The many existing forms of advertisement on the Internet have widely different distribution and acceptance. There are significant opportunities in this area as no-one has yet 'cracked the code' and found the perfect solution to advertising on the Internet.

The traditional banner advertisement

The Internet's most widespread and commonly used form of advertising is the banner ad. This is a graphic element with a fixed size and a fixed position on the website. The banner ad is effective at several levels – the user can see the advertisement, click on it and get onto the advertiser's website. In certain cases the user can participate in an interactive game, etc., on the actual banner ad. Below are some examples of conventional banner ads.

As with all other forms of advertisement, banner ads have undergone a dramatic development in recent years. Several different sub-categories have appeared.

Traditional banner ads

Animated banner advertisements

Banner ads can be designed as animated advertisements in the style of a simple cartoon – still with text and the facility to click onto a website. They are usually designed to take up as little memory as possible (as a rule a maximum of 10–15 kB). Animated banners are the most widespread type of banner now on the Internet as they attract more attention than traditional static ads. Additionally, they do not require special technologies to develop or execute them. Sometimes the animation lasts a maximum of a few seconds, in other ads the animation can loop (repeat itself).

Interactive banner advertisements

Interactive banner advertisements are a further development in Internet marketing, giving the user the opportunity to participate in interactive games or amusements – these are incorporated into the actual banner ad itself. The interactive element increases the advertising possibilities dramatically. Now when the user looks at the banner ad he or she is drawn play against it and thus clicks onto the underlying website.

Provisional figures show that interactive banner ads increase the click rate by several hundred percent – up to 600 percent! – in comparison to static banner ads. However, not all websites allow this form of banner ad.

Context-sensitive banner advertisements

These advertisements are also called search word banners. This banner type appears to the user as a conventional banner advertisement. The difference is that the individual banner ad is targeted at the specific user. The context-sensitive banner ad is found today primarily in search engines. The advantage it has there is that this type of banner is made context-dependent, so that each time a user searches for a word in the database, a banner ad appears for the company which has purchased that word.

If, for example, the user searches for the word 'car', 'motorway', 'tyres', or the like, an advertisement will appear for a car manufacturer. If the user searches for holidays, a banner ad will appear for a travel agent, and so on.

Today the major search engines, such as AltaVista and Yahoo!, offer words for sale. Most search engines are also able to check what country the user comes from and then display an appropriate version of the banner ad. Therefore don't be surprised to come across American banner ads on foreign websites – it is only Americans who will see them!

Search-word banners are at present one of the most targeted marketing tools available on the Internet. American studies show that the chance of a user clicking on a banner advertisement is more than 60 percent greater than normal if the banner is related to the search the user has in progress.

Rich media banners

Of course, everything should be tried on the Internet, including transmitting video via a banner ad. New banner technologies, such as d-html, Java and Flash, introduce new possibilities with regard to the content and creativity possible in the banner. Today banners can integrate small games, streaming news, sound and video clips. You can even download files and print discount coupons or product information from a banner. Enliven.com is one of the companies that have specialised in producing these rich media banners.

It's not all plain sailing, however. Some of the problems with these new areas of development are that the advertisements become rather ponderous and they usually need special technology to be installed on the user's machine, or require the most recent versions of browsers before they can function properly.

In addition, today it is possible for users to install a little program that removes all banner ads from the Internet page viewed. It is therefore important for online marketing people to continue to explore the options with banner ads, so that these are regarded as interesting and relevant to the individual user, instead of an irritating waste of bandwidth.

Shifting the banner

US research suggests that shifting the location of the banner (or button) to new locations on a web page increases the click rate. This is to be expected, as users will view a change with more interest. However, as new positions become the norm, the incremental increases in performance will be reduced. It may also prove detrimental to the host site as users question the stability of its interface.

How banner marketing works

Once a company has decided to advertise on the Internet, the first problem arises: What should the banner ad look like? You can generate many accurate measurements of how well banners perform. You can measure impressions, click-throughs and even how many of the users who clicked performed the desired action.

A number of design rules have directly contributed to many forms of banner ads now presented by advertisers. Common to the design of all banners is that a banner ad is designed to get as many appropriate – targeted – people as possible to click on it in order to reach the relevant place on the company's website. However, the company must have decided what it wants to do with these new leads before launching the banner ad, and must have prepared itself to handle the response. First, a quick review of the practical details:

The size of banner advertisements

The market is still fairly new so there are very few conventions or standards in the field of banner advertising. This will undoubtedly change as the market matures.

The size of a banner ad can be measured in several ways:

1. How much data must be downloaded onto the user's machine in order for the advertisement to be viewed (measured in kilobytes).
2. How long a banner ad's animation lasts (measured in time, seconds).
3. How much of the screen the banner ad takes up (measured in pixels).

Below we show the most common formats (IAB/CASIE standard creative sizes, in mm):

120 x 60

125 x 125

468 x 60

At the address
www.webreference.
com/dev/banners
there is a report
describing a study
of the placement of
banner ads and the
effect of this. One of
the things the
report says is that
in trials there was a
228 percent
improvement in
performance when
the banner was
positioned on the
right-hand side
rather than at the
top of a web page.

What do we want to know and what can we measure?

One of the practical aspects of the Internet is that almost anything at all can be measured, once the systems for this are integrated into the website. In the long term information about the users and their profile will be one of the most important sources of income on the Internet, as it gives advertisers the ability to target their messages in a way which is quite unprecedented. However, very high traffic is required before target group related advertising can be provided, so it will probably be some time before this can be carried out effectively.

Hits – the pernicious weed of Internet measurements

The term 'hits' is as difficult to eradicate as the most pernicious weed. This is probably because the measurement of hits provides such impressive figures. They are just not saying anything relevant, because each time a little bit of graphics is downloaded it counts as a hit. This means that a page which contains many different graphic elements will generate perhaps 20 to 30 hits, while another page will only generate a few. The figure is different from page to page and therefore this unit of measurement is unusable.

Number of pages displayed

This unit is much better, or it was. This is because today most websites are designed without the use of static HTML, that is to say that the pages do not exist in reality but are generated from a database at the time a user requests them, so as a result the concept of a page is very vague. Nor has the introduction of frames, that is the division of a page into several segments, made it any easier, as each frame counts as a separate page.

Number of exposures

The measurement of exposures, that is, the viewings of

a given advertisement, is known from traditional advertising. It is quite possible to measure how many times the ad's graphic element is downloaded. However, this unit of measurement also has its problems, as parameters such as position (visible or not visible on the screen without scrolling), size, whether users have specified that they want to see the advertisement (via search words) or whether it has been seen by chance, will all be of significance for its effect. In addition, the multiplicity of types of banner ad makes the unit of measurement more complex. In spite of this, the number of exposures will continue to be one of the most important units of measurement on which people rely.

The click rate – how many actually click on the advertisement

Campaign statistics usually include the amount of impressions and click-throughs. Everything indicates that this measurement, probably in combination with the exposure figure, can be converted most accurately into a concrete value for the advertiser and will therefore be the most valuable. The problem for advertisement sellers, however, is that poorly designed banner ads have a much lower click rate, and thus much poorer income, than good ads. When designing a banner ad try to optimise the click rate. The same applies to the planning and drawing up of a media plan.

Post click – what happens after they click?

Adserver technologies, such as DoubleClick's DART, allow advertisers to determine what happens to individual users after they have clicked a banner through to your site.

This is the 'look to book' factor. Conversion data allow advertisers and media buyers alike to determine the most cost-efficient sites in terms of business and revenue generation. This should however be limited to direct response campaigns, as it is no measure of the effectiveness of branding or longer-term business generation.

What it costs to advertise on the net

Many parameters determine what an advertisement costs and it is still something of a shanty-town market, consisting of many small sites where the difference between list price and the actual price paid can vary by up to 50 percent. Nevertheless, the larger websites are becoming more professional. The established advertisement networks on the Internet, such as DoubleClick or 24/7 Media, are contributing to a more mature and structured pricing of Internet advertisement.

The better the position, the more expensive

The more visitors who have access to the ad, the more expensive it will be. A rule of thumb is that the higher the banner is located in the website's hierarchy, the greater the exposure it will get and the more expensive it will be. Therefore the front page is typically the most expensive location on a website. The price depends upon the website and the position in the hierarchy.

Unsold inventory

The major portals have significant site inventory that will remain unsold. It is therefore possible to secure very cost-effective rates on a run-of-network basis, as sites are simply offloading advertising they could not sell. Expect to pay $10–$30 per thousand.

Exposure as price parameter

Another important sales parameter is the time the banner ad is exposed to a given user. Generally most advertising sellers offer sales over set periods of time, typically on a weekly, fortnightly or monthly basis. The price varies according to the season and the demand. However, there are a number of problems associated with this placement for a period of time. When an advertisement has been seen on the net just three times by the same user, it will have lost its value – a problem which is called banner burnout or banner blindness. The user notices the ad but doesn't 'see' it. In addition, if users have not found the banner ad interesting enough for a click after having seen it three times, then they will probably never click on it! Nevertheless, this is still the most widespread form of sale. The most common forms are:

- *Permanent banner placement*
  A permanent banner ad is seen each time a user enters the page in which the advertisement is placed. This type of banner is found typically in a site with low traffic, as the price charged, on a cost per thousand basis, would be too low to cover the administration cost. It is also found where areas of a website are very niche and extremely competitive. Hence advertisers will purchase on a monthly basis to ensure no competitors gain access to it.
  Price: about $1,000 per month for low traffic sites.

  Per Thousand Basis
  The most popular of models, advertisers purchase a set number of impressions (pages). This means a set number of eyes will be exposed to an advertisement. It is popular as it allows advertisers to gain access to high traffic sites without having to commit to all pages. It further allows advertisers to choose sections of a site that are most relevant and test their efficiency with minimal budgetary commitment

- *Run of site*
  Run of site advertising is a relatively cheap way to get exposure for banner ads. The advertiser typically buys a number of exposures over an agreed period of time and the banner is displayed in the places that are not sold to permanent advertisements. There are many exceptional deals to be had here, as this incorporates unsold inventory.
  Price: about $10–$30 per thousand.

- *Targeted placement*

  A large number of websites offer a variety of targeting possibilities such as frequency (how many times a user is exposed to a banner), geography, domain (from which country the user is connected), SIC codes, browser type (especially relevant in rich media campaigns), operating system and service provider. Time-determined banner placement is where the banner ad only appears on the website at selected times of the day. For example, if an advertiser has a banner targeted at the family, a choice can be made to show the banner between 6 p.m. and 9 p.m. – the time when families most frequently use the net. This form of sale enables the advertiser to target the banner campaign and is specially used by advertising networks, where a campaign may run on several different websites.

- *Hybrid pricing*

  Hybrid agreements are typically negotiated individually. The advertiser pays a smaller price per impression and in return pays a given amount per click-through or fixed percentage of the turnover generated. Performance-based agreements are equally becoming more common. Valueclick.com is one of the advertisement networks that have specialised in selling 'pay per click' campaigns.

- *Sponsorships*

  One of the most popular advertising options is sponsoring sites or sections. This allows powerful branding and potential content integration. Sponsorships tend to deliver high click-throughs and, as such, charge a significant premium. However, strong consideration must be given to the impact this has on your advertising campaign. Over-reliance on sponsorships limits the number of sites one can use and this ultimately retards reach. Compromising reach works to the detriment of raising awareness.

The click rate is the
most relevant form of payment

A sales form which so far has not been very widespread is payment per lead, that is, per visitor who is brought to the advertiser's website via the advertisement – also called the click rate.

This way the advertiser buys a fixed number of visits and pays a pre-set price per click. The banner ad will remain on the website until the agreed number of visits is attained, just as at present GRP (Gross Rating Points) can be bought – as exposures to the desired target group – on television. These forms of sale are much more precise than sale per set period of time, and pressure from new advertisers is expected to result in payment forms where buying a particular number of exposures or leads is predominant in the future. According to IAB, CPM or impressions-based deals account for 41 percent of total advertisement spending.

Combination advertising

A final sales form that is used to a great extent, particularly by Australian newspapers and magazines, is combination advertising. Here the advertiser is offered several types of advertisement in connection with the same advertising campaign. For example, an advertiser can be offered a combined package consisting of a whole page in a magazine, a demo-program on the magazine's front cover CD-ROM, and the opportunity to have job advertisements placed on the magazine's website where the advertiser is also offered a month's web advertising. Several newspapers have also introduced Internet classified advertising which is linked to Internet advertising in order to achieve synergy. The price varies considerably depending upon extent, time and the advertising seller.

The price of a visit

The price of a banner ad varies considerably, but it has

not been abnormal for a company (sometimes unwittingly) to have paid 15 cents for an advertisement exposure and one to two dollars for a visit to the company's website!

These amounts will decrease in line with increasing understanding on the part of companies as well as the entry into the market of media agencies and specialised net agencies. A more professional attitude to advertising on the net, as regards both place and price, will ensure a fair and acceptable contact price. However, for a while yet a visit to a website will cost considerably more than a traditional exposure in other media, partly because it is worth much more – provided the company is fully prepared as to what it wants to say to the visitor and what offers it has ready!

Advertising networks

In the USA increasingly it is companies such as DoubleClick and 24/7 Media that handle the sale of advertising space for a number of websites. The advantage of this is that they can centralise the management, making it more efficient, and in this way can offer many differentiated services. They can also target the advertisement to a much greater extent than is the case for advertising on one website. When advertising with DoubleClick advertisers never know where the advertisement will be shown; they just pay for the desired performance. With DoubleClick an advertiser can pay for a number of exposures or for a number of click-throughs. Today DoubleClick has more than 1500 websites in their network in more than 20 countries.

"The really difficult part of building a network is that you have got to have enough diverse inventory and enough ad offers for a system to become efficient."

Kevin O'Connor, president, DoubleClick

When the advertisement is shown it takes into account the browser type and version, operating system and version, what plug-ins the recipient has and what service provider is used.

DoubleClick permits the use of every kind of technology on websites, corresponding to more than 100 million exposures per month, so that it is possible to use sound, create interactive banner ads, etc. The way in which DoubleClick targets the advertisement is by continually gathering information about the user in a database and by matching the web page with advertising criteria.

A number of new networks such as Aaddzz (www.aaddzz.com) and ValueClick (valueclick.com) use the same procedure but go for smaller websites so that while they can take longer to amass a sufficiently large number of exposures, they can on the other hand offer considerably lower prices.

www.aaddzz.com
valueclick.com

Ten design rules to make banner advertisements more effective

All Internet agencies designing banner ads have their own theories about what works. A number of these guidelines are also available on the net. Some are obvious, others more doubtful. This is no exact science but rather an indication of what appears to increase traffic.

1. Advertise where the target group is to be found

There should preferably be a connection between the place where the advertising occurs and the product or the company the advertisement concerns. The greater the targeting, for example, by means of the purchase of search words or by profiling the users on the advertisement website, the better the effect. In the long term much greater targeting will be possible, so that a company will be able to define precisely the target group for its advertising on the net.

2. Ask questions

The way people's minds work, if they see a relevant and exciting question to which they would like to know the answer, they will click in order to find it out. Make sure that users are not disappointed by failing to provide the answer when they reach the website. Good teasers can increase the click rate by up to 15 percent.

3. Use bright colours

Some advertisements are more attractive than others. Bright colours and a nice design will always give a better click rate than some cramped text that looks amateurish. Studies show that green, blue and yellow work best, while black advertisements are the least effective.

4. Encourage action

Something as simple as a request to 'click here' appears to give a higher click-through rate. However, more elegant requests can also be used. Take into account the product and the target group when determining the tone of the message.

5. Cryptic messages arouse curiosity

Here again care must be taken not to entice the wrong users onto the company's website. However, used correctly a cryptic message can arouse users' curiosity and get them to click.

6. Animated banner advertisements work better

Forrester Research estimates that animated advertisements are about 25 percent more effective. The reason is quite simply that there is greater attraction in movement than in stillness. Consequently most banner ads are now animated.

7. Interactive banner advertisements work even better

Although this can still only be implemented on certain websites, the use of sound and interactivity can really increase the click rate, partly because it is still a new experience.

8. Test banner advertisements

As with all other advertisements, some work better than others. It is therefore recommended that advertisers develop a number of different banner ads with different messages and test these either on typical users before they are launched or directly on the advertisement website during the first days of the period of exposure so that they can select the best. The latter method requires frequent changes to be made to the website for the first few days, for example, three different advertisements a day for three days, and also the ability to record the different click rates for the different advertisements. It is recommended to dedicate 10 per-cent of the total budget to testing the banner cam-paigns before the real campaign starts.

9. Monitor the effect

If an advertiser spreads out the advertising over a large number of websites rather than selecting a central (but also expensive) placement, it is important that the effect is continuously monitored. In this way the advertiser can find out which advertising websites are working and which are not. The advertising strategy can then be continuously refined, omitting those websites with the poorest click rate and at the same time trying new ones. However, it is not always possible to measure the click rate, although this is vital if advertisers are to know when they should replace their banner ads.

10. Change the banner
advertisements frequently

In Internet circles they talk of the 'banner burnout effect'. The company Double Click carried out a study which showed that the likelihood of clicking on a ban-ner ad falls by more than 200 percent from the first exposure to the fourth exposure. By this time the ban-ner ad is not delivering the goods. In order to make best use of the resources available for advertising, the banner ads should therefore be changed at intervals dependent upon the user composition of the advertising site (how often the same users return).

The above guidelines are not exhaustive and additional guidelines will be formulated in the future. For example, it is not always the case that an advertisement must lead to the front page of a website. It can make good sense and save the user time if it takes the user straight to the order page. In addition, there are more and more companies in the USA that are satisfied with the familiarity that is built up by means of exposure on the net and therefore do not give any through-click ability at all. However, there is no doubt that it will be advantageous to follow the 10 tips above when developing banner ads.

CHAPTER

New forms of advertising

*"Banner ads aren't working yet and websites are
desperately trying to find the combination that will work."*

Bill Doyle, senior analyst, Forrester Research

Banner ads are far from being the Holy Grail of advertising – in fact they are relatively boring – but we will probably continue to see them for years to come. However, designers are already looking for other, more elegant, forms of Internet advertising. Of recent developments, some look promising from the user's point of view, while others are more doubtful.

Sponsorship

A form of advertising that is rapidly gaining ground on the Internet is sponsorship. In the first quarter of 1999, 28 percent of media advertisement on the Internet in the USA was used on sponsorships, according to Forrester. Sponsorship is the exposure of a brand, logo or product, typically for a longer time than an advertisement. This is similar to television where, for example, sports transmissions are sponsored by big advertisers. The sponsorship can apply to all or part of a website, and the position of the sponsorship announcement can also vary. Sponsorships generally get more exposure than banner ads and are best placed where are highly targeted, in order to offer the users a relevant product or experience.

Gatorade sportsdrink is an example of an integrated sponsorship, where product and sponsor go well together. Gatorade sponsor nfl.com and nba.com's virtual GM game, where web users are offered a relevant web experience, such as competitions.

Microsites

Microsites are in some ways comparable to sponsorship. A microsite is a limited area on the web supplier's graphic environment where the content is managed and paid for by an external advertiser/company. Kraft Interactive Kitchen has successfully run a sponsorship and microsite for Kraft holiday recipes in co-operation with www.foodtv.com online holiday promotions.

Companies such as Armani and Gap have also used the technique. For companies selling low-interest products, or impulse-buy products, microsites are particularly relevant. In particular, makers of soft drinks, candy and the like shouldn't build large websites as it is expensive and difficult to generate traffic to them. An insurance company can be fairly sure its website won't be much visited, as users will only look for the company when they are thinking specifically about insurance – very seldom. But by being where the users are to be found when they do need insurance, more interest can be created around an otherwise low-interest product. The insurance company could, for example, create a microsite on used-car databases, list 10 pieces of advice for buyers of used cars and at the same time offer a good insurance deal. This achieves a much more precise and relevant exchange of information than could ever be done on the company's own website.

www.nba.com

mini CASE

*Visa – it's
everywhere you
want to be.*

www.visa.com

www.rankit.com

Visa is currently an important player on the Internet as it is one of the most frequently used means of payment on the net. Visa's strategy for online marketing primarily serves the purpose of supporting Visa's other marketing mix which consists of sponsorships, marketed products and Visa's two websites: Visa Expo and Rankit (aimed at students).

The aim was to have Visa's logo placed on the best possible websites within sport, entertainment, restaurants and travel so that when users saw Visa's logo it would either be on, or would lead to, a place they would like to be. Visa's US sponsorships included the Olympics in Atlanta, the NFL, the US skiing team and the three major horse-races which together make up 'the Triple Crown'. Visa developed the first ever microsite on Yahoo! under the name Siteseer. Each week Visa presented here the 10 best links within three different relevant areas, such as skiing, NFL trainers, music, St Valentine's day holiday locations, good shopping sites in the run-up to Christmas, etc.

Visa has developed similar microsites and sponsored content on other websites, such as Geocities, Epicurious, ESPNet, NFL.com, Sportsline, etc., with everything from restaurant guides to competitions and a chance to chat to America's top chef. The program has been very extensive and very successful. Visa has not only 'occupied' particular areas of the Internet but has also won a position as a leader in the use of digital media. The policy was to have activities in places where the users were to be found rather than on Visa's own websites. The overall web strategy was developed by BBDO New York and has already won four international prizes for innovative marketing on the Internet.

Interstitials or intermercials

One of the newest forms of advertising on the Internet is interstitials or intermercials. These are advertisements shown between page changes on a website – they are also known as 'pop-ups' – are increasingly being used in the USA. On www.bezerk.com 'You don't know Jack', brief advertisements appear between the pages for companies who sponsor the online game.

At the website www.msnbc.com, which continually tries out the latest Microsoft-specific technologies such as Active Server Pages and dynamic HTML, this advertising can be seen if you go to the sports page.

A very recent advertisement form is browser ads, where a window in the user's browser displays ads. The ads are thus continuously visible on all webpages and the user actually earns money while surfing in return for running the browser ads. Alladvantage.com downloads a viewbar to users where ads are displayed targeted to the user, who earns in return 20c–$1 per hour.

The CD-ROM magazine *Blender* decided in autumn 1997 to cease production of CD-ROMs and instead convert the product to the web. At www.blender.com a special Blenderbrowser can be downloaded after which the user can watch videos and full-screen advertisements in the form of 10-second interstitials with sound. In addition *Blender* offers content sponsorships.

Alliances and affiliate programs

The reason that large companies producing or supplying complementary products join together on the net is because the task of updating a user-oriented website that revolves around the user in a given situation can seldom be managed by one company alone.

Experience shows that if market leaders from different branches join forces, as far as brand-building is concerned there will be a synergy and a rubbing off of one company's set of values on the other's in a way which is beneficial for all the parties concerned.

'Consumers don't like looking at blank screens. If you can give them something to look at, they actually like it.'
Robert Lee, CEO, Streamix

www.msnbc.com

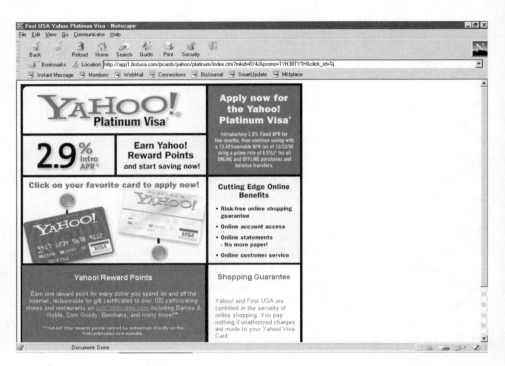

One company that has had huge success in creating alliances on the net is Amazon; through its co-operation with Yahoo! it has been able to increase sales considerably. AOL also has alliances with other companies regarding the creation of content and the sale of goods.

Another version of alliances is affiliate programs. This concept was introduced by Amazon back in 1997, and has proved a major reason for the online bookstore's success. As the Internet today has more than 40 million websites, a strong distribution strategy is essential for successful e-commerce. Amazon has more than 350,000 distributors of its books, all based on its affiliate program. A website focused on cigar smoking might recommend books about the topic. These books can be bought via the Amazon affiliate bookstore that is placed on the local cigar site. The owner will earn a percentage of the total sales generated via the site. The Internet appears to be tailor-made for this type of alliance, where companies that do not overlap or compete too much, join forces.

Guerrilla marketing

The purpose of guerrilla marketing is to brand and generate traffic to a website, or motivate specific calls or actions, by word-of-mouth or other untraditional means of marketing. An example of guerrilla marketing is offline sampling of branded merchandise in highly frequented places such as airports, train stations or places where it is easy to meet the target group, such as sports clubs and schools. Other examples are offline/online event marketing, untraditional outdoor marketing or viral marketing, where Internet users are offered incentives to forward promotional e-mails.

As part of the relaunch of Yahoo! Denmark, 5,000 Yahoo! apples were distributed on the busiest train station in Denmark with the message that in the next hours a trip to New York could be won on their site. As well as the word-of-mouth this marketing created, Yahoo! managed to get it mentioned in newspapers.

Push advertisements

A relatively new advertising concept, so-called push advertisements, was born in the USA. It invites users to register for a kind of advertising service based on a number of companies being linked to a database to which the Internet user has access. Users can select specified advertisers/companies about which they would like to receive further information. The selected advertisers send advertisements via e-mail either as text, graphics or short films. Thus the users select their own advertisements and not the other way round. The advantage is that the advertising is targeted, reaching a recipient who is already involved and interested in the product. At present several companies are working on this technology; Backweb is a leader in the field.

Agent-based forms of advertising

It is anticipated that before long agents will appear in the form of animated figures moving freely around the screen, and even outside the browser. The ads will be programmed to enter into a primitive dialogue with the user, as independent entities with their own personalities, giving a completely new perspective to advertising on the Internet. The technology is so new that it has still not been seen on commercial sites. It is, however, expected to be developed within a short time, so that the first 'advertisement mouthpieces' of this type will be in use within the next six months. These types of advertisement are described in detail in Chapter 14.

Direct e-marketing

www.gvu.gatech.edu

Among those on the Internet, e-mail is by far most popular activity. According to GVU (www.gvu.gatech.edu), e-mail is the number one 'indispensable' Internet technology. Today already three times as many e-mails are being sent than letters in the USA per day.

e-marketing is cheap

We are talking about a few cents instead of a few dollars. 1-800-Flowers say that communicating with their customers via e-mail rather than snail mail offers a 75 percent cost savings.

e-marketing is measurable

When a customer signs up to receive your newsletter by e-mail, you know you have a reader. If delivery has failed this is immediately apparent to the sender and the mail can be resent. This guarantees total coverage of the target audience. And if HTML tags are embedded, when and how many recipients respond can be measured. The response on an e-mail newsletter can be as high as 25 percent.

e-marketing can be highly targeted

In theory a database can create individual e-mails for each receiver without any extra cost!

e-marketing is enormously adaptable
It is possible to offer a straight text message of a full-colour mailing that looks exactly like a web page and at the same time uses an interactive component that allows interaction with the content.

Opt in

The response rate from an opt-in newsletter driven campaign can be up to 10 times the response on banner ads. Pennmedia.com offers opt-in e-mail newsletters and sends about 200 different newsletters to over 11 million users. The response on a newsletter will invariably depend on the specific offer, presentation, technology and not at least the ability to...

Target, target and target...

By integrating a database-driven site within e-mail, messages can now be targeted more precisely. For example, for a company e-mailing 1,000 users, it is now possible to send out hundreds of unique e-mails with various mixes of advertising, offers, editorial content, and so on. Flonetwork.com is an example of a company handling permission-based e-mail programs.

At the other end of the targeting spectrum is collaborative filtering, which allows e-mails to be sent with relevant offers based on information about a particular user's prior purchases and overall user purchase patterns. Collaborative filtering can also use demographic information and domain name data to target e-mails more effectively. In addition messages can be sent in different formats, depending upon the e-mail program the customer uses. And this is just the beginning. Tracking the consumer's reaction to these campaigns allows incredibly complex predictive modelling, giving the ability to know what consumers want to hear about almost before they know themselves.

Direct e-marketing is the second generation after spam. It is a more intelligent way of creating a dialogue with consumers who 'want' to be contacted and has matured as spam campaigns have become less effective. GVU user services show that 61 percent of all consumers who were receiving unsolicited e-mails last year were deleting them before reading them! These figures are very similar to those of classic (paper-based) junk-mail – the difference is that we now are in the twenty-first century.

Five percent of all spam is gone!

The fight against spam has become stronger and stronger. Today, thousands of organisations around the world are fighting for a cleaner cyberspace. The first visible result was achieved by EuroCause, an Internet-based lobby group that managed, with support from the EEC, to ban spam completely in Europe in 1998. The problem is that 95 percent of spam comes from the US!

The trend is obvious: spam will fade away and be replaced by far more sophisticated direct e-marketing campaigns, all database-driven and based on consumer permission.

Integration with other marketing activities

Integration between online and offline campaigns are not established by labelling the web address on the television or print ad. Integrated marketing requires the offline and online campaigns to be based on the same creative platform and communicate similar messages. Done right, a lot of synergy can be gained.

The campaign should ensure long-term brand building, generation of traffic and sales across online and offline advertisement. It is still a common misconception with many companies that it is sufficient to label a web address on television and print advertisement.

However, this misconception is more widespread in Europe than in the USA. For .com companies whose business is only on the Internet, integrated marketing has become a standard element of ad campaigns. These companies use both offline and online media in an integrated mix to create awareness, generate traffic and ensure sales. There are traditional offline companies with marketing or sales activities on the Internet who early on saw the value in marketing their online activities offline. Honda and Armani have won prizes for their whole-page advertisements for web activities in the magazine *Wired*, and CNN, clnet, MSNBC and others with access to television channels run television advertisements for their websites at all times of the day.

The reason why to date few innovative advertising concepts have been developed which combine different media is probably that designers in the traditional agencies have still not recognised the huge potential of the Internet. We are now beginning to see advertisement agencies that specialise in marketing .com companies and integrating offline and online marketing. We can expect that these companies will introduce quite different, newly developed advertising concepts utilising several media in conjunction and focusing upon the strengths of the individual media in relation to each other.

When M&M's were going to launch a new colour for their sweets in Denmark, it was decided there should be a vote by the customers. This was to take place in the shops where voting slips were handed out with M&M's point-of-sale material announcing the M&M's election. At the same time it was decide to run an interactive election campaign on the Internet between the three colours pink, mauve and blue. The voting could be followed on the net as three glasses filled with the appropriate amount of M&M's in the respective colours

mini**CASE**

M&M's blue advertising

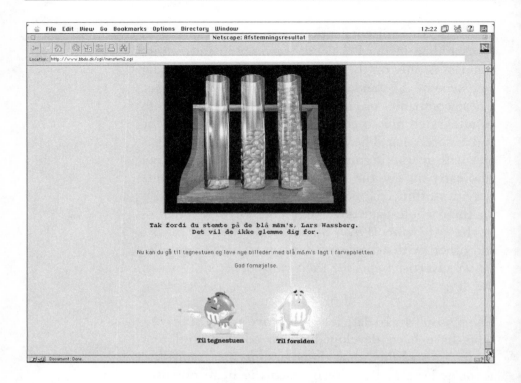

Tak fordi du stemte på de blå m&m's, Lars Wassberg.
Det vil de ikke glemme dig for.

Nu kan du gå til tegnestuen og lave nye billeder med blå m&m's lagt i farvepaletten.

God fornøjelse.

Til tegnestuen   Til forsiden

Document : Done.

Blue wins the vote at M&M's website.

corresponding to the current position in the election. When the colour election took place on M&M's website, feedback was received about how many had voted and for what colours. At the same time the election had the result that afterwards in M&M's painting competition the selected colour was added to the colour palette. During the month in which the election was held, drawings contained the colours mauve, pink and blue, which had not been possible before. When the election was over, more than 5,000 people had cast a vote on the Internet, considerably more than had been cast in the shops. The final choice was the colour blue, which was celebrated in all kinds of ways on television, on the Internet, in the shops and in the M&M's packs, which now also contained blue M&M's. At the same time blue became a permanent colour on the painting palette.

Whole-page advertisement from the launching of www.news.com in the San Francisco Chronicle.

Television, point-of-sale material and the Internet had combined in a completely new way and the three media had each supported the campaign and created an innovative way of launching a new product. Sales were tremendous and M&M's later won the respected Direct Mail Prize in 1996 for the Internet part of the campaign – the first time this prize had been awarded to a campaign that did not include paper and stamps!

CHAPTER

When the browser becomes invisible

"The days of navigating the web using a 'web browser' are numbered. Can you imagine accessing all the information that is stored in your computer's hard disk through one multi-purpose application? No? Well that's what we do today on the web!"

Ariel Poler, founder, I/Pro

Today the Internet makes a number of demands of users of the medium. These can be categorised as two main types of difficulty:

1. It is difficult to get started
The first obstacle is the technical and understanding barrier which still makes it difficult for many people to get started.

2. It is difficult to find your way around and to find relevant content
The second obstacle is the need to know how to find the way around the web, an environment which is continuously growing in size, with several thousand additional websites being added each week.

The work on eliminating or reducing these obstacles is in full swing. A number of innovative companies have already found how to turn these problems into an advantage that can be used actively in marketing. New products and new ways of doing things are appearing all the time and before long the Internet will have a completely different appearance and a different interface that will revolutionise its use – yet again!

These changes will have great significance on the way companies market themselves on the Internet of the future.

Warning – access for nerds only!
As the Internet is used today, every single session requires a number of factors to be fulfilled. The user needs to have access to a computer, it needs to be switched on (up and running), which can easily take a couple of minutes, and a user has had to go to the trouble of installing a so-called browser program that provides access to the World Wide Web (a program market which is dominated at present by Netscape Navigator and Microsoft Explorer). Finally, the user needs to have a phone line to an Internet Service Provider (ISP) and

needs to be successful in getting through.

The obstacles to access to the Internet are in fact quite high in comparison to traditional media such as television and radio, particularly as the installation of a modem and browser is still something that requires a relatively high degree of technical knowledge.

Furthermore, it costs something to be on the net, both in the form of an annual subscription to the ISP and in ongoing telephone call charges, though the price is becoming lower every year.

It is all the more impressive that in spite of this the Internet has a growth rate on practically all parameters of 50 to 100 percent per year.

Work is being carried out urgently to remove the technical barriers so that the use of the Internet is made easier. This chapter will, however, only deal with initiatives that are of significance for a company's presence on the net.

Welcome to the net – here is your personal newspaper

Most net users feel a greater or lesser degree of dejection and confusion. 'I know that there is relevant content somewhere out there, but I can't find it!' New behavioural studies show that 50 percent of frequent users no longer surf the net, but instead visit the same sites each time they log on. The strength of the Internet has become its weakness. A number of companies are trying to solve this problem. By integrating content from a number of sources and making this content configurable, they are trying to create the ultimate place to start, where it is easy to find exciting relevant content, where users are kept up to date with the things in which they are interested and where they are at the same time surprised by content they had not expected. Search engines such as Excite and Yahoo! have had these kinds of Internet starting places for a while

www.myyahoo.com

live.excite.com

www.planetdirect
.com

www.zdnet.com

**www.snap.
com
the perfect
place to start**

(www.myyahoo.com, live.excite.com). Other initiatives are from companies such as Planet Direct and Ziff Davis (www.planetdirect.com, www.zdnet.com). Several of these sites are offered through ISPs as the first place you come to when you open your browser.

One of the more successful starting places is from the company c l net, which launched its service www.snap .com in autumn 1997. The site has received good reviews and is forecast to be a huge success. More than 50 different alliances are included so that users can obtain content from NBC, CNN, CBS and from c l net's own websites, which were already much visited. Users can tailor this starting place to their own needs, so that they are saved having to travel around on the net in order to find different content and instead has it all delivered to one address which is the first they see when they go on the net. c l net has also entered into agreements with seven of the largest ISPs in the USA to have www.snap.com as the first page their users see. A CD-ROM-based manual is also provided which makes it easy for users to get started.

Recently Disney jumped on the bandwagon with its portal GO (www.go.com). The launch of GO was also the starting signal of one of the most impressive and massive offline campaigns created entirely for a website.

These portals, or starting places, will be very interesting websites to own and very attractive places for companies to market themselves, as they will be visited very frequently. All ISPs should therefore consider making this form of service available, as it could become one of the areas of competition in the future.

When online and offline merge

One way to make access to the Internet easier is to use a different and more familiar medium, for example CD-ROM, to which many people have now become accustomed. This is done by several ISPs in order to

Snap! Online's website.

have a physical product to sell (in contrast to the immaterial Internet subscription).

Another example of the combination of CD-ROM and the Internet is *Launch*, a music magazine which primarily exists on CD-ROM but which combines the Internet with the offline product in very interesting ways. This also applies to the advertisements in the magazine.

In the future the interface will probably be on the Internet while the CD-ROM will hold a lot of high-bandwidth content such as sound and video which is not suitable for the Internet at present. By using the CD-ROM as a container, companies can supply a more dynamic presentation and at the same time achieve topicality by having the dynamic data such as prices and availability of goods, press releases, etc. come from the net. The weakness of this solution is that the CD-ROM has to be inserted in the machine.

On the other hand it would be possible for the CD-ROM producers to integrate not just Internet access but also content from the Internet in the actual

CD-ROM solution. Hybrid solutions of this kind lead to a number of problems, but provided companies are willing to send CD-ROMs out to their customers it will be possible to integrate the Internet into the solution.

The browser as part of the operating system

Another technological breakthrough which will make the Internet more accessible is the integration of Internet technology with existing computer programs and even with the operating system. The newest operating system from Apple, MacOS 8.0 integrates the Internet with the desktop (the background image you always see on the screen). Everything is pre-installed and e-mails and the World Wide Web are available at the touch of a button. New Java programs and web objects provide different access to information from the net and the most popular applications (primarily from Microsoft) all have integrated net access.

The newest version of Windows, Windows 98, will also have the Internet integrated in it. Microsoft plans to incorporate a new channel paradigm so that from the desktop you will have direct access to the most important channels of information. For companies this means that access to customers is moving closer and that information will flow to them even when they have not asked for it. But this also means that the traditional way of creating websites will have to become much more user-oriented.

The Internet as part of television

For a long time it was a subject for discussion whether the television or the computer would win the battle for the consumers' attention. The computer won, but it is going to change its appearance so that it is hardly distinguishable from a television, provided it is put in the living room, at any rate. At present there are a number of trials under way regarding the installation of cable modems – small decoder boxes which give access to the Internet via a network of cables. This has been technically possible for a long time but it has required very large investment at the cable network's nodes in order to convert the existing network from a one-way to a two-way network. However, there is no longer any doubt that it will come eventually. In the USA estimates from the consultants Kinetic Strategies show that by the start of the new millennium there will be 2.9 million US homes connected to the Internet via their television network. Microsoft has made a large number of acquisitions in order to prepare the company for the day when the Internet is generally available in the living room. One of Microsoft's acquisitions is the company WebTV which sells a box costing $99 that makes it possible to surf the net from those places where WebTV has set up servers. There are two reasons why these connections are so interesting:

Speed

Accessing the Internet via the cable network will give speeds of about three hundred times that of a 28.8 kbps modem which at the moment is the de facto standard. For this to work the rest of the Internet also needs to be made faster. Content stored on the cable network in special servers will, however, be available very quickly.

Easy accessibility

Unlike traditional computer access, access via the television and cable network of the future will be immediate. Users will switch it on, just as they switch on the television today.

Internet access via television can be compared to a form of interactive teletext. Users will be able to find out the films showing at the cinema on any given day and then book a ticket. They will be able to obtain local weather forecasts and communicate with the meteorologist via e-mail and print out an individual weather map.

If this form of connection becomes popular, all talk of the Internet's penetration will disappear at a stroke, and the Internet will be the most attractive medium to use for marketing purposes. Once again, however, it will mean that all the content that is found on the Internet today will have to be modified, as the higher speeds will offer a number of new opportunities waiting to be utilised, and also because the resolution and the screen format will be different.

At present there are many initiatives attempting to get the Internet out of the browser and into the computer in order to integrate the Internet with daily life, without the user having to make a conscious effort. At the same time some of these solutions are starting to resemble the television medium as it is known today – a more passive experience where the information is provided without any particularly active input on the part of the user.

mini CASE

Push technology and webcasting

In 1996 Pointcast started to provide a program which could be downloaded free of charge from the net. The package consisted of two items: a client program which could be adapted individually and a screensaver which brought news and headlines that suited individual adaptation (that is, the user's interests).

The client program consisted of a number of channels, each of which is comparable to a television channel such as Discovery or EuroSport. The users decided which channels they wanted, choosing between sport, weather forecasts, news, business information, gossip, etc. Each channel could also be tailored to suit the interests of the users – what sports they wanted, what parts of the USA they wanted weather forecasts for, what companies they wanted to follow, etc. In connection with the individual setting up of the client, the user was also invited to answer a number of demographic questions, all of which would help to make the selection of information more precise. Afterwards the user could decide how often the client was to update its information – every hour, a quarter of an hour before work, during the lunch break, etc.

At these set times the client program downloaded a sufficiently large tailored package of information onto the computer from the Internet. When the user, for example, came back from lunch, the client was ready with updated relevant share prices, news, sports results, etc., all available on the computer, so that the traditional waiting periods on the net were eliminated.

Updated advertisements were also downloaded with the information – so-called smart ads. These could, as a result of being stored in the computer and not on the Internet, take up more space and therefore be more dynamic. Like the content, the advertisements were selected in accordance with the individual user's profile. Both the information and the advertisements were linked to the Internet, so that by a single click it was possible to jump to further information or to the website of the advertising company. Pointcast has been a great success. Today more than two million people have downloaded and installed the Pointcast client on their machines.

The number of channels in Pointcast has increased considerably, so that today there is a much greater range of information to choose from, and as a result the value to the individual user has also increased. Pointcast is currently working on a future version of the program and on the possibility of enabling large companies to give their employees access to the net in a more controlled way by using Internet clients. Pointcast is clearly developing in the direction of resembling a network of different channels – a metaphor which is very reminiscent of today's television. The fear expressed by many people is that as a result the Internet will become just as passive as television.

Pointcast is no longer alone in the market for this type of push-based solution. Many new players have appeared

Pointcast's website.

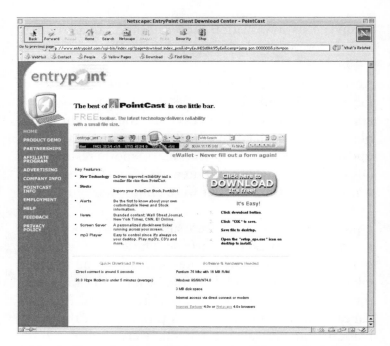

with similar solutions, the most significant of which are Marimba and Backweb. Other examples of push technology can be found at the following addresses:

- www.marimba.com (Castanet tuner)
- www.infomarket.ibm.com (IBM Newsticker)
- www.intermind.com (Intermind Communicator)
- www.netdelivery.com (Netdelivery)

When the Internet reaches ubiquity

Today we see all kinds of hand-held devices which are integrated with the Internet: mobile phones through the WAP (Wireless Aplication Protocol) browsers; digital radios through DAB (Digital Audio Broadband); PDAs like Palm and Windows CE devices. And it looks like we´re going to be connected anytime, anywhere through a host of devices. At that point we will stop talking about being on the net, like we don't talk about being on the telephone net! The Internet will become as integrated in our daily life as electricity and it will be taken for granted by all kids growing up today.

CHAPTER **XIV**

The intelligent website

"Imagine your personal mentor – an agent whose sole aim is to help you to become better informed, wiser, richer and able to act more quickly ... This mentor already exists in cyberspace – it's called an infomediary!"

Anon.

In line with increasing use of interactivity on the Internet a new phenomenon has appeared: the intelligent website. There is no doubt that optimal interactivity is achieved by targeted dialogue, but how is it possible to achieve targeted dialogue with 100,000 users, all at once? Even if a website in theory is targeted at, for example, people aged 12 to 18 years, there is an enormous difference in the users' behaviour and preferences. Eighteen-year-olds will hardly like to be talked to as if they are 12 years old! The intelligent website has proved to be the solution to this problem. In practice an intelligent website is not just one website but many individual websites or items of information that are generated based on the user's behaviour, preferences and profile. The individual website can be compiled on the basis of a vast number of different observations which together make up a clear picture of the user.

The anonymous consumer disappears

The problem with the individualisation of communication on the Internet so far has been obtaining information about the user. In theory Internet users are almost 100 percent anonymous until the time they voluntarily provide information about themselves. Only the browser type and the client origin can be recorded – data that does little to help to paint a picture of the user. The wish to know the user better has led to the use of two tools, the final results of which can be used to individualise/personalise the website, namely the questionnaire and the club concept.

The questionnaire

Since the introduction of the World Wide Web, the questionnaire has been the most frequently used technique for surveying consumer's behaviour and preferences. The response percentage for questionnaires is, however, now very low, as the technique has been greatly overused. The users quite simply find it difficult to see what they get out of constantly providing personal information.

The club concept

The setting up of 'clubs', where the answering of one or more questions acts as an entrance card to the website, has proved successful. This is primarily because there is usually a balance between what the users have to give (information about themselves) and what they get (access to an attractive website). The club concept is also attractive to the web providers, as user behaviour can be identified at an individual level. This permits in-depth research into a particular user's behaviour on the website and extensive individualisation.

The first agent took over in 1966

As early as 1966 Eliza was born at the Massachusetts Institute of Technology. A 240-line program, it created a virtual psychologist who could answer questions with other questions. Although Eliza is now a museum piece, the program set the scene for a new generation of websites which has emerged over the past two years. This phenomenon is called agents or 'bots'. The name is derived from the word 'robots' and covers a new type of intelligent program which not only builds up static individualised websites, but also dynamic individualised websites which learn from the user's behaviour and design themselves accordingly. The two program types – 'agents' and 'bots' – are, however, not identical. Agents filter information online based on the users' wishes, for example, by specialising in being able to find the cheapest airline ticket. Bots are programmed to carry out actual tasks, learning from the users' behaviour and drawing conclusions. In the future the two concepts will probably just both be called agents.

The lifestyle agent broke the ice

One of the weaknesses of agents has so far been that they could only act on the basis of information gathered via questionnaires or keyed-in search words, but this problem now appears to have been solved. In 1997 Andersen Consulting developed the world's first lifestyle agent. This was not built up on the basis of information provided by a questionnaire but from a series of pictures from which the individual user made a selection. Each series of pictures identified an area of the user's behaviour or preferences – for example, how the user preferred to travel – with a picture of a plane, a car, a caravan, a train or a bus. By just asking a few behaviour-describing questions it was possible for the agent, in combination with an American behaviour database that has charted Americans' behaviour for years, to draw up a precise profile of the user. This profile could ultimately lead to an accurately targeted communication between advertiser and user.

The agents' functions have changed during the past five years, from originally just being able to act on the basis of the users' wishes, to today being able to act on the basis of observations gained over a period of time. For example, if it is found that a user visits the same website dealing with Singapore several times on the same day, this can be an indication that the user is planning to travel there. On the basis of this observation, the agent can offer to carry out a search for the cheapest flights to the Far East. Amazon is today using a similar technique when the site compares the visitor's individual author-choice with other user author-choices, then recommends a particular title. The agent observes and draws conclusions, increasingly acting as the user's personal secretary. The agent's observations can also be used in other contexts, such as when a user visits a commercial website after having shown interest in a particular subject many times. The result will not be an enquiry from the agent but a reorganisation of the structure of the website. From originally having been configured based on the behaviour of an 'average' user, the subsequent pages that the user visits will be 100 percent tailored on

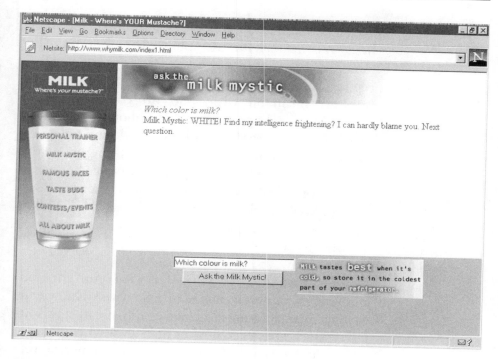

the basis of the user's profile. The icons that represent the options in the website will be put in order of priority according to the user's interest and not according to general principles.

www.whymilk.com unfortunately isn't active any longer. The site was taken down in 1998.

It is basically a question of creating the optimal communications tool, a tool that can create a quality dialogue with the users for as long as possible. The fewer reasons the user has for leaving the website, the greater the likelihood of the user becoming involved in the content and message of the website. www.whymilk.com was a good example of the fact that the technology can strengthen dialogue between the brand and the users. In 1997 the talking agent, the Milk Mystic, was developed to advise users about milk. The agent based its responses on numerous frequently asked questions. These were answered automatically after the user had keyed in the whole question. The reply was not just a response to the key word, which is typical of such programs today. When a question was asked, the agent automatically generated a tailor-made reply, based on the way the user phrased the question. For example, if the robot was asked, "Who made you?", it replied, "No-one made me – I am just me!" If the questioning continued with, "So do you not have a mother?", it replied, "Don't ask me about my mother – that has nothing to do with milk – and I am only built to talk about milk!" The fascinating thing about this agent was that it also had a sense of humour. For example, if it was asked what colour milk had, after a few seconds it would reply, "Did you really ask that? Milk is white of course! Haven't you got any more complicated questions?"

www. knowledgeinsight. com

Insight Technologies (www.knowledgeinsight.com) specialising in development of Enterprise Knowledge Management solutions has managed to create new software, which goes even further than www.whymilk.com. The software is able to automatically summarise, recommend and hyperlink millions of Internet pages, and create a personal website for a user with a summary. If you, for example, choose to type in the question: "Why is milk white?", the software will search the whole Internet, choose the best answers and create a short summary of the conclusions for the user. This new technology creates a range of new opportunities for the Internet user.

In the future every consumer will have an agent!

Film actors know they've reached a certain level of accomplishment in their career when they attract the services of an agent. Good agents know almost everything about their actors. Their history, their preferences and their acting skills – they know the actors so well that they can almost act on behalf of the actor. What if consumers had an agent who was able to 'listen, learn and react' to their 'master'? When choosing insurance, the agent could help by providing the insurance company with all necessary information, run the comparison process, negotiate the best price and advise the 'master' about the preferred choice. Based on the 'master's' choice, the agent would learn even more about the preferences, which would be reflected in the next action, which in theory would be even more precise.

In the future agents will not just exist as agents for websites, but as proper personal agents. Personal agents will be owned by the individual users, with the sole purpose of helping the users operate on the Internet. The name of the new trend is infomediary – a consumer advocate that constantly learns about consumers' preferences and acts on their behalf in an objective way. The infomediary will learn what travel preferences the users have and also what types of hotel they prefer, which 'frequent flyer' clubs they belong to, and be informed about the credit card if necessary. In theory the agent is no longer an agent but a reflection of the user on the Internet.

The dawn of the infomediary

The trend is obvious. The days when consumers had to type in the same data every time they visited the Internet have reached an end. Infomediaries – databases with one set of centralised consumer data – have started to appear more and more. The purpose of the infomediary is simply to administrate and protect the consumer's private information. When visiting a website the site will request a set of data from the user. The user will then refer back to a particular site to which the user has typed in all personal data. The site acts as a consumer custodian; it will evaluate the requested data every time. If the value of the data requested by the site is high, the consumer custodian site might negotiate a special discount for the user as payment for the data.

The value of the site is not only that the consumer will gain more privacy protection, it will also make life a bit

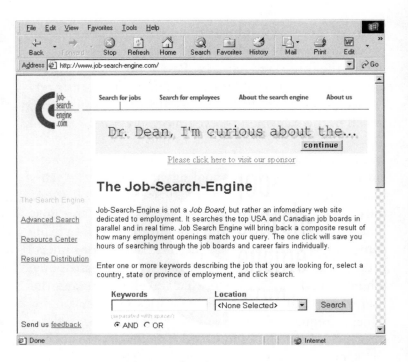

File Edit View Favorites Tools Help

Back Forward Stop Refresh Home Search Favorites History Mail Print Edit

Address http://www.job-search-engine.com/ Go

Search for jobs   Search for employees   About the search engine   About us

Dr. Dean, I'm curious about the...
continue

Please click here to visit our sponsor

The Job-Search-Engine

Job-Search-Engine is not a *Job Board*, but rather an infomediary web site dedicated to employment. It searches the top USA and Canadian job boards in parallel and in real time. Job Search Engine will bring back a composite result of how many employment openings match your query. The one click will save you hours of searching through the job boards and career fairs individually.

Enter one or more keywords describing the job that you are looking for, select a country, state or province of employment, and click search.

The Search Engine

Advanced Search

Resource Center

Resume Distribution

Keywords   Location
                              <None Selected>   Search
(separated with spaces)
Send us feedback   ⦿ AND ○ OR

Done   Internet

www.job-search-engine.com claims to be the first infomediary website in the world.

easier as it won't be necessary to retype data. The website owner will also gain, as data collected will be high quality, being monitored and updated from a central database. Today's portals will probably not exist 12 months, thanks to infomediaries like www.job-search-engine.com, www.lumeria.com and freeonline.com.au. Portals will have to offer more than stock quotes and horoscopes. They will have to be infomediaries, achieving true communication between brands and consumers.

Portals like AOL, Yahoo! and Lycos are trying to position themselves as a 'first stop' for access to the Internet, where people can quickly and conveniently find useful resources. In reality, these enterprises are on the way to becoming infomediaries, focusing on capturing information about customers and, using this, helping customers connect with vendors. The difference between them and real infomediaries is that portals today aren't necessarily using the captured information to deliver better service in the future. This, however, will change.

The people-dead Internet
This could lead to a completely new phenomenon, namely an Internet without human participation, which at present seems like science fiction. Taken to its conclusion we could end up with an Internet where most of the traffic is generated by infomediaries and not by people. The Internet could thus come to play a completely different role than that we know today, namely a role where all known marketing rules suddenly have to be redefined, for how does a website influence or persuade an infomediary?

The above is not just science fiction but almost a reality as can be deduced from the number of types of 'classic' agents that can be found today on the Internet. Below is a short list of the most frequently used agents (robots/bots) the average surfer may encounter. Characteristic of the agents listed below are that they all represent elements of an infomediary but haven't yet managed to represent the essence of a real infomediary. Most of the agents listed will be invisible to users unless they know the agents' actual behaviour very well.

Agent
A virtual secretary which typically searches the Internet for relevant information at the request of the owner. This could concern cheap prices, best flights or the like.

Clone robot
An agent which 'steals' a user's identity by observing the user for a period of time in, for example, chat rooms. The clone robot throws the 'real' user out of the system when it feels able to take over the dialogue and thereafter continues the dialogue independently – without the involvement of the user who is now completely unable to influence what happens.

TIP

Visit
www.botspot.com/
and get an update
on the latest bots
on the market.

Guard robot

The opposite to the clone robot, namely an agent which ensures that the above does not take place. The robot's purpose is to keep chat rooms free of clone robots. Today it is estimated that about five percent of all chat rooms have guard robots. According to the publication *Netbots*, in the middle of 1997 there were 600 agents on the Internet, and the number is increasing by three new intelligent agents (bots) each day.

Mail robot

Filters incoming mail for the owner on the basis of the user's behaviour when reading previous e-mails and draws up a prioritised order for reading the mail.

Cancel robot

An agent which searches for news groups where it delivers a pre-programmed message and deletes messages which according to it are not in accordance with particular political or religious convictions. This agent is often used by hackers of an opposing political conviction who want to undermine an opponent's dissemination of a particular belief.

Chatter robot

Answers questions and gives assistance, without users who are communicating with the agent necessarily being aware that they are actually communicating with an agent.

The agent – a threat or an opportunity!

Agents already have a comprehensive multi-faceted role, and the roles will become even more diverse in the future with the introduction of the infomediary. That currently the agent's influence is relatively harmless does not mean that the technology should not be taken seriously. In the middle of 1997 Andersen Consulting developed the retailer's worst nightmare – a program (an agent) called Waldo the Web Wizard. This agent could independently gather and compare prices. If you typed in the name of a CD you wanted to buy, the agent visited 15 selected websites in order to shop around for the best price. Just a few days after its introduction, three department stores boycotted the agent by denying it access to their websites.

In the short term the department stores which decided to deny the agent access to their websites won, as the only basis of decision was the price. In the long term, when the agent has become generally available, all indications are that the very same stores will be the losers. Only two years after the launch of Web Wizard more than 100 international websites have established their presence on a similar technique. Most well known are www.priceline.com and www.excite.com which both offer to compare well-known brands on price.

The disadvantage of the agent is that it only searches by price and does not take into account special offers or trading parameters which the goods in questions may well have. Therefore, if a store has a special offer of the type 'Buy three CDs for the price of two', a simple version of Waldo the Web Wizard will not register this. The counter to Waldo the Web Wizard has, however, already been developed by the retailers. The trading agent, as the opponent is called, negotiates with agents such as Waldo the Web Wizard. When Waldo the Web Wizard visits a store, the trading agent will ask Waldo about the user's profile and will work out a relevant offer based on this. If it is a question of an attractive customer with, for example, a profile showing that they are a major customer of a competitor, a loyal customer of the store concerned or a gold credit card holder, the offer will be designed to be especially attractive. If the person concerned has expressed an interest in a particular type of product, for example, video films or hi-fi equipment, the agent compiles a special offer. The offer does not necessarily consist of goods on which there is a discount, but a discount is given provided all the products are bought at the same time. It is likely that every website in the future will include an invisible part in addition to the visible part. The invisible underlying part of the website will be a veritable army of individual trading agents. These will be designed to attract other agents and thereby create the desired exposure to the users who are represented by the agents. The role of the infomediary, which will represent the second generation of the classic agent, will be to act 100 percent on the consumer's behalf. They will be able to, in a more intelligent way, negotiate on behalf of the consumer and ensure that the result of the negotiating process will lead to a result that reflects the consumer's preferences and requirements.

Where is the money?

Data is worth money; updated knowledge about the consumer is worth gold. Until now consumers haven't had a real possibility to trade with their personal set of information. An address line and a phone number have been valued exactly the same no matter who typed in the data: rich or pure, targeted or non-targeted. The dawn of the infomediary will change the rules. One of its main roles will be to gain as much value out of the consumer data as possible. In return the consumer will get a better deal reflected by a larger discount, better service or no extra fees.

Serious business

The fact that agents are taken seriously can be seen from the large amount of resources that are allocated to this field. A few years ago Andersen Consulting established the Center for Strategic Technology Research (CSTaR®), IBM set up the 'Intelligent Agent Software Technology Center' and Microsoft set up the 'Microsoft Agent Center'.

Companies have great plans for the infomediary in the

TIP

Tip: Some classified ads are starting to be driven by bots. AdHound at Classified Warehouse (www.classifiedware house.com) will search more than 150 newspapers in the US for the best match based on your search criteria. The next step will be classified ads driven by an infomediary.

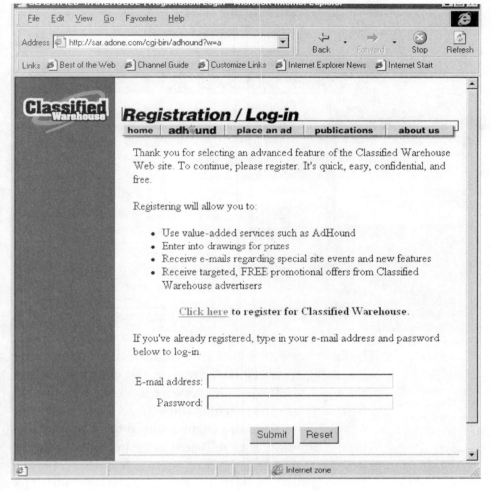

future. IBM's vision is to construct an infomediary which remembers what the consumer likes and also knows the user's behaviour, lifestyle and taste. The vision is that the infomediary would, for example, be able to describe with great precision how owners live without having had their home actually described, so that if the owners wanted to buy a bookcase the agent could tell whether the bookcase would suit the home or not, as far as taste was concerned.

Microsoft has launched an infomediary that can listen to the user's (verbal) speech and can also answer in

Classified Warehouse is a free service searching more than 150 newspapers for the best classified match.

If the user keys in film and music preferences, the agent helps to find films which users with similar tastes have enjoyed.

ordinary speech. There are a number of versions of this infomediary available today with the ability to change the voice production and appearance, but this is just the first step towards agents which have a personal style and behaviour and can change with time. The first successful attempts at taste-oriented agents have, however, not yet reached the level of a real infomediary. One of the concepts closest to the essential infomediary idea is www.firefly.com, a virtual community for which membership is required.

Firefly invites visitors to record their tastes in music and films by selecting their favourite films, songs and artists. On the basis of other users' tastes, the website can draw conclusions regarding which other film genre or types of music the user should acquire. The agent constructs an 'average taste' for each music genre and then makes an individual music or film suggestion. At the same time the agent refers to other members who have the same tastes and who are currently online.

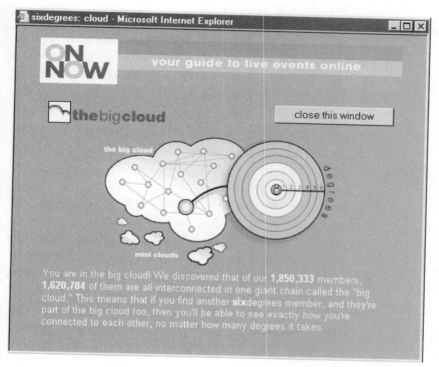

You are in the big cloud! We discovered that of our **1,850,333** members, **1,620,784** of them are all interconnected in one giant chain called the "big cloud." This means that if you find another **sixdegrees** member, and they're part of the big cloud too, then you'll be able to see exactly how you're connected to each other, no matter how many degrees it takes.

Firefly is one of the best attempts at developing an intelligent taste agent and today it has over one million users. Membership is free as the running costs of the concept are covered by the advertising income and the sale of records and films. Firefly gives an indication of how the personal agent will look in the future.

We are all connected within six degrees

Your Sixdegrees Stats

User: martin@lindstrom.com (as of 03/03/00):

Contacts

Total 1st degree contacts:	4
Total 2nd degree contacts:	26
Total 3rd degree contacts	236
Total 4th degree contacts	2159
Total 5th degree contacts:	14385
Total 6th degree contacts:	52485
Total 1st-6th degree contacts:	69295

A current membership status from www.sixdegrees.com

Another example of an agent driven website which could easily be turned into an infomediary is Sixdegrees. www.sixdegrees.com is one of the most successful database-driven websites. Based on detailed consumer data it matches people with each other all around the world. Today more than two million people are members of the network (creating access with people up to the fifth degree, typically covering more than 50,000 related people per person).

Several other media have entered into the area of the agent. PlanetAll is an American community run by a group of companies including Reuters. PlanetAll is an electronic newspaper, which is tailored to suit the needs of individual users and also updates them daily with relevant news via e-mail – free of charge! After having recorded the user's electronic profile, the agent works out which items of news are of interest. Another feature is that users can supply the system with information

For a small fee ewatch (www.ewatch.com) will watch what people are saying about your brand name world-wide on the Internet

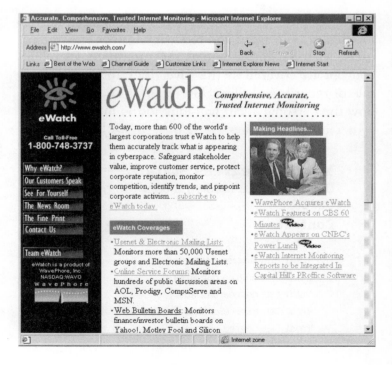

about their lives, for example where they went to school and what clubs they have been a member of. On the basis of this data the computer can track down old classmates and inform the user of any changes of address. And the computer also compiles a personal daily horoscope.

The survival for agents will be the infomediary

In spite of agents' many positive characteristics, it is too early to guarantee that the phenomenon will be a success. In the same way as with the penetration of credit cards in Australia, the penetration of agents could stagnate due to people's reluctance to register. The benefits cannot be denied, but the emotional factors often have greater weight. In order for agents to be a success they must be given a human face, like the milk robot described earlier, and at any time act on behalf of the consumer like a real infomediary. The key to an agent's success is its ability to build and practise trust. It is very important that it interprets the consumer's requirement to real action. If the infomediary concept sets the trend, it is very likely that agents, in a much more advanced version than the one we know today, will have a future on the Internet.

The significance of infomediaries for society

The above examples are characterised by being founded on push-based communication. The information comes to the user in a customised version. If this form of information becomes prevalent on the Internet there will once again be a change in our communication patterns.

Whereas in the 1970s and 1980s, users were passive in their search for information, in the 1990s they are active. Users search for information on the Internet. With the introduction of customised communication the scene will change yet again. In line with steadily increasing individualisation of the flow of information, the users will to a greater extent define what information is relevant for them. The consumer will make a selection of the infomediary from those best able to meet the user's actual information requirements, combined with the agent's brand profile. If the consumer's first choice is a source, which customises the communication 100 percent to suit the user, there is very little chance that the user will change infomediary. The user has chosen 'one god', or one information provider, and the user has thereby become yet again a passive recipient of information.

If users who are interested in sports choose to let an infomediary, sponsored by Nike for example, filter information for them, the users' behaviour changes from being active to being passive. The users have become loyal to one medium (or one brand) in the area of information concerned. Typically users will rely 100 percent on this medium once it has been 'approved' as an information filter. The loyalty to the infomediary will have a self-reinforcing effect as the first selected infomediary, Nike, will make it difficult for other competing infomediaries to make their presence known. A real example of the above imaginary cases is NewsDude (www.ics.uci.edu/~dbillsus/NewsDude). NewsDude is a simple example of an infomediary that learns about a user's interests in daily news stories. It can download news stories from the Internet and read these stories to the user. The user can provide feedback for the stories that the system retrieved, which allows News Dude to learn a profile of the user's interests. This profile can then be used to compile a personal news program specifically tailored to the user's interest.

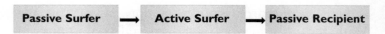

Infomediaries will change
the role of analysis agencies

Whereas in the 1970s target groups were segmented on the basis of consumers' demographic and geographic criteria, in the 1980s and at the beginning of the 1990s they were segmented on the basis of psychological characteristics, that is, the consumers' lifestyle (for example, determined by AC Nielsen's RISC analyses or Roy Morgan's segmentation model). In the future it will be possible to survey consumers' preferences and lifestyles in a much more precise and varied way based on the information provided by the infomediary. Consumers' behaviour will be able to be charted by means of scanner codes in supermarkets, credit card use and frequent flyer points, and also by what information the users obtain from the Internet. Several supermarket chains will shortly launch concepts which integrate the consumer's 'Frequent Buyer Points', customer card and purchasing patterns in order to be able to simulate the consumer's behaviour before it is actually carried out. This will enable the launch of virtual shopping lists which continuously 'learn' from the buying patterns of the individual user and other users in order to be able to produce the 'perfect' shopping list based on this data. In practice this will mean that it can work out when it is time to buy Colgate or feminine hygiene products. In addition it will be able to work out which potential products could be suitable for the user; a conclusion it can draw based on what thousands of other users with similar buying patterns have revealed. The opportunities for increased sales are obvious. If Pepsi wants to win a share of the market at the expense of Coca-Cola, it will be able to buy access to the system and offer the user a particularly attractive offer at precisely the time when there is no Coca-Cola left in the fridge.

In addition to purchasing data, the new technologies open the door to more precise recording of the user profile, not at segment level but at an individual level.

It is already possible to see how long a user stays on a website, how often the user returns to the website and how many pages the user looks at, etc. If this information is correlated with the content of the individual pages, it is possible to paint a clear picture of the user's specific interests and also a picture of how these are prioritised in relation to each other. This information opens the door to a whole new world, where a consumer's visit to a website can be simulated even before the website has been constructed, exclusively on the basis of the data which has been accumulated over the years concerning the consumer's reaction to other websites. Information of the above type will be able to be used in connection with the development of particularly well-defined marketing strategies and also in the development of more individualised user-adapted products. Whereas today, apart from in the service industries, there is predominantly mass production of standardised products, in the future there will be mass production of individualised products, probably on the basis of knowledge obtained from the Internet. And whereas today the directly visible consequence of the agent is the individualisation of advertisements, in the future the agent will be behind massive changes in patterns of consumption, changes which it is impossible to predict at present.

Privacy will be the real test of the infomediary concept

No matter what direction the development of the infomediaries will take in the coming years, consumer privacy has emerged as a major concern among Internet users.

- How far will the websites be allowed to go using consumer data?
- Can consumer data be sold without the consumer's consent?
- Can data from various databases be mixed?

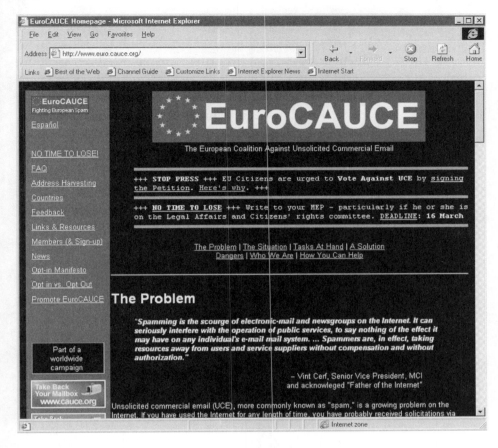

The browser window shows:

EuroCAUCE Homepage - Microsoft Internet Explorer

Address: http://www.euro.cauce.org/

EuroCAUCE
Fighting European Spam

Español

NO TIME TO LOSE!
FAQ
Address Harvesting
Countries
Feedback
Links & Resources
Members (& Sign-up)
News
Opt-in Manifesto
Opt in vs. Opt Out
Promote EuroCAUCE

Part of a worldwide campaign

Take Back Your Mailbox
www.cauce.org

EuroCAUCE

The European Coalition Against Unsolicited Commercial Email

+++ STOP PRESS +++ EU Citizens are urged to **Vote Against UCE** by signing the Petition. Here's why. +++

+++ **NO TIME TO LOSE** +++ Write to your MEP - particularly if he or she is on the Legal Affairs and Citizens' rights committee. DEADLINE: 16 March

The Problem | The Situation | Tasks At Hand | A Solution
Dangers | Who We Are | How You Can Help

The Problem

"Spamming is the scourge of electronic-mail and newsgroups on the Internet. It can seriously interfere with the operation of public services, to say nothing of the effect it may have on any individual's e-mail mail system. ... Spammers are, in effect, taking resources away from users and service suppliers without compensation and without authorization."

– Vint Cerf, Senior Vice President, MCI
and acknowleged "Father of the Internet"

Unsolicited commercial email (UCE), more commonly known as "spam," is a growing problem on the Internet. If you have used the Internet for any length of time, you have probably received solicitations via

A 1996 direct survey found that 83 percent of those surveyed said there should be a law requiring an opt-in procedure for names to be included on direct mail lists.

A 1998 *Business Week* poll found that 53 percent of respondents said governments should pass laws about how personal information should be captured and used online, a figure three times higher than the number of consumers who supported the idea that governments should let trade groups develop voluntary privacy standards.

Today there is no international law on the Internet protecting the consumer from data misuse. The fact that almost every country in the world legislates for individual privacy laws indicates that a uniform world-wide

EuroCAUCE (The European Coalition against Unsolicited Commercial Email) is one of the first European organisations that has managed to create rules about spamming.

rule will be almost impossible to introduce. Several organisations have however tried to lobby for the introduction of sets of international rules. This includes EuroCAUCE (www.cauce.org), which in 1998 managed to ban e-mail spamming in Europe via support from the European Union (EU). Just as television, radio and cinema have their own set of rules in most countries, the same is to be expected for the Internet in the interests of protecting the consumer. Will the dawn of the infomediary be the solution to the problem or be like petrol on a fire when privacy issues become a major consumer concern? Only time will tell.

The future belongs to the consumers

"Our attention is worth something — completely analogous to the value of our labour. It is a very interesting and enormous idea to put forward, but I believe that we will be forced to recognise that our attention will have a very high value in the years to come."

Tor Nørretraanders, scientific author

"If you love someone – set them free."

Sting

When the customers take power

It may sound like a cliché, but the indications are that in the future companies will be surrendering power to the customers. Imagine a shopping centre giving a choice of 100 shoe shops – where would you buy your shoes? You might prefer a particular shop you already know, you might look for the best bargain or the best service, perhaps choose the shop closest to the entrance or the one with a really special selection. A lot of factors will be decisive when it comes to choosing. On the Internet the situation is the same, but here it is not just 100 shops but 10,000 to choose from. There are now over 13,000 online shops selling music CDs! Being attractive in such a competitive situation, being in a position to attract customers and retain their loyalty, are the great challenges of the future. This demands integrity and mutual respect. Customers do not want to be owned, they want freedom of choice. In the future companies will have to create a universe where customers can come and go freely, discuss products among themselves, find product-related information and haggle about the price. It is even possible to imagine a situation in which the company will pay to be visited – it will suddenly be a question of reversed admission fee.

In the October 1996 issue of *Wired*, Nicholas Negroponte wrote about a woman who went to buy a car. The salesperson convinced her she should buy a $19,500 Ford Taurus. She said she would sleep on it, but instead used the Internet to find out whether there were other people nearby who also wanted a Taurus. By next morning she had found 15 others. A good deal of e-mail traffic followed, but she was soon able to return to the dealer and tell him that she was ready to buy, but the price ought to be $16,500. The reduction of $3,000 was so large that the dealer thought there must have been a misunderstanding. "No, it's just that I forgot to mention that I'm buying 16 cars!" she replied – and the deal went through with no problems. It is not known whether the story is true, but it is a fact that users on the net have the ability to form a new type of purchasing cartel. And today this is in widespread use: visit www.letsbuyit.com or www.accompany.com.

Websters – the consumers of the future

It is possible that the current generation of managers will not experience major revolutions and changes. These may take place when the generation of websters – the children who have literally grown up with the Internet as an integral and natural part of their daily life – come to power. For them all the barriers of ignorance will have broken down. Tolerance of foreign cultures and different minority groups will be much higher than today and the power of the experts will have disappeared. (On the other hand the top honcho at Toys'R'Us was fired because he hadn't reacted fast enough on the Internet, and Etoys went public with a market capitalisation 40 percent higher than his company – after only 3 years of existence.)

The great changes will only take place when the generation of websters has grown up.

The fact that this will lead to great changes can already be felt today. Television, particularly in families with children, is having to make way for another medium. It is said that in the USA up to 25 percent of prime-time television viewing (7.30 p.m. to 9 p.m.) has been replaced by the Internet. It is impossible to predict exactly what will happen when the medium and our understanding of it eventually mature (as has happened with other media), but it is certain to change the way products and brands are marketed.

Aspects not covered by this book

When we say that the Internet will change the whole of our society, it is clear that such a change will have many more consequences than just those connected with marketing, with which this book is primarily concerned. Even though other aspects do not at first glance appear to have an effect upon a company's communication with its customers, it will still be very important to understand the effect of, for example, the ethical aspects concerning the Internet and also education and legislation, as ultimately the way in which these aspects are handled can be decisive for the further development of the Internet – both nationally and internationally.

Is private life threatened?

In 1997 a US company managed to build up a database containing very detailed information about the private lives of more than 50,000 US families. The database was built up with help from the families' children. They could obtain a free game from the company in return for telling the company details about their families: what car they drove, their interests, what brands they bought, etc. Each time the children wanted to get to the next level in the game, they were asked for further details in order to gain access. In the end the company was in possession of an incredibly detailed picture of a family's life, information which was worth its weight in gold for marketing purposes. Even though this means of collecting information was and is in breach of US law, there was nothing that could be done as the server was based in the Bahamas!

Less unusual information recording currently takes place innumerable times during each Internet session and without infringing any legislation. Users voluntarily provide lots of information on the net, both consciously and unconsciously. Today there are few companies able to make effective use of this data, but this situation will change rapidly. Most companies will adhere to the net's ethical regulations and treat the data as confidential, but others will be much less scrupulous. There is a real danger that consumers will suddenly find themselves extras in a very realistic version of George Orwell's *1984*, and this may put a stop to the further development of the Internet.

Is legislation ready for the new picture of the world?

We are on the brink of a media explosion which will have great legal consequences. When everything can be copied, amended and distributed all over the world at the speed of light, then it will be an almost impossible task to control and regulate information in accordance with the existing copyright concepts. The respected American researcher Esther Dyson said in autumn 1997 that she believed that authors in the future would have to live off media appearances and lectures rather than off the copyright to their material. And it obviously takes only minutes to download, for example, the Aqua hit 'Barbie Girl' from the net -- even in those places where the physical record is sold out in the shops.

It only takes a few minutes to download 'Barbie Girl' from the net.

There is already enormous digital trade occurring. The amount of transactions and deals taking place in cyberspace is so large that many people say that concepts such as trade balance and gross national product are now more at home in the museum of economics rather than in countries' accounts. The problem is that many products are being converted from atoms into bits (shares, literature, music, software, information, entertainment, etc.) which means that reproduction is free and the warehouses unlimited. At the same time we are nearing the day when digital pseudo currencies will start to arise, either in the form of electronic money, loyalty points, local club schemes or pure and simple digital barter. In addition, the way we measure a product and its value will change considerably in the future.

When it is possible to buy the right to a digital game or a piece of music for a limited period and pay with the consumer's presence on the net or with other goods, the existing laws and economic traffic regulations will have to be abandoned. In the USA people are already talking about the 'New Network Economy'. When a company such as Netscape can become worth an inconceivable sum in less than two years by giving away 50 million copies of its core product, this indicates something about the extent of the economic changes to come. The time is therefore ripe to have a closer look at the existing legislation.

We are educating our children for a linear society which does not exist

A fundamental problem facing most countries today is that the education system is simply not geared to the new network-oriented picture of the world. In many cases the pupils, even in the younger classes, know more about the technology than their teachers. Education is simply not adapted to the situation that all the world's information will be available via the Internet and that in the future it will be possible to search through all this material in just a few seconds and get answers in this way.

The problem also exists at institutes of higher education where there are problems in training the people who are in demand in the new information industry. New skills are required at an increasing rate and a basic understanding of the new economy and the network way of thinking will be a natural requirement of all graduates from schools of economics and universities.

On the brink of two new Internets

All the changes that have occurred due to the Internet during the past 4–5 years come from relatively slow, unstable, unsecure connections. So imagine what will happen when we see the next generation of Internets, which are being built right now. First out is the Mobile Internet, which is carried through mobile telephones on the commonly accepted standard WAP (Wireless Application Protocol); IDG expect 1 *billion* mobile phones to be sold during the next three years, with 50 percent of them being WAP-enabled. That means there will be at least twice as many users on this new

Internet as we have on today's net. But they will be different users, and will have totally different behaviours and ways of using the net. However, the result will be impressive changes. Secondly we are seeing new broadband connections being built. In Sweden, for example, about 1 million households (30 percent of total households) will soon have 10 MB symmetric Internet connections installed. Broadband will allow the possibility of every website sending full-screen digital video over the net, and we will be close to what was earlier called 'The Information Highway'. Again, broadband connection will have dramatic consequences on the way people interact.

Metaphors such as browsing will be redundant.

In addition, doubtlessly the TV media will change a lot. New measures will create an invisible integration between media controlled by the user (interactive media) and media that control the user (media where the user is passive). The versatility and the combination of different media and forms of presentation will combine into a multimedia soup – which means that the presentation of information as it is known today will appear antediluvian. Within the networked media metaphors such as browsing and leafing will also be redundant. Instead there will be content which it is not possible to leaf through.

In the future we will have interfaces that follow users on their journeys, for example from the office to the car, where they may discreetly recommend a visit to nearby exhibition that has just opened, while keeping the user up-to-date with the latest results from the football – a service of course sponsored by Coca-Cola. Users will be notified via their watches if there has been a accident on the normal route home, and at the same time will be advised to visit a newly opened sushi restaurant in the next street which has a special offer that they can enjoy while waiting for the traffic to return to normal. At home the computer can use the same system to provide ongoing news reports via the screen saver, while at the same time share prices from selected companies appear in the top corner of the screen combined with latest press releases from the same companies. All brought to you and sponsored by known brands and peppered with a suitable quantity of relevant advertisements.

Metaphors such as web pages, clickable links and search engines, all part of the 2D universe, will eventually change as well and be substituted with other conventions. The media of the future will not need a computer; push media will not wait for the user's click. Information will be fluid and will find a user, at any time and in any place via anything, for example, mobile phones and pagers. The new net will be a medium that is always there, bringing updated information to a user whether it is asked for or not. All kinds of hybrids will arise in a fluid combination of pull and push media. How? Television programs will provide links to underlying content, where users can participate in quizzes, debates, obtain further information or test themselves on the program's subject matter. Websites will integrate longer or shorter audio or video clips. Traditional EDP programs such as calendars and spreadsheets will integrate information from the net, both live while the user is working with the program and automatically without the user being present …

Is there an end to all this?

Probably not. The one sure thing is that development will continue. In Chapter 3 we discussed the three stages in a company's development on the Internet, and the last few chapters have been very focused on the changes created by the net in company's valuechains, logistics, processes, organisation and so on. This area has been dubbed e-business, and it is a good term since it makes clear that the Internet is about the whole business. But the challenges facing business will remain the same: in the future, when these new developments are in place, the competition will again turn to how to create and retain the best relations with consumers. Here, the brand will always play a very important role.

It is very difficult to make predictions further into the future, but there could well be a fourth distributed and fragmented stage which might be called 'the push phase', where a company's presence becomes more fragmented and much more integrated in the users' daily life – in the television they watch, in the appliances they use, and in the content and the communication they encounter every single day. It will be up to the company to be where the users are – physically, contextually and psychologically.

Being on the Internet as a company is a project that is only finished the day the company disconnects from the net. However, that day is unlikely to come, as the Internet becomes more and more integrated in the things people create. Therefore companies would be wise to accustom themselves to a much more changeable existence, where an ongoing allocation of resources to digital commitments will ensure that the company adapts itself to the expectations of its customers. As one of Ford's managers said to the employees: "If our company is not customer-driven, our cars won't be either!" There is not much time for preparation, as this trend is continuing with undiminished vigour.

The ten Internet commandments

1. Know your mission on the Internet.
2. Be everything for someone – not something for everyone.
3. Give the users something to take home.
4. The company's solution must be based on a strategy.
5. Utilise the possibilities of the Internet.
6. Make sure that the company is intellectually on the net.
7. Involve the users in the design process.
8. Test your solution.
9. Give the users power and control.
10. We have only just begun - be prepared for change!

1. Know your mission on the Internet.

It is better not to be on the Internet at all than to be there and not know why. There is a great danger that a badly conceived website will create more ill-will than goodwill. Being on the Internet is no longer good enough, it imposes obligations.

2. Be everything for someone - not something for everyone

Even though the Internet is a world-wide medium, this is not to say that a target group does not need to be defined - quite the reverse. The more precise the dialogue between the sender and the recipient, the greater consumer involvement can be achieved.

3. Give the users something to take home

The consumer pays to be exposed to advertisements on the Internet. The cost is not measured just in financial terms, but also in time and a blocked telephone line! These high 'consumer costs' create expectations, therefore a website should reward the user either with relevant information, discounts or good entertainment.

4. The company's solution must be based on a strategy

Within a couple of years for most companies the Internet will not just be an extra element in the marketing plan, but an activity which in many cases will change the whole company. A strong Internet strategy should be based on a carefully planned strategy which fits in with the company's other development plans.

5. Utilise the possibilities of the Internet
So far we have only just seen the tip of the iceberg. Innovation is invaluable. Just think of Interflora, amazon.com and FedEx!

6. Make sure that the company is intellectually on the net
Involvement of all stages of the company pays for itself. It has always been the case that the success of a marketing campaign only becomes apparent when the whole organisation is behind the measure - right from the board of directors to the sales team out in the field. The same is true for the Internet.

7. Involve the users in the design process
At present too many websites are developed by programmers or designers who have forgotten how a 'typical' user thinks and reacts. A user-friendly interface design is the be-all and end-all of a good website. Remember that the designers of the website are practically never part of the target group!

8. Test your solution
Several hundred browsers and several thousand different types of computer have meant that the end user will probably obtain a completely different experience of the website than was originally intended.

Testing both the technical aspect and the way it is experienced are essential in order to ensure that the final product lives up to expectations.

9. Give the users power and control
The more freedom the user experiences, the greater the involvement attained. The behaviour of users cannot be controlled, but only guided. In the final instance it is up to the user whether the website is rejected in favour of that of a competitor.

This option is only a 'mouse-click' away.

10. We have only just begun - be prepared for change!
The Internet is only four years old. TV has a history of more than 50 years and is still developing. The development process in cyberspace has only just begun. You can choose to be a participant - or just a spectator!

Recommended links

The Internet is full of exciting sites connected with the subject of this book. Below is a list of links (by no means exhaustive) which we use ourselves to keep up to date and at the forefront of developments.

www.ebrandwidth.com
www.thestandard.com
www.forrester.com
www.eiu.com
www.popco.com
www.info-strategy.com
www.webweek.com
www.wired.com
www.abcnews.com
www.cnn.com
www.news.com
www.computerworld.com
www.intemet.com
www.cnet.com
www.cnnfn.com/digitaljam
www.pathfinder.com
www.fastcompany.com
www.scientificamerican.com
www.edoc.com
www.adage.com
www.keynote.com
www.globaltrack.com
www.adtrack.com

www.adbot.com
www.TSRS.se/products/
    netcheck.htm
www.bpai.com
www.accessabvs.com/webaudit
www.accessabc.com
www.decisive.com
www.mediacentral.com
www.pscentral.com
www.cyberatlas.com
www.idcresearch.com
www3.mids.org/mn/605/usergrow
    .html
www3.mids.org/weather/eu/
    index.html
www.jup.com
www2000.ogsm.vanderbilt.edu
www.cc.gatech.edu/gvu/user_
    surveys/User_Survey_Home.html
www.nielsenmedia.com
www.ora.com/research/users/
    index.html

Glossary

Agent
> An electronic program reminiscent of artificial intelligence on the Internet. Agents can independently perform an action on the basis of repeated (typically uniform) actions on the part of the user. An agent is often invisible to the user.

America Online
> Major online service, covering all the USA and some European countries.

ARPA
> (Advanced Research Projects Agency). A project, which was started by USA's defence after the Second World War. The project resulted in the construction of ARPAnet, which later developed into the Internet.

ATM
> (Asynchronous Transfer Mode). ATM makes possible a much faster transfer of information and may well become the next generation data transmission method, permitting sound, text and pictures to be transmitted in real-time.

Attachment
> A document (or other kind of file) attached to an e-mail.

Bandwidth
> The amount of information, which can be transferred via a particular channel of communication.

Baud
> The number of times per second a modem modulates the computer's signal.

BBS
> Bulletin Board System. An electronic notice board, where mail can be sent, discussions carried on and files exchanged.

Bit
> The smallest unit which can be transmitted, namely a number 0 or 1.

Bookmark
> Also called favourite page. A bookmark is recorded via a function incorporated in the browser (Netscape), to enable you to have quick/direct access to a particular page at a later time.

Bots
> From the word robots. Electronic programs reminiscent of artificial intelligence on the Internet. Bots make possible independent action on the basis of repeated uniform actions on the part of the user.

Bps
> Bit per second - specifies a modem's speed.

Brand-building
> The strengthening of brand names.

Branded product

A product which is mass-produced with the same name and graphic identity. Often a branded product is sold at a higher price than a corresponding 'unbranded' product. A branded product often gives the user a guarantee of 'quality', which offsets the often 'higher' price.

Brand loyalty

How loyal a user is to a brand. Indicates whether the user buys the same brand every single time or changes between several brands within the same category.

Browser

A program which 'reads' data on the Internet and transforms this into pictures, graphics and text. One of the world's first browsers was Netscape. (See also navigation program).

Byte

There are eight bits in a byte. A byte corresponds to one symbol, for example a letter.

Cancel bot

An agent which looks for news groups, to which it delivers pre-programmed messages and deletes other messages which according to it do not agree with particular political or religious convictions. The agent is often used by hackers of opposing political convictions, who want to undermine opponents' dissemination of a particular belief on the net.

Chat room

Internet Relay Chat (IRC) - popularly called chat room or chat forum - is a virtual room on the net, where users can communicate with one or more other users in real-time. Chat forums work principally like news groups, but in real-time and not necessarily with a predefined subject as the topic of the communication.

Chatter bot

Answers questions and gives advice – without the person who is communicating with the agent necessarily being aware that he is connected to an agent.

Clicks-and-mortar

Combination of online and offline businesses.

Clone bot

An agent which 'steals' a user's identity. It observes him for a while, e.g. in chat rooms, then throws the real user out of the system when it feels able to take over the dialogue. The clone bot thereafter carries on the dialogue independently, without the user's involvement. The user is now completely without influence over what happens.

Code

A program text (also called program code) that carries out an action in a program or website.

Community

A meeting place. Often used in connection with websites, where several users can meet each other or obtain relevant information on a particular subject.

CompuServe

American online service with

approx. 300,000 users in Europe.

Cookie

A short program code which records on the user's hard disk the user's behaviour at a particular website.

Cyberspace

A term which is used to describe the virtual reality. Sometimes used as a synonym for the Internet.

Originally invented as a term by the science-fiction author William Gibson as a description of a parallel reality, where time, place and space have completely new meanings.

Data

Information. The word is often used in connection with computers or in contexts where large amounts of information are involved.

Direct marketing

The term covers all activities where a message is sent directly to one or more recipients via traditional or electronic mail. Direct marketing is based on a carefully planned segmentation strategy, which aims at ensuring that the message and target group match and ultimately have the desired effect (increased sales, changed attitude, greater awareness).

DM

Abbreviation of the expression: Direct marketing. (See also under Direct marketing).

Domain

Each computer on the Internet has a particular address. The address usually consists of two parts. These are a domain name and a top-level domain name. For example: www.companyname.dk, which is www.domain.toplevel-domain. The domain name is a computer name. A top-level domain name for Denmark is dk. Other common top-level domains are .edu, .com, .org, etc. The domain name is identified by the server. When a new computer is connected to the Internet the name has to be registered. Each country has its own body which is responsible for the registration.

Download

The transfer of program codes from one computer to another over the telephone network via a modem. Often used in connection with downloading a web page.

Dynamic adverts

Adverts which continually change appearance or message, for example on the basis of the users' reactions, new product launches, the time or other factors related to the advertised product.

Electronic post

The word covers all electronic communication. This applies both to e-mail and internal message systems such as cc mail and Quick Mail.

E-mail

Electronic mail. An e-mail is a message which is sent between different users on the Internet. Various files (for example Word documents) can also be attached to an e-mail.

FAQ

Stands for Frequently Asked Questions. BBS's, list servers, websites and discussion groups have typically an FAQ-file, where you can find the most commonly asked questions. A good place to start when you come to a new site.

Favourite page

Also called bookmark (see this). A favourite page is recorded via a function incorporated in the browser (Internet Explorer), to enable you to have quick/direct access to a particular page at a later time. The function can be compared to an 'electronic' bookmark.

FIDO-net

International network which links many BBS's.

Flame war

When a debate on the Internet becomes heated and the contributions become snide and personal, it is called a flame war.

Frequency

The term is used in a marketing context and indicates how often a user is exposed to a particular website, web address or advert.

FTP

(File Transfer Protocol) is an Internet protocol which makes it possible to move data files to and from computers. By FTP is meant sometimes the programs which make this transfer possible.

Goal

In a marketing context the term often covers what concrete (quantitative as well as qualitative) results the company wants a website to lead to.

Gopher

Forerunner of the World Wide Web. Gopher can be described as an information service or a tool based on a simple menu system. Via Gopher you can also download files onto your computer. The information on a Gopher server is hierarchically structured. The information was originally text-based, but today Gopher is also available with a graphic interface.

Guard bot

This is the counter to the clone bot (see this) - namely an agent which protects against clone bots. The robot's purpose is to keep chat rooms free of clone bots. Today it is estimated that about five percent of all chat rooms have guard bots. According to the publication *Netbots*, in the middle of 1997 there were 600 agents on the Internet, and the number is increasing by three new intelligent agents (bots) each day.

Hits

A hit is the same as the number of elements a user downloads during a visit to a particular (web)page. If the user visits a website (a page), which consists of seven illustrations, the user generates seven hits. If the user visits another page on the same web address, the total number of hits will increase by the number of elements which are downloaded.

Home page

By a home page is meant the introductory page for an organisation on the World Wide Web. If an organisation or a company has a World Wide Web address, it is the home page the user reaches by writing the address. From here there are usually links to the organisation's other pages.

Hot-list

A list of popular World Wide Web addresses.

HTML

(Hypertext Markup Language). The language in which the information pages on the World Wide Web are constructed. An HTML document can in principle be read by any text processing system. However, to obtain full benefit you need to use a browser which can translate the HTML-file's representations of graphics, layout codes and links.

HTTP

(Hypertext Transfer Protocol). A standard which ensures that text, pictures and sound can be transferred to an individual document on the World Wide Web. HTTP permits links to other documents and parts of documents. All World Wide Web addresses begin with http://

Hyperlink

A hyperlink is a function which ensures that the user can move from one World Wide Web page to another by clicking on an underlined word or a picture. A hyperlink is often also called just a link.

Hypertext

A digital text format letting users jump around in text using links.

Icon

A symbol in a website that often leads to a particular action if the icon is activated.

Infomediary

A third-party search engine collecting data on its user and acting on the user's behalf to gain benefits on the net. It can handle the millions of data necessary to create true one-to-one communication.

Internet

The worldwide network of networks.

Internet account

To get on the Internet you have to start an account with an Internet Service Provider.

IP

Internet Protocol. A communication standard or language for networks on the Internet.

IRC

Internet Relay Chat. A forum for text-based discussions in real-time. (See also chat room.)

ISOC

Internet Society. The closest the net comes to a governing body. Handles operations and new protocols.

ISP
  (Internet Service Provider). A
  company which provides connection to the Internet. In Denmark
  the largest ISP or Internet
  Service Provider is Tele
  Danmark.

Lifestyle agent
  An agent which on the basis of a
  little information can predict a
  user's behaviour on or off the
  Internet.

Link
  A connection between two different pages (or in principle two different websites). A shortcut to
  another place on the Internet.
  Links are usually found in the
  text, but pictures and animation
  can also be links.

Log-on
  Your user name. Used typically
  together with a password when
  you log on to BBS's, a computer
  or an online service.

Mail bot
  The bot filters incoming e-mails
  for the owner based on the
  owner's behaviour when reading
  previous e-mails and from this
  draws up a prioritised order for
  reading.

Mailing list
  A mailing list consists of a number of e-mail addresses of people
  who subscribe to the list. When a
  message is sent to the list's own
  e-mail address, it is automatically
  forwarded to all those who subscribe to the list.

Medium
  A channel of communication

with the sole purpose of sending
a message from one or more
senders to many recipients.

Modem
  A modem is the hardware which
  makes it possible to connect a
  computer to other computers via
  a telephone line. A modem
  transforms the computer's digital
  signals to fluctuations (modulation) which can then be sent
  via the telephone network.
  Demodulation is the reverse
  process and modem is
  an abbreviation of modulator
  demodulator.

Navigation program
  A navigation program gives the
  user access to the World Wide
  Web. Another word for this is
  browser (see also browser). The
  most widely-used programs
  today are Netscape Navigator
  and Internet Explorer, which are
  available for both PC and
  Macintosh.

Netscape Navigator
  A popular navigation program on
  the World Wide Web. Using
  Netscape you can also participate
  in news groups and download
  files from FTP-servers, etc.

News group
  A news group is an electronic
  conference, a discussion group,
  on the Internet.

Offline
  When the modem is not connected to another modem.

Online
  When the modem is connected
  to another modem.

Online service
Means in principle only that services are provided electronically either via the Internet or via the telephone network.

Own brands
A 'branded product', often owned by a supermarket or department store and which typically can only be purchased in the supermarket's or store's shops. An own brand is often cheaper than traditional branded goods, but has often exactly the same characteristics.

Password
Your code word which is used together with your user name (log-on), when you are setting up a connection to a network service.

Personal agent
A program which learns from the user's actions and after a time can carry out the same actions itself.

Plug-in
An independent program which the user can download free of charge which makes it possible to carry out or see special activities - typically animations and sound effects.

Promotion
Often used in connection with a campaign which is supported by various advertising activities. Often this covers marketing activities in the shops such as signs, events and demonstrations.

Protocol
A 'set of regulations' for how computers communicate with each other.

Reload
To download a web page once again. If the data is sufficiently dynamic or if something goes wrong while a page is being downloaded, you can reload the page.

Revisit
How often a user comes back to the same website.

RISC
A registered trademark of A.C. Nielsen. An analysis method which enables the charting of the user on the basis of his or her behaviour.

Robot
See agent.

Search agent
A program which makes it possible to search for particular information on the Internet. A search agent is represented in the form of search pages, for example, www.yahoo.com or www.altavista.com.

Server
By a server is meant a computer which stores information and programs, and which gives other computers access to the information via the network.

Shockwave
Shockwave belongs to the category: plug-in programs (see also plug-in). An independent program which the user can download free of charge. Shockwave is a program developed by Macromedia, which makes it possible for the user to play games,

listen to music or move graphic elements around on a page. Shockwave can be found on www.macromedia.com

Site

See website.

Surfing

Surfing is slang for using the Internet and the World Wide Web.

Target group

Which type(s) of people a website is aimed at. Often similarities between the types of people can be categorised in a main target group. The people in the target group usually have the same characteristics.

TCP

(Transmission Control Protocol). TCP handles the data transfer. Together with IP (see IP), TCP forms the communication standard on the Internet.

Telnet

Telnet gives you remote terminal access - that is, you can connect to other computers across the Internet and control them as though you had a directly-connected terminal.

Trade marketing

Strategy for how a product is to be marketed in retail trade. Trade marketing management controls the consumers' access to the product.

Transmission speed

The effective speed of the connection. Can be slower or faster than the modulation speed. Data compression increases the speed,

while serial ports and poor connections reduce it.

Trend

Often a tendency in society which points towards a general social development which only a few have begun to follow and act upon.

UNIX

The most common operating system for Internet servers.

URL

(Uniform Resource Locator). The place which identifies an address on the Internet. A URL is the same as an address on the World Wide Web.

Usenet

Usenet is a name for a collection of electronic conferences or discussion forums on the Internet. These can be compared to a large notice board, divided into a number of different headings, i.e. news groups, each of which deal with a particular subject.

USP

Unique Selling Point. A concrete product benefit which is often used to distinguish one product from other competing products in a particular market.

Value centre

A value centre is a section of a website which is built up around a number of uniform values, with together are intended to support the overall profile/image of the brand. Often a website consists of five-six different value centres. A value centre supports between three and six different values.

Visit

A person who visits a website is recorded as a visit. If the user repeats his visit, it is recorded as another visit. 'Unique visits' differ from visits in that the user is only recorded once, regardless of how many times the user visits a particular website.

The Web

The World Wide Web.

Webcrawler, Yahoo!, AltaVista

Search tools for the World Wide Web.

Webmaster

The person who is responsible for a website.

Web page

The name of the page which the user sees when he uses the World Wide Web. Each web page has a particular address. (See also website).

Webserver

By a webserver is meant the computer on which the World Wide Web information is stored.

Website, site

By a website is meant a place on the World Wide Web which has its own name. A company can, for example, have its own site - either on its own server or on a web hotel operated by an Internet Service Provider. (See also web page).

WebTV

A registered trademark for a new product which gives Internet access via TV. This is carried out via a special WebTV-box which in principle consists of a computer and a modem.

World Wide Web

One of the Internet's standards. The World Wide Web is a large network of documents, which among other things contain hypertext and pictures. WWW is hypertext-based and makes it possible to organise the information in a user-friendly way. The information, which can be in the form of text, sound, pictures and/or animation, can be found on one computer or on different computers, but is easily accessible via a so-called hyperlink.

WWW

Abbreviation for World Wide Web. Another is W3.

References

Our major source of inspiration has without doubt been the Internet itself, but referring to the many articles we have obtained from the Internet will be meaningless. Instead, in the section 'Recommended links', we have listed the addresses of the many websites which we visit regularly and subscribe to in order to keep ourselves up to date. Below is therefore only a list of the printed material which has served to provide inspiration for this book.

Armstrong, Arthur G. & John Hagel III: *Netgain*. Harvard Business School Press 1997.

Baecker, R.M. & W.S. Buxton: *Human Computer Interaction: A Multidisciplinary Approach*. Morgan Kaufmann 1987.

Bayer, D.: *A Learning Agent for Resource Discovery on the World Wide Web*. MSC Project Dissertation, University of Aberdeen 1995.

Benedikt, Michael: *Cyberspace*. MIT Press 1991.

Boyer, M. Christine: *CyberCities: Visual Perception in the Age of Electronic Communication*. Princeton Architectural Press 1996.

Bremser, Wayne: *Escape from Banner Hell*. Interactivity, Sept. 1997.

Caglayan, Apler & Colin Harrison: *Agent*. Wiley Computer Publishing 1997.

Coupland, Douglas: *Microserfs*. Harper Collins 1995.

Cronin, Mary J.: *Banking and Finance on the Internet*. Van Nostrand Reinhold Publications 1997.

Csikszentihalyi, M.: *Flow: The Psychology of Optimal Experience*. Harper & Row 1990.

Csikszentihalyi, M. & I. Selega: *Optimal Experience - Psychological Studies of Flow in Consciousness*. Cambridge University Press 1988.

Falk, Thomas & Nils-Göran Olve: *IT som strategisk resurs. [IT as strategic resource]* Liber-Hermods AB 1996.

Franklin, S.: *Artificial Minds*. MIT Press 1995.

Franzen, Giep: *Advertising Effectiveness*. NTC Publications 1994.

Gibson, William: *Neuromancer*. Ace Books 1984.

Gilder, George: *Microcosm: The Quantum Revolution in Economics and Technology*. Simon and Schuster 1989.

Goldberg, Athomas: *Avatars and Agents, or Life Among the Indigenous Peoples of Cyberspace*. Addison-Wesley 1997.

Gould, J.D. & C. Lewis: *Designing for Usability: Key Principles and What Designers Think*. Communication of ACM, vol. 28 no. 3, March 1985.

Hafner, Katie & Matthew Lyon: *Where Wizards Stay Up Late: The Origins of the Internet*. Simon and Schuster 1996.

Hale, Constance: *Principles of English Usage in the Digital Age*. Hardwired 1996.

Jones, Steven G.: *Cybersociety*. Sage Publications 1995.

Kelly, Kevin: *New Rules of the New Economy*. Wired, Sept. 1997.

Kiesler, Sara: *Culture of the Internet*. Lawrence Erlbaum Associates 1997.

Kristof, Ray & Amy Satran: *Interactivity by design*. Adobe Press 1995.

Kunde, Jesper: *Corporate Religion*. Børsens Forlag 1997.

Lanier, Jaron: My *problems with Agents*. Wired, Nov. 1996.

Leonard, Andrew: *The Origin of New Species*. Hardwired 1997.

Lewis, C.: *'Thinking Aloud' Method in Cognitive Interface Design*. IBM Research report RC 9265, Feb. 1982.

Lewis, C. et al.: *Testing a Walkthrough Methodology for Theory-Based Design of Walk-Up-and-Use Interfaces*. CHI'90 Proceedings, April 1990.

Lidsky, David: *Tomorrow's Web today*. InternetUser, Aug. 1997.

McLuhan, Marshall: *Understanding media - The Extension of Man*. MIT Press 1964.

Mok, Clement: *Designing Business*. Adobe Press 1996.

Molich, R. et al.: *Brugervenlige EDB-systemer. [User-friendly EDP systems]* Teknisk Forlag 1986.

Negroponte, Nicholas: *Being Digital*. Alfred A. Knopf 1995.

Nielsen, L: *Hypertext and Hypermedia*. Academic Press 1990.

Nørretranders, Tor: *Stedet som ikke er - fremtidens nærvær, netværk og Internet. [The place that doesn't exist- the presence, network and Internet of the future]* Aschehoug 1997.

Pearce, Celia: *Beyond Shoot your Friends: A Call to Arms in the Battle Against Violence*. Addison Wesley 1997.

Reid, Robert 1I.: *Real Revolution*. Wired, Oct. 1997.

Rheingold, Howard: *Virtual Community*. Addison-Wesley 1993.

Schneiderman, B.: *Designing the User Interface: Strategies for Effective Human-Computer Interaction*. Addison-Wesley 1987.

Schuler, Douglas: *Wired for Change*. Addison-Wesley 1996.

Siegel, David: *Creating Killer Websites*. Hayden Books 1997.

Skelly, T.C. & D.D. Thiel: *The Development of Seductive Interfaces: Empowering People*. ACM CHI'90, Tutorial Notes 1990.

Stephenson, Neal: *Snow Crash*. Bantam 1992.

Szeto, Butterick, McKirchy-Spencer et al.: *Designing Interactive Web Sites*. Hayden Books 1997.

Turkle, Sherry: *Life on the Screen: Identity in the Age of the Internet*. Simon and Schuster 1995.

Vassos, Tom: *Strategic Internet Marketing.* QUE 1996.

Wallace, James: *Overdrive.* John Wiley & Sons Inc. 1997.

Wayner, Peter: *Digital Cash: Commerce on the Internet.* AP Professional Publications 1997.

White, J.E.: *Mobile Agents.* AAAI Press/MIT Press/Software Agents 1996.

Williams, Joseph: *Bots and other Internet Beasties.* Sams Publications 1996.

Zeff, Robbin & Bradley Aronson: *Advertising on the Internet.* John Wiley & Sons 1997.

About the authors

Over 10 years of interactive brand management expertise and a passion for e-marketing and the Internet led Martin Lindström and Tim Frank Andersen to write this book. The authors feel that traditional marketeers have not yet harnessed the Internet to extend brands into cyberspace. With the launch of one of the world's first digital advertising agencies, BBDO Interactive (now Fremfab Inc.) in Europe in 1995, Lindström and Andersen set the scene for brand management on the Internet. Today Fremfab Inc. is the largest online agency in Europe and is internationally renowned for its many award-winning campaigns.

Lindström founded BBDO Interactive Inc., Australia/Asia (later renamed ZIVO Inc.) in 1997, which has become the region's largest web development company. He established eBrandwidth.com in 2000 to advise Fortune Top 500 companies on international clicks and mortar strategies. Companies seeking Lindström's advice include Pepsi Co., Fosters, Microsoft, Visa, M&M's, Snickers, Hewlett Packard, ABC, Mercedes-Benz, Cable & Wireless, LEGO, Yellow Pages, SmithKlineBeecham and Quicken.

In 1996 Lindström co-authored Europe's first book about the trade marketing. In 1997, with Andersen, he wrote the first book on Internet brands, and in 1999 *Brand Building on the Internet* was published in Asia and Australia. Lindström regularly contributes to leading international newspapers and magazines. The *Australian*, *The Times*, *US Today*, *Business Review Weekly*, *Wired*, Internet.com and ClickZ.com are among those to seek his comments on the future of the net.

Since graduating as an engineer Tim Frank Andersen has worked with interactive media for the past seven years, first in charge of interactive media with Baltica, and then as advertising manager for both Baltica and Danica. Tim has also served as manager for the consultants at integrated Media productions. He was responsible for the digital development in the BBDO-group and is today the director of Networkers A/S, managing a client portfolio of key European and international brands such as; ABB, DSB, FONA, LEGO, M&M's, Tel Danmark, Magasin, Realkredit Danmark, Snickers in Sweden and Store Brand in Norway.

The authors can be contacted by email on:

    Martin Lindström   martin@lindstrom.com
    Tim Frank Andersen   tfa@networkers.dk